Strategy and Security in the Caribbean

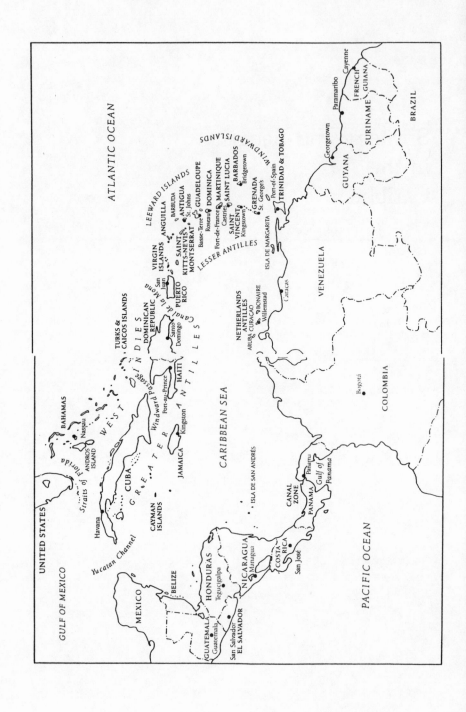

Strategy and Security in the Caribbean

Edited by
IVELAW L. GRIFFITH

PRAEGER

New York
Westport, Connecticut
London

Library of Congress Cataloging-in-Publication Data

Strategy and security in the Caribbean / edited by Ivelaw L. Griffith.
     p.   cm.
  Includes bibliographical references and index.
  ISBN 0-275-93830-1 (alk. paper)
    1. Caribbean Area—Strategic aspects. I. Griffith, Ivelaw L.
  UA609.S78 1991
  355'.0330729–dc20   91-7208

British Library Cataloguing in Publication Data is available.

Library of Congress Catalog Card Number: 91-7208
ISBN: 0-275-93830-1

First published in 1991

Praeger Publishers, One Madison Avenue, New York, NY 10010
An imprint of Greenwood Publishing Group, Inc.

Printed in the United States of America

The paper used in this book complies with the
Permanent Paper Standard issued by the National
Information Standards Organization (Z39.48–1984).

10   9   8   7   6   5   4   3   2   1

To

Shakina Aisha, Ivelaw Lamar
and
children of the Caribbean everywhere

Contents

Preface

Looking ahead to the year 2000, I see a gestation period over which scholars with primary interests in economics, sociology, political science, peace studies, psychology, ecology, and a few other areas offer the fruits of their individual and collective endeavors to deliver Caribbean security studies as a healthy interdisciplinary infant.

This process would require appropriate conceptual and theoretical definition and redefinition of security, establishing interdisciplinary boundaries, some common methodological currencies, and maintaining security issues on the research and publication agendas of Caribbeanists. Some of this has already started, perhaps in an unconscious way. Our selected bibliography gives a sample of this foundation, which is also evidenced by the increasing analysis of security issues by scholars and policy practitioners — in the media, in scholarly books and journals, and at professional conferences.

The idea of producing this book itself, a small contribution to the evolution I talk about, was an offshoot of a conference. The Caribbean Studies Association held its Fourteenth Annual Conference during May 1989 in Barbados. Three of the chapters here, now revised, were presented at the conference — those by García Muñiz, Phillips, and mine on perception. Other members of the panel were Pablo Maríñez of Universidad Nacional Autonoma de Mexico and Neville Duncan, a contributor to this volume.

The favorable response to the Barbados panel and the continuing importance of security issues prompted me to pursue this book as a contribution to the security debate and to the foundation of Caribbean security studies. The success of this project, however, is attributable to the assistance of many people, only some of whom can be named here. Humberto García Muñiz and Dion Phillips offered encouragement and useful advice. Barbara Haywood typed and retyped the major portion of the final manuscript. All contributors received the support of several people and institutions at different stages of their work. And my wife, Francille, and my students Alvin Mitchell, Rennie Greenidge, Clive Walker, Lulu Cruz, Rosemarie Trotman, and Shaun Brown assisted me with several chores, both big and small. I'm grateful for the help of all those named and unnamed, none of whom bear any responsibility for any shortcoming in this work.

Introduction

Studies on national and regional security tend to have a "big power" orientation. They look at challenges to large and powerful states and how their actions and reactions affect global peace and security. Examination of small state security dilemmas is undertaken invariably as a tangent to the concerns of the large and powerful or when small state security problems present actual or potential threats to the security interests of the big powers. This low priority of the security problems of small states in their own right has led to considerable misunderstanding about their security problems, policies, and measures.

This book seeks to clarify some of the misunderstanding in relation to the Caribbean, particularly the English-speaking Caribbean. Appreciating the national and regional security circumstances of Caribbean countries requires coming to terms with several factors. One is perception. How Caribbean political leaders interpret their internal and external security challenges is crucial to understanding the kinds of policies and strategies they adopt. Caribbean countries have a feature in common with small states elsewhere. The institutional basis for their decision making is very narrow, and it facilitates the dominance of one or two leaders. In such circumstances the perceptions of those leaders guide security policies and initiatives, making the perception factor all the more important.

Understanding the resource base of Caribbean states enables us to appreciate both the nature of some of the problems and the reasons why some security measures are feasible and others are not. A few Caribbean states — Barbados, Guyana, Jamaica, and Trinidad and Tobago — have strategic materials such as bauxite and oil, but resources in the region are generally limited. However, it is well established that meaningful national and regional security requires that states own or have access to appropriate security resources. External threats tend to become more credible where security resources are minimal. And resource capacity not only influences elite perceptions about the intentions of others; it also helps determine how policy choices are made.

The geopolitics of the hemisphere is such that Anglophone Caribbean states are subordinate to the interests of others. They are vulnerable to U.S. national interest pursuits and to those of middle powers in the area, such as Brazil, Mexico, and Venezuela. Some of the security problems, therefore, relate to the geography of the region and to the power politics being played in the hemisphere and internationally. Consequently, the range of credible options open to states in the region is influenced by the geopolitics of the area.

Internal political instability, militarization, and intervention have been among the major security dilemmas to confront Caribbean countries over the past three decades. The experiences of Jamaica, Grenada, and Nicaragua between 1970 and 1990 are examples of instability related to ideological disputes and political factionalism. In Nicaragua there was an added factor — U.S. covert and overt action. In Haiti, El Salvador, and Surinam instability has been linked either to the military's intrusion into politics through coups or to its cooptation for political rule by civilians. The instability in Guyana in the 1960s was due to racial conflict. And the economic deprivation in parts of the region has contributed to the eruption of violence that often threatens internal peace and stability.

Two kinds of militarization have existed in the Caribbean. The first was along a "problem-solution" continuum for some states. Some leader, for example, in Grenada and Guyana, rationalized militarization as a credible response to actual or potential national security threats. But with the passage of time and changed circumstances, it became a problem. There were huge imbalances in the allocation of scarce resources, and the military was used as an instrument of political rule. This itself led to threats to domestic security. The second kind of militarization derives from the U.S. military presence in the region. The United States considers the Caribbean Basin to be its southern flank, its strategic rear. And as Chapters 1 and 2 show, it therefore maintains military forces there, principally in Puerto Rico, Panama, and in Guantanamo, Cuba. In the Anglophone Caribbean there are also installations and facilities, in Antigua, the Bahamas, Bermuda, and the U.S. Virgin Islands, plus military advisory groups and attaches throughout the area.

Caribbean states have also experienced intervention. In 1953 the British sent troops into Guyana to quash a nationalist movement. Guyana also experienced intervention in 1966 with Venezuelan military action in Ankoko, part of the territory they claim, and with Venezuela's role in the 1968 insurrection in Rupununi, also in the part of Guyana claimed by Venezuela. There was U.S. intervention in Guatemala in 1954 and in the Dominican Republic in 1965. U.S. action in Grenada in 1983 was precipitated by a domestic crisis that gave the United States the opportunity to pursue a long-held desire to sabotage the then Marxist government in Grenada. And in December 1989 the United States intervened in Panama, ostensibly to protect U.S. lives, help restore democracy, capture General Manuel Noriega to bring him to justice on drug trafficking and other charges, and preserve the integrity of the Panama Canal Treaty.

Caribbean countries enter the 1990s with economic problems presenting some of the gravest security threats. As we will see in this volume, economic problems have a current high threat-value. But they also have a latent threat-value in that current problems can precipitate political and military problems later. For example, the high debt burden — primarily an economic security matter — has far-reaching military and political consequences. For in attempting to manage their debts, states run the risk of jeopardizing their internal security because of labor, business, and other reactions that such measures precipitate. Guyana, Trinidad and Tobago, Venezuela, Argentina, Chile, Panama, and Colombia are among states in the hemisphere that experienced this in 1988 and 1989 with strikes, riots, public demonstrations, and arson and vandalism against public property costing millions of dollars. In Venezuela 300 people were killed in the spring of 1989, and there was a coup attempt in Trinidad in July 1990 with strong economic undercurrents.

Given this background, it is understandable that countries adopt different security measures to safeguard their national (sometimes meaning regime) security interests. Some states militarize. Some seek security guarantees from powerful friends, like Belize with Britain. The countries in the Eastern Caribbean have pursued a form of collective security by creating the Regional Security System in 1982. And economic integration and alternative economic strategies in Guyana, Jamaica, and elsewhere are all partly intended to buttress economic security and forestall military-political threats caused by economic deprivation.

The selections in this volume permit us to understand some common as well as unique aspects of the region's security circumstances. Part of our task here is to help explain and interpret them and, we hope, to aid efforts to deal with them. Part I looks at issues of relevance to the entire region. Chapter 1 focuses on what Caribbean leaders define as their main internal and external security concerns. This reveals a range of issues in the military, economic, and political spheres. Some issues stand out, among them drugs and the foreign debt. I examine some factors that influence how Caribbean political elites interpret security issues and suggest a few implications of working with some existing disparities.

In the next chapter Humberto García Muñiz discusses the historical and geopolitical factors surrounding the use of Caribbean territories for maintaining U.S. security installations. He explains the concern with having security networks for geostrategic purposes as well as to ensure domestic political order. And García Muñiz details the dilemmas in which Puerto Rico finds itself as an important cog in both the geostrategic and the internal security wheels. Chapter 3 offers a comparative analysis of internal security problems springing from political violence. Neville Duncan examines relative deprivation and ideological and other factors that led to episodes of violence in the region over the last 50 years. He criticizes some colonial and postcolonial approaches to conflict management and advocates innovative measures to resolve conflicts without derogating from civil and political rights consistent with a democratic political framework.

The Eastern Caribbean comes under scrutiny in Chapter 4. Clifford Griffin shows the linkages among political security, economic security, and military security in the subregion, paying particular attention to Grenada. He argues that the postinvasion economic strategy suggested for Grenada and touted as exemplary for the region stands to undermine the very domestic political order it was intended to protect.

Part II offers four case studies. Dion Phillips traces how successive governments in Barbados have shaped that country's defense policies and planning since independence in 1966. He finds both continuity and change over time, occasioned mainly by the nature of the domestic political environment, events in the region, and U.S. foreign and defense posture toward the area. Alma Young examines the Belize-Guatemala territorial dispute, offering insights into both the historical and the contemporary dimensions of that intractable dispute. The economic, military, and internal political ramifications of the controversy are explored, and Young shows how the refugee problems in Central America have complicated matters in Belize.

In Chapter 7 I look at Guyana's military in the context of changes introduced in the country since the death of Forbes Burnham in 1985. Attention is paid to the roles ascribed to the Guyana Defense Force and other military outfits — regime political security, the military defense, and economic and diplomatic security — and the degree to which some have been accentuated over the years. Jannette Domingo provides an analysis of the geopolitical considerations that guided U.S. involvement in the Virgin Islands and shows the changing relationship over the years. She looks at the link between economic dependency and political self-determination there and outlines the economic factors shaping the debate about decolonization in the Virgin Islands. Domingo also examines options available to the islanders as they ponder the evolution of relations with the United States.

This collection addresses several aspects of the instability problems in the region, the intervention and the militarization it has experienced, and the economic, political, and other vulnerability from which it suffers. No attempt was made to impose a single theoretical approach on contributors. Use is made of geopolitical analysis founded essentially on realist theory, political economy frameworks, political psychology notions, and conflict theory. This suggests both the multidimensional nature of the security circumstances of the Caribbean as well as the variety of perspectives from which problems of strategy and security in the region can be viewed.

I REGIONAL SECURITY ISSUES

1　Security Perceptions of English Caribbean Elites

Ivelaw L. Griffith

Like leaders elsewhere, Caribbean political elites formulate and execute policies partly in response to their perception of issues and problems. Kenneth Boulding's assertion more than two decades ago still holds true:

> we must recognize that the people whose decisions determine the policies and actions of nations do not respond to the "objective" facts of the situation, whatever that may mean, but to their "image" of the situation. It is what we think the world is like, and not what it is really like, that determines our behavior.[1]

Over the past decade there has been considerable attention to security problems and policies in the Caribbean. This attention has revolved around four main themes: U.S. militarization of the region in pursuit of its political and strategic interests; drugs, political instability and other security challenges; increased emphasis on domestic military and para-military institutions in parts of the region; and assessment of the Regional Security System (RSS) as a collective security mechanism.

Although much of the analysis is policy oriented, very little exists on the perceptual backdrop against which security initiatives in the Caribbean are undertaken. Some studies do comment on elite thinking, but to the extent that there is perception analysis, it is always tangential to other things.[2] To help fill this void I examine the perception-security nexus by looking at elite concerns about military, political, and economic aspects of the region's security. First I identify the relevant elites. This is followed by a profile of security perceptions. I then suggest some factors that influence these perceptions and consider a few implications of the profile.

CARIBBEAN ELITES

The ultimate security and foreign policy decision-making unit of a state is usually one of the following: predominant leader — a single individual with power to make the choice and to stifle opposition; single group — a set of interacting individuals all of whom are members of a single body, having the ability to select a course of action and secure compliance; multiple autonomous groups — groups or coalitions of important actors, no one of which, by itself, can decide and force compliance on the others; or no overarching body in which all the necessary parties are members.[3] The foreign policy and security elites of the Caribbean may be defined broadly as the political officeholders and senior appointed officials involved in the formulation, execution, and evaluation of foreign and security policy for their states. This definition suggests that the elites operate in the context of a single group decision unit — the Cabinet.[4]

Closer scrutiny, however, reveals that the single group decision structure is more form than substance. The reality is more a situation of predominant leaders operating in single group frameworks. Several reasons explain this. First, irrespective of leadership type (charismatic or rational-legal), or foreign policy orientation, the political culture of the Caribbean has accommodated strong and decisive, though not tyrannical, leadership. Many of these leaders — Eric Williams (Trinidad and Tobago), Norman Manley and Alexander Bustamante (Jamaica), Errol Barrow (Barbados), Forbes Burnham (Guyana), and Vere Bird, Sr. (Antigua) are the most noteworthy — were or are acknowledged political giants in their own societies as well as within the wider region. Their political beliefs, political styles, political experiences, and the histories of their societies all combined to facilitate their exercise of predominance. This pattern persists although the era of the charismatic leader is waning.[5]

Second, foreign and security policy making is the preserve of the executive branch in the Caribbean. In most societies with coequal or roughly coequal branches of government — for example, the United States with the executive, the legislature, and the judiciary — foreign and security policy roles are played by at least two of the branches. Taking the United States again, although executive branch preeminence in foreign and security policy is established, the Congress has well-recognized capabilities in these areas, which it utilizes and cherishes.[6] All Caribbean states have governments with multiple branches — executive, legislative, judicial — although these operate differently than in the United States.[7] Yet foreign and security policy making is the sole preserve of the executive. Some parliaments have committees with foreign and security policy mandates. They are, however, either emasculated by the executive or have abdicated such roles, all in the context of political environments where the predominance of the leader of the ruling party and head of the administration is the norm.

Moreover, a combination of practical circumstances (for example, small size or dearth of skills) and political desire creates situations of multiple role performance, especially in the Eastern Caribbean. Thus, many prime ministers are also defense ministers. Some also hold the foreign affairs portfolio as well as others. For example, in the Cabinet line-up in St. Vincent following the May 1989 elections, Prime Minister James Mitchell retained power over the Ministries of Finance, Defense, and Foreign Affairs. After the March 13, 1990, elections in Grenada, Prime Minister Nicholas Braithwaite took control of National Security, Information, and Carricou Affairs. As of September 1990 in St. Kitts, Prime Minister Kennedy Simmonds also held the portfolios for defense, finance, home affairs, and foreign affairs. Elsewhere in the region Belize Prime Minister George Price is responsible for finance, home affairs, and defense. And in Guyana, although President Desmond Hoyte reassigned responsibility for home affairs, he continued the tradition of being responsible for defense. In addition, all the prime ministers — president in Guyana's case — are leaders of their respective political parties. This fusion of power enables them to exercise clout even in cases where single groups seem firmly operational. As Searwar says, "the ruling group, in the case of the Caribbean, nearly always reflects the perceptions and views of a dominant leader."[8] Braveboy-Wagner is also correct: "In particular, crisis decisions tend to be personal decisions with little attention paid to opposition sentiment and not enough alternative information and opinion solicited."[9]

The multiple autonomous group decision structure has not been featured in independent Caribbean nations. The closest thing to this is perhaps in Guyana. There the Central Executive Committee of the ruling People's National Congress has subcommittees for foreign affairs and other subjects, paralleling some of the decision structures of the executive branch of the government. But then the doctrine of Paramountcy of the Party that guides political affairs there — especially during the Burnham era — detracts from the autonomy of multiple groups in subordinating government bodies to party ones. Moreover, Burnham exercised hegemony over all policy agencies in a way that permitted no real autonomy. Members of the subcommittees, therefore, do little more than influence some of the decisions of the paramount leader.

"Leaders' personal characteristics are more likely to influence foreign [and security] policy decisions if the leaders are predominant in their government."[10] This is certainly true of the Caribbean. One study by Basil Ince on Trinidad and Tobago showed Prime Minister Eric Williams to be the consummate decision maker; more *deus inter homines* than *primus inter pares* within the Cabinet.[11] Dr. Williams's erudition, charisma, intellect, and political style may have made Trinidad and Tobago a special case. But then the Caribbean has had, and still has, other leaders who, although not fully comparable with Williams, have towered over their societies intellectually and or politically. The late Forbes Burnham (Guyana), Robert Bradshaw (St. Kitts), and Errol Barrow (Barbados) were among them. And there is Michael Manley (Jamaica), Vere Bird, Sr. (Antigua), John Compton (St. Lucia), and Lynden Pindling (the Bahamas).

The predominance of these leaders in security, foreign policy, and, indeed, all other matters makes the consequences of their perceptions and subsequent actions loom larger in relative terms compared with states where other models prevail. This is partly because the institutional context in which decisions are presented magnifies the images of the leaders. The consequences of misperception or inexpedience could, therefore, be severe. As one international politics specialist points out:

> The failings and errors of leaders of great powers can be disguised and compensated for by the organizational and material resources they can bring to bear. Even the awe in which they tend to be held may suffice. But the errors of the leaders of a minor power [small state] have immediate and unmistakable consequences and are only too often beyond repair; and there is no disguising them.[12]

The existence of the predominant leader model in the Caribbean, however, accommodates the involvement of other entities and individuals in decision making, primarily as decision influencers. Some leaders give credence to the principles of Cabinet government and consult their Cabinets before making decisions. Others use their Cabinets to give official imprimatur to essentially personal decisions, if only because under the terms of their constitutions and in the context of parliamentary government, the Cabinet is a key institution. In some places, like Guyana, entities such as the Central Executive

Committee and the General Council of the ruling party also play some role. Indeed under the doctrine of Party Paramountcy there, emphasized more during the Burnham era, especially between 1973 and 1985, the Cabinet as a government entity is subordinate to bodies such as the Central Executive Committee and the General Council of the ruling party.

Bureaucratic elites also influence some security decisions. Included in this group are the permanent secretaries, chairmen of constitutional bodies like the Public Service Commissions, the Police Service Commissions, and the Judicial Service Commissions, and the heads of public corporations in places like Guyana, Jamaica, and Trinidad and Tobago, which have large public sectors. In some cases decision influencers are also to be found among the business elite, labor and religious leaders, and in the foreign diplomatic corps where one or two diplomats "have the ear" of the prime minister or the president. Of course the extent to which such individuals are influential depends on their access to leaders and the leaders' willingness or obligation to act on their advice.

The security policy elites of the Caribbean are, therefore, the sum of the president, prime ministers, foreign ministers, and defense ministers of the various states.[13] These leaders operate ostensibly within Cabinet decision structures with supporting bureaucratic mechanisms, but the reality is less of single group and more of predominant leader situations. They operate in policy-making frameworks that oblige them to be mindful of internal and external considerations. Their decisions and initiatives hinge on several factors; the most important are

assumptions about the Caribbean, the hemisphere, and the international milieu;

the manner in which threats to the regime, the society, or to both are defined;

the response to threats, and opportunities for the threat or use of force, or other measures;

the force levels and weapons systems for appropriate responses to actual and potential threats;

the human, material, and other capabilities required to respond to external security needs while meeting internal socioeconomic demands;

public opinion and political support for regime and national objectives and policies;

the creation of incentives and controls to ensure the support of objectives by the security establishment.

SECURITY PERCEPTIONS

Although some Caribbean leaders are inclined to view security in traditional military terms, most subscribe to the view that the protection of their nations requires a broad definition of the term to account for the dimensions from which the most critical threats emerge — the economic and the political. Thus, in the Caribbean, security is defined to encompass military, political, and economic dimensions. Expectedly, for some leaders there is greater emphasis on some dimension(s) than on others. For example, Trinidad and Tobago, Dominica, and Barbados have experienced mercenary and coup attempts at undermining the stability of their polities. The leaders in these countries are, therefore, very sensitive to actual or potential threats coming from those directions.[14]

Military Dimension

Many Caribbean elites are sensitive to potential military threats. But overt military threats are the least of their concerns. Terrorism as experienced in Europe and the Middle East is not a matter of great import, but the potential for terrorist action related to the drug trade is a matter of grave concern. Guyana and Trinidad and Tobago are the states with the greatest racial pluralism. Both have seen racial strife. Guyana's in the late 1950s and early 1960s developed to dangerous proportions. Both societies have improved in terms of racial harmony, but political polarization and economic disparity related to race still exist.[15] However, civil war there or elsewhere in the Caribbean is not likely.

There is some concern about U.S. military operations in the region. The United States has a record of military interventions in the area — Guatemala in 1954; Dominican Republic in 1965; and several times in Haiti and Nicaragua earlier on. The 1983 Grenada invasion was the first in the English Caribbean. It is etched indelibly in the memories of West Indians, both of those who supported it and of those who opposed it. It was not, however, the latest intervention episode. The latest was in Panama in December 1989. The United States justified the action on four grounds: the need to protect U.S. lives; help restore democracy; preserve the integrity of the Panama Canal Treaty; and bring General Manuel Noriega to justice for drug trafficking, among other things.[16]

Thus, even for those states that supported the U.S. action in Grenada and in Panama as being beneficial to the Caribbean, the prospect of intervention, whether for pure U.S. national interests or in pursuit of U.S.-Caribbean interests, is a consideration not entirely dismissed. The

Grenada action signaled the low tolerance of the United States for Marxist pursuits in the area. This has contributed to the eclipse of radical politics in the region. There are, therefore, no "Grenadas" in the Caribbean to occasion similar U.S. action (although a "Grenada" is not the only possible basis for intervention); neither are any on the horizon.

Concerns about the United States also derive from another factor. As the U.S. strategic rear and a key element in the Western defense mechanism, the Caribbean Basin has a considerable U.S. military presence.[17] The principal force concentrations are in Puerto Rico, at the Atlantic threshold of the Caribbean; in Panama, at the southern rim of the Caribbean Basin; and in Cuba, at Guantanamo, on the northern perimeter. According to the Pentagon's *Department of Defense Base Structure Reported for Fiscal Year 1989,* the U.S. Navy maintains a strength of 5,004 in Puerto Rico. There is also a tactical fighter group of 406. In Panama there is a 961-member naval presence, and an air force personnel strength of 3,101 in addition to the army's Southern Command's force of 17,000 there. The naval operations in Cuba have a personnel establishment of 3,711.

The United States also has military installations, facilities, and personnel in Antigua, the Bahamas, Bermuda, and the U.S. Virgin Islands and military advisory groups and attaches in various parts of the region. This military network is designed to secure the region from external and internal threats to U.S. security interests. The concern of Caribbean elites about the possibility of becoming embroiled in conflicts of an East-West nature because of the region's linkages to the Western defense is thus not unfounded, even in the context of cooled Soviet-U.S. tensions. As such, a threat to the United States becomes, by extension, a potential threat to the Caribbean.

Cuba has a significant military capability — an active army of 175,000, a reserve force of 130,000, and a sophisticated inventory — and once actively pursued relations with English Caribbean states.[18] These matters are of interest to Caribbean leaders. But they have been of comparatively greater concern to Americans. Some Caribbean leaders have been known for their strident anti-Communist enunciations and their distaste for Castro's political overtures. Among them are Mary Eugenia Charles of Dominica and John Compton of St. Lucia. Former Prime Minister of Jamaica Edward Seaga and the late Herbert Blaize of Grenada were also in this group. However, the kinds of concerns voiced in the United States about probable military adventures by Cuba in the Caribbean are not paralleled within the Caribbean. As one example, North American statesmen and scholars have attached much more premium to the MIGs and the surface-to-air missiles in Cuba and to their potential threat to the area than have leaders in the Caribbean.

A realistic, although latent, concern based on East-West politics, however, exists. Any conflict between the two superpowers may draw Cuba into the picture, either initially by the Soviets or by U.S. pre-emptive action. Caribbean leaders worry about the inevitability of military spillovers into the area in such scenarios. Moreover, some feel that because the United States perceives Cuba as a threat, Cuba becomes an indirect threat to the Caribbean. The cases of Guyana (under Burnham), Jamaica (under Manley, 1972–1980), and Grenada (under Bishop) show how close contacts with Cuba can result in the kind of economic ostracism, diplomatic hostility, and military intervention from which the entire region can suffer.

Venezuela has territorial claims against several states, among them Guyana, Trinidad and Tobago, and Dominica. That against Guyana is the largest and most significant — for five-eighths of its territory. And in pursuit of that claim, Venezuela has used aggression (in 1966) as well as political and economic intimidation.[19] Fears of military intervention up to the early 1980s were not unfounded, and they can never be entirely dismissed. Since 1985, however, relations have been improving, with heads of states visits, economic and technical assistance by Venezuela, and Venezuelan investment in Guyanese mining and oil exploration ventures.[20] Thus, although military intervention cannot be ruled out, it is doubtful that Venezuela would use such methods to settle its claims.

The experiences of some states in the region cause them to be sensitive to military-political threats stemming from mercenary adventures or coup attempts. In 1970 Trinidad and Tobago was the scene of a military uprising. In October 1976, a conspiracy to topple the Tom Adams government in Barbados was exposed. In March 1979 Eric Gairy was removed by force in Grenada. In April 1981 there was a failed coup attempt against the Eugenia Charles regime in Dominica. It was led by U.S. and Canadian mercenaries in collaboration with ex-Prime Minister Patrick John. In December of the same year, another coup attempt involving former Dominica Defense Force (DDF) members was foiled. This led to the disbanding of the DDF.

The six-day bloody coup attempt in Trinidad and Tobago in July–August 1990 is the region's latest internal military-political crisis. The grim drama began on July 27 when Abu Bakr, a black Muslim leader and 113 members of his Jamaat-al-Muslimeen (Group of Muslims) took control of the parliament building and held Prime Minister Robinson and 15 other government officials hostage. The police headquarters in

Port-of-Spain was fire bombed, and the headquarters of Trinidad and Tobago Television was occupied, with 25 hostages taken there. Massive looting, arson, and vandalism left 23 people dead, 300 wounded, about 4,000 people unemployed, and property damage estimated at TT$300 million.

Abu Bakr explained that the action was intended to replace the government with a different regime. He blamed the Robinson government for Trinidad's continuous economic deprivation and for the corruption and mismanagement there. During the seizure Bakr secured an agreement from Robinson to vacate office, have Deputy Prime Minister Winston Dookeram serve as interim ruler, and prepare elections within three months. Up to the time of writing, the governments seemed unwilling to honor that agreement. Bakr and his rebels surrendered on August 1. Treason and other charges were filed against all 114 of the participants in the affair. Bakr himself was charged with 15 offenses, including treason, 9 counts of murder, firearm possession, and hostage taking.[21]

These experiences color the political histories of Caribbean societies and are not easily expunged from the memories of the present elites. In spite of the 1990 coup attempt in Trinidad, however, no evidence suggests that the region is generally in jeopardy of such threats.

Especially in the Eastern Caribbean, leaders perceive their security problems primarily in terms of drugs and of thwarting potential subversion from within. They consider U.S. support to be an ultimate resource for meeting security threats. Speaking in Washington at the James Monroe Memorial Foundation in April 1987, Dominica's Mary Charles argued that the Monroe Doctrine was an appropriate framework for Caribbean countries to invite U.S. security assistance. She contended, "I have no doubt that the Monroe Doctrine was applied fittingly in this [the 1983 Grenada intervention] case. . . . We in the Caribbean who see ourselves as allies of the Americas wish to maintain that tradition and uphold the Monroe Doctrine as it has developed over the ages."[22]

Other leaders are less specific in naming potential invitees. Barbadian Prime Minister Erskine Sandiford went to New York in August 1990 shortly after the Trinidad incident. And in a speech at the Fifth Anniversary Breakfast of the Caribbean-American Chamber of Commerce and Industry, he was frank about the willingness of Barbados to invite outside assistance if an eventuality similar to Trinidad's developed. Without naming countries, he declared, "if there were a threat or an attempt to overthrow a government of Barbados, a democratically elected government of Barbados by force, I would have no hesitation in seeking support from friendly governments in the region or outside the region."[23]

Political Dimension

Political factionalism has featured in the political histories of Caribbean states. Jamaica, Trinidad and Tobago, Dominica, Grenada, Antigua, the Bahamas, and St. Kitts have all known the kind of factional politics and elite infighting that can rupture the fabric of a society. Factionalism has arisen from conflicts among strong willed leaders. It has also correlated with race. And in Trinidad and Antigua it cast a cloud on politics that still lingers and could disrupt their peace and security. It is, therefore, a matter to which leaders are very sensitive.

Destabilization seeks generally to change either the regional balance of power or, relatedly, the ideological posture of particular states. There have been destabilization efforts by Caribbean Basin states — Venezuela against Guyana in 1968 and in 1980–1982. But destabilization attempts have generally been made by the United States. U.S. geopolitical interests in the region, coupled with its record of interventions, make the prospect of U.S. destabilization a political reality that the Caribbean must live with. U.S. destabilization has been both overt and covert. It is usually the result of a perception by the United States of actual or potential threats to its national interests by Cuba, Cuban surrogates, or from Cuban-Soviet pursuits in the region.

Caribbean states have responded differently to destabilization. Grenada under Maurice Bishop adopted the Popular Mobilization approach where the ruling New Jewel Movement conducted political education campaigns on the nature and objectives of their political changes and on the antipathy developed toward them by the United States and some states in the region. Extensive use was made of workers, professionals, and other interest groups to help persuade Grenadians to prepare to "defend the revolution" politically and physically. The Defensive/Reactive Diplomacy approach was used by Guyana under Forbes Burnham and by Jamaica under Michael Manley (1972–1980).[24]

These nations used their diplomats to sensitize the international community to threats to their sovereignty and to garner support and sympathy. They operated particularly within the Non-Aligned Movement, the United Nations, G-77, and the Caribbean Community and Common Market (CARICOM). One analyst concluded that generally, the response of Caribbean states to the problem of external destabilization has been piecemeal. He argues that where there is consensus, the response is nevertheless inadequate to meet challenges by the most powerful international actors. And he suggested that "perhaps the most significant problem undermining effective responses to external destabilization is the tendency toward political disunity or ideological fragmentation of the region."[25]

Some Caribbean leaders harbor muted suspicions about Venezuelan pursuits in the region. It is felt though, that judging from the nature of their present conduct, any ulterior motives by Venezuela would be more economic in direction than anything else. Cuba's achievements and its firm stands in dealing with the United States are popularly admired in parts of the Caribbean. But many leaders, especially in the Eastern Caribbean, are wary of Cuba and the likelihood of their being victims of Cuban destabilization. Former Barbadian diplomat Charles Skeete presents what is perhaps a sentiment of most Caribbean leaders: "While we believe that Castroism may be good for Cuba, we have our reservations as to whether Castro is entitled to spread his ideology to our region."[26]

This is in spite of Cuba's new rapprochement with the Caribbean. Diplomatic relations were restored with Jamaica in July 1990 after nearly a decade of mutual hostility between the two following Edward Seaga's victory in 1980. And at the July–August 1990 CARICOM Summit in Jamaica, Caribbean leaders looked favorably on Cuba's request for observer status in the regional institution. Guyana, the country with closest ties to Cuba, was mandated to follow up on the matter. CARICOM leaders have several concerns and conditions about the observer request, one of which is Cuba's nonrecognition of any government in Grenada since the 1983 U.S. intervention.

Drugs present perhaps the single most critical security challenge to the region. Prime Minister Sandiford has called it "perhaps the most serious problem for the region in the next decade."[27] The problems relate mainly to drug production, trafficking, use, and money laundering. It is no longer a problem for a handful of countries. All Caribbean nations are implicated in some way, some more than others.

A sample of some recent statistics suggests the extent of one aspect of the problem. In May 1990 a record 620 kilos of cocaine valued at US$124 million was confiscated in the Cayman Islands. In February of the same year, 50 pounds of cocaine valued at TT$60 million was seized aboard the cruise ship *Cunard Countess* in Trinidad. The Guyana police reported that cocaine seizures and arrests for 1988 have surpassed those for the previous year. In 1987, 66,364 pounds of marijuana and 400 grams of cocaine were confiscated. In 1988, the marijuana figure was down to 44,127 pounds, but that for cocaine rose to 3,575 grams.

Better news came from the Bahamas. In August 1990 National Security Minister Paul Adderley reported that whereas 12,306 pounds of cocaine had been seized in the first six months of 1988 and 10,261 pounds for January to June 1989, the figure for the same period in 1990 was merely 1,119 pounds. Seizure in international waters adjacent to the Bahamas for the same period in 1988 totalled 840 pounds. For 1989 it was 6,964 pounds, but there was a drop to 2,198 pounds for the first half of 1990. Adderley suggested that Mexico, Guatemala, Belize, Haiti, the U.S. Virgin Islands, and other countries are replacing the Bahamas as a major smuggling route from Colombia to the United States.

The drug problem is one with military, political, and economic dimensions. Its effect on the values of Caribbean societies is a major cause for alarm. Drug money has been used to finance the operations of political parties, and unbridled corruption has developed in some places. The observation by one commentator on the report of a 1986 inquiry in Trinidad has regionwide validity:

> The publication of the Scott Drug Report highlights a problem that threatens to undermine the sovereignty and security of the young nation. The Commission makes clear that the corruptive power of narcotics has, like a cancer, for some time been growing at the very entrails of the local community, hooking within the vice of drug abuse school children, teachers, and even a couple of Cabinet Ministers of the previous administration.[28]

Perhaps the most notorious case was in the Bahamas. Continuous allegations about high-level drug-related corruption involving the prime minister and other government officials prompted an official inquiry in 1983. In its 384-page report the Commission of Inquiry noted that widespread transshipment of drugs through the Bahamas had adversely affected almost all strata of the society. Several top officials were indicted. The commission noted several questionable practices by the prime minister and the fact that between 1977 and the time of its inquiry his expenditures and assets far exceeded his official income. Nevertheless, there was no firm evidence of his being on a drug payroll as alleged. The commission reported:

> We were also alarmed by the extent to which persons in the public service have been corrupted by the illegal trade. We have given our reasons later in this report for concluding that corruption existed at the upper and lower levels

of the Royal Bahamas Police Force and we have concluded that certain Immigration and Customs officers accepted bribes. We were particularly concerned to discover that those corrupting influences made their presence felt at the levels of Permanent Secretary and Minister. . . . In our opinion, the whole nation must accept some responsibility. Apathy and a weak public opinion have led to the present unhappy and undesirable state of affairs in the nation.[29]

The commission's report and the implementation of some of its recommendations have improved the picture in the Bahamas, but the drug problem still looms large there. In his March 1989 Statement of Explanation for the Bahamas to Congress — part of the foreign assistance certification procedure — President George Bush noted "while the Government of the Commonwealth of the Bahamas is more active in investigating allegations of corruption, we are concerned by reports that corruption still exists. Prime Minister Pindling and his ministers must forcefully address this issue." The statement also called for "stronger unilateral efforts to curb drug trafficking and consumption within the Bahamas."[30]

In August 1988 I had an extensive interview with Cuthbert Phillips, then police commissioner of St. Lucia, on security concerns in the Eastern Caribbean. The drug problem consumed much of our attention and the commissioner waxed eloquent in declaiming against the drug barons and those who aid them. Less than a month later Phillips was fired for being implicated in drug-related corruption and inefficiency in the Royal St. Lucia Police Force. Much of the drug corruption springs from greed and a dangerous acquisitive streak in parts of the Caribbean. However, some of it relates to the relative economic deprivation in parts of the region and the difficulty of some government officials to resist the temptation to earn easy money to supplement their meager incomes.

A former Antiguan diplomat highlighted some practical realities. Antigua is one of the more economically comfortable islands in the Eastern Caribbean. But the average monthly salary of a police officer there is US$456 whereas the police commissioner earns about US$2,000 a month. Junior customs officials get about US$365 per month, and senior officers, US$483. One could thus appreciate the susceptibility to bribery, considering that these officials could make four or five times their monthly income for facilitating one transaction. For example, the average pilot reportedly earns about US$5,000 per kilo for his services.[31]

The drug trade is now a billion-dollar international business, valued at about US$500 billion, and Caribbean countries are being drawn into it.

One recent example of how Caribbean countries are becoming implicated is sufficient to indicate the justifiable concern by Caribbean leaders.

A shipment of ten tons of arms with an estimated value of J$8 million arrived in Jamaica on December 22, 1988. It was to be airlifted later to Colombia. The shipment, from Heckler and Koch of West Germany, included 1,000 G3A3 automatic assault rifles, 250 HK21 machine guns, ten 60-millimeter commando mortars, and 600 rounds of high explosive 60-millimeter mortar shells. The planned transshipment involved West Germans, Englishmen, Panamanians, Colombians, and Jamaicans. Interrogation of the conspirators on January 4 and 5, 1989, revealed that the arms were destined for a leftist insurgent group called the Revolutionary Armed Forces of Colombia (FARC). The operation was underwritten by Colombian cocaine dealers who finance FARC. The arms were financed by an earlier special drug shipment to Europe.

The affair ended on January 6, 1989, when the arms were put on board a Colombian military aircraft and sent to Bogota. The foreigners were extradited and the Jamaicans were held on a variety of charges. This successful interdiction operation was the culmination of diligent work by the Jamaican police, defense force, and custom officials, in cooperation with private sector security officials. The Jamaican national security minister quite rightly said, "This incident once again illustrated the critical need for the highest vigilance on the part of our security forces."[32]

Several countries have found it necessary to introduce draconian legislation to deal with aspects of the problem. Among these are Jamaica, Trinidad and Tobago, St. Kitts, Guyana, St. Lucia, and St. Vincent. These laws generally impose stiff fines and terms of imprisonment for drug use and trafficking. They also provide for confiscating property acquired through drug trading and create or expand institutions to deal with different aspects of the problem. In Guyana, for example, the March 1988 Narcotic Drugs and Psychotropic Substances Act imposes heavy fines and prison terms, sanctions seizure of drug-acquired property, and allows bail for drug offenders only under special circumstances. In Barbados, the 1990 Drug Abuse (Prevention and Control) Act and the Proceeds of Crime Act establish similar stringent measures.[33]

Economic Dimension

The aspect of the region's security on which there is greatest elite image convergence is the economic. For most Caribbean leaders, the economic problems gripping their societies present the greatest security threat. The economic security dimension has both manifest and latent elements. Economic problems are seen as likely precipitants of later political and military challenges. Many leaders would endorse the position of the Prime Minister of St. Vincent and the Grenadines, James Mitchell:

Fundamentally, in my view, the sores of poverty in our region cannot be cured by military therapy. I lead a popular government and I need to deliver the goods. Opportunities for subversion will emerge when the people are frustrated again. It is the collapse of social institutions that creates avenues for international intrigues. If the people's expectations are not fulfilled through the channels that people like me create, we will, in due course, be inviting the colonels or the commissars. And the more arms we have available in the country, the greater will be the temptation to solve our problem with a coup.[34]

Economic vulnerability is a critical security dilemma for most small states.[35] The economic vulnerability of the Caribbean is an increasingly burning issue.[36] It is not merely a functional vulnerability. It is also a structural vulnerability where Caribbean economies suffer from, among other things, heavy reliance on foreign trade, limited production and export diversification, low savings, heavy reliance on foreign capital, and a dearth of capable economic and commercial management skills.

One respected Caribbean economist has characterized the region's economies as suffering from dependent underdevelopment.[37] And CARICOM, on which many hopes lay to mitigate the situation, has not fulfilled expectations. There are several reasons for this. First, the expansion of CARICOM trade has been frustrated by import restrictions, especially by the larger states, a situation occasioned by their adverse balance of payments situations. Moreover, CARICOM states have failed to agree on industrial allocation policies. This has stymied efforts at industrialization and economic diversification. Further, until the implementation of the Grande Anse Declaration signed at the 1989 summit in Grenada, the limited regional labor mobility will continue to affect the region adversely. In addition, regional trade expansion has been unable to generate the foreign exchange required for imports from hard currency areas.

A major problem is the high indebtedness of Caribbean countries. According to the Caribbean Development Bank, Jamaica's debt for 1988 was US$3,995 million; Trinidad and Tobago had US$1,328 million; and Guyana, US$893 million. In recent times St. Kitts has had the smallest figure, US$22 million.[38] Servicing the debts is a major headache because debt ratios run very high. In 1988 the ratio of Jamaica's debt service to exports was a dramatic 52 percent. The debts are not only a great economic burden, but in attempting to manage them, states run the risk of jeopardizing their internal security because of popular, labor, business, or other reaction. Both Guyana and Trinidad and Tobago found themselves in this situation in 1988 and 1989 with riots, strikes, public demonstrations, and arson and vandalism against public property costing millions of dollars.[39]

Former Prime Minister Edward Seaga of Jamaica has argued that the ability of the developing world to meet necessary welfare considerations while servicing their external debt requires real economic growth. Quite rightly, he feels that the priority should be to achieve sustainable economic growth in the medium term.[40] One can hardly challenge this proposition. But there seems to be a chicken and egg dilemma: can such countries strive for growth before seeking debt solutions, or should efforts be concentrated on debt crisis solutions at the expense of real growth? Both approaches have serious implications for economic and political stability. Firm decisions on these issues are difficult. Most leaders — especially those of Guyana, Jamaica, and Trinidad and Tobago — are working on half measures or on coping strategies in collaboration with regional and international bodies.[41]

INFLUENCES AND IMPLICATIONS

Elite perception is a function of several factors, some within a society and others in the political environment in which it exists. The educational levels of leaders, their previous political and professional experiences, their class relationships, their interpretation of history, and their beliefs about their nations and about their roles in them are all among the internal factors.[42]

With few exceptions, Caribbean leaders have all had tertiary-level training. The exceptions are Vere Bird, Sr., of Antigua and George Price of Belize. Bird was unable to go beyond high school. Price was forced by family exigencies to prematurely end his religious training at St. Augustine Seminary in Mississippi. Most leaders had their higher education in British or North American universities. The exceptions are Dr. Kennedy Simmonds of St. Kitts, who received his medical degree from the University of the West Indies (UWI), and Nicholas Braithwaite, who received his B.A. in education from UWI. Some have studied at both regional and foreign institutions. Sandiford of Barbados, for example, got his B.A. in English from UWI and his M.A. in Economics from Manchester University.

Caribbean leaders generally make a career of politics and act as though they are indispensable to the political survival of their nations. As such some of them tend to see little distinction between the security of their regimes and that of the nation. In some places, therefore, leaders seek to entrench themselves in power through fraudulent means. Grenada, under Eric Gairy, and Guyana are examples of this. Nevertheless, before entering politics, most of the current leaders had professions to which they can return if ousted from office or when they retire from politics. For example, Lynden Pindling of the Bahamas, Mary Charles of Dominica, Desmond Hoyte of Guyana, John Compton of St. Lucia, and A. N. R. Robinson of Trinidad and Tobago are lawyers. James Mitchell of St. Vincent is an agronomist, Kennedy Simmonds of St. Kitts is a medical doctor, and Erskine Sandiford of Barbados and Nicholas Braithwaite of Grenada are educators.

Vere Bird, Sr., and George Price apart, Caribbean leaders have middle-class origins. However, some of them, such as Maurice Bishop, Forbes Burnham, and Michael Manley, develop working-class sympathies and advocacy over the course of their political lives. They are more inclined than the others to interpret local and international issues using democratic socialist or Marxist conceptual lenses. While some socialist sentiment still exists under great disguise in Guyana and Jamaica, contemporary Caribbean leaders are essentially capitalist in ideological orientation and pragmatic in political strategies, a marked contrast to ten to fifteen years ago. They espouse social democratic principles and place premium on civil and political rights, such as freedoms of speech and association and free and fair elections. They endorse free enterprise and actively seek foreign investment.[43]

Caribbean states exist in a geopolitical milieu that makes them subordinate to the interests of more powerful states, such as the United States and Venezuela in the hemisphere, and to others elsewhere.[44] They accept that their power is inferior to that in the dominant state system and realize that changes in the dominant system have greater effect on them than the reverse. As such the international political environment has considerable impact on how leaders in the region define and interpret issues.

Much of the interplay between elites in subordinate and dominant states described generally by Paul Johnson is true for the Caribbean. Johnson talks about "ideological, cultural and other normative mechanisms of manipulation," explaining:

Essentially I am referring to those recurrent social processes whereby decision-making elites in subordinate states come to share the values, beliefs and attitudes of the elites in the hegemonic power, and hence are spontaneously disposed to identifying their own and their country's interests with those of the hegemon and to devise their own policies accordingly. These elites of subordinate states may be educated abroad, rely on foreign technical experts, read mass media dominated by imported wire service reports, attend movies imported from the hegemonic country, travel extensively there, associate with the foreign diplomatic community, adopt a foreign life-style, and so on.[45]

The perception profile offered above suggests that there is both image convergence and divergence in the Caribbean. This reflects similarities and differences among Caribbean elites as to the nature and intensity of threats. The greatest convergence lies in the economic area; the divergence is in the military and political ones. Political histories, present political and economic circumstances, and the nature of Caribbean leadership do not permit the definition of a single regional security perception.

Although Caribbean nations share several common historical, political, and other features, there are still strong definitions of national and subregional interests that often jar against what seem to be manifestly regional ones. Thus, for example, there is common recognition of military, political, and economic vulnerability, but there is divergence in perceptions regarding the source and intensity of threats. The Organization of Eastern Caribbean States (OECS) places a premium on drugs and potential threats from internal subversion and mercenary action. And they seem more disposed than the others to invite the United States to deal with actual and potential threats to their security. Jamaica worries justifiably about the political violence there, and, along with the Bahamas, it is finding the drug problem to be intractable. Guyana and Belize, the mainland states, have cause to worry about potential political, and possibly military, problems stemming from the Venezuelan and Guatemalan claims, as well as about drugs.[46]

Three related implications flow from this profile. First, although the disparities are not critical in all areas, they could necessitate the use of precious time and already scarce resources in attempting to narrow the range of differences. Second, because external security measures by these states individually hold few prospects for success, collaboration is important. However, collaboration needs consensus, if not unanimity, to be credible and successful. Divergences of the kind noted above can present obstacles to this.

Third, Caribbean states stand to create greater scope for others, such as the United States, Venezuela, and Cuba, to determine the nature and direction of events in the region. In such circumstances, they stand to lose the initiative and act by default, progressively being carried by the turn of events and the interests of other states, rather than by their own volition and in pursuit of their own interests.

Events related to the October 1983 Grenada intervention dramatize this last point. The failure of Caribbean leaders to adopt a decisive position at the emergency summit in Trinidad, coupled with the inclination of some leaders to facilitate extraregional initiatives, helped accommodate the pursuit of U.S. interests. The United States may have intervened regardless. But at least Caribbean leaders, by avoiding acts of omission and commission and a loss of initiative, could have prevented being facilitators.

The differences among the elites, however, are not conflicting enough to prevent the development of working consensus in crucial areas. Some of the security policies and strategies in recent times derive partly from these perceptions. Among them are the creation of the Regional Security System (RSS) in 1982; a strengthening of military and paramilitary establishments in Guyana and Jamaica over several years; and a repression of leftist parties and interest groups in Grenada, Dominica, and St. Lucia, particularly after 1983.

There have also been increased military purchases, assistance, and training from the United States by Jamaica and Eastern Caribbean countries following the Grenada intervention; a deemphasis on the military in Barbados following the Democratic Labor Party's return to power there in 1986; the formation of the Caribbean Democratic Union as a conservative ideological coalition in 1986; calls for regionwide participation in the RSS after the 1990 Trinidad coup attempt; and strengthening of security around Parliament in Barbados, Jamaica, and elsewhere in the region following the 1990 military-political crisis in Trinidad.

NOTES

1. Kenneth Boulding, "National Images and International Systems," in James N. Rosenau, ed., *International Politics and Foreign Policy* (New York: The Free Press, 1969), p. 423.

2. As far as I know, the only other recent work where perception is the central and not a peripheral concern is by Anthony Maingot. See his "Security Perspectives of Governing Elites in the English-Speaking Caribbean," *Essays on Strategy and Diplomacy No. 4,* The Keck Center for International Strategic Studies, 1985. Maingot looks at internal and external security. He points to the region's vulnerability, caused by both indigenous and exogenous factors. He finds that Caribbean leaders are

conscious of the geopolitics of the region that make them subject to U.S. dictates, but they do not accept the Caribbean as the United States' *mare nostrum*. Neither do they harbor false expectations about U.S. protective capabilities. Maingot examines the dynamics of Cuban-Caribbean relations, the development of the Adams Doctrine, and the sensitivity to security matters that has developed in parts of the region.

3. See Margaret Hermann, Charles Hermann, and Joe Hagan, "How Decision Units Shape Foreign Policy Behavior," in Charles Hermann et al., eds., *New Directions in the Study of Foreign Policy* (Boston: Allen and Unwin, 1987), esp. pp. 311–18. Also see Margaret Hermann and Charles Hermann, "Who Makes Foreign Policy Decisions and How: An Empirical Enquiry," *International Studies Quarterly* 33 (1989): 361–87.

4. For a discussion of Cabinet leadership see Stanley de Smith, *Constitutional and Administrative Law* (London: Penguin, 1977), pp. 144–75.

5. On the question of leadership in the Caribbean see Archie Singham, *The Hero and the Crowd in a Colonial Polity* (New Haven: Yale University Press, 1968); George Danns, "Leadership, Legitimacy, and the West Indian Experience," *Working Paper Series No. 1,* Institute of Development Studies, University of Guyana, 1978; and Percy Hintzen, "From Idealism to Pragmatism: The Evolution of Political Leadership in the Anglophone Caribbean," Paper presented at the 12th Annual Conference of the Caribbean Studies Association, Belize, May 1987.

6. See Marc Smyrl, *Conflict or Codetermination: Congress, the President, and the Power to Make War* (Cambridge, Mass.: Ballinger, 1988); Charles Kegley and Eugene Wittkopf, eds., *The Domestic Sources of American Foreign Policy* (New York: St. Martin's Press, 1988), pp. 1–11 and Chs. 8, 11; and Robert Art, "Congress and the Defense Budget: Enhancing Policy Oversight," *Political Science Quarterly* 100 (1985): 227–48.

7. The form of government in the Caribbean is parliamentary. Although Guyana has an executive presidential arrangement, and Dominica and Trinidad and Tobago have ceremonial presidents, there are modifications of parliamentary operations in all three. See Francis Alexis, *Changing Caribbean Constitutions* (Bridgetown, Barbados: Antilles Publishers, 1983), pp. 50–159; and Fred Phillips, *West Indian Constitutions: Post-Independence Reforms* (New York: Oceana Publications, 1985), esp. Chs. 1–7.

8. Lloyd Searwar, "Dominant Issues in the Role and Responses of the Caribbean Small State," Paper presented at Workshop on Peace, Development, and Security in the Caribbean Basin: Perspectives to the Year 2000, Kingston, Jamaica, March 1987, p. 4. A revised version of this paper appears as Chapter 1 of Anthony Bryan, J. E. Greene, and Timothy Shaw, eds., *Peace, Development, and Security in the Caribbean* (New York: St. Martin's Press, 1990).

9. Jacqueline Braveboy-Wagner, "Caribbean Foreign Policy," *Caribbean Affairs* 1 (1988): 86. She also adds a salutary note in recording her observation of a decrease in personalism and increased bureaucratic and interest group influence.

10. Margaret Hermann and Charles Hermann, "A Look Inside the 'Black Box': Building on a Decade of Research," in Gerald Hopple, ed., *Biopolitics, Political Psychology, and International Politics* (New York: St. Martin's Press, 1982), p. 4.

11. Basil Ince, "Leadership and Foreign Policy Decision Making in a Small State: Trinidad and Tobago's Decision to Enter the OAS," in Basil Ince et al., eds.,

Issues in Caribbean International Relations (Lanham: University Press of America, 1983).

12. David Vital, *The Survival of Small States* (London: Oxford University Press, 1971), p. 12.

13. A few states have different portfolios and individuals for external security (defense) and internal security (home affairs and national security). Two such states are Guyana with Home Affairs Minister Stella Odie-Ali and Jamaica with National Security Minister Keith Knight. Jamaica's defense minister is Prime Minister Manley. That of Guyana is President Hoyte.

14. The analysis that follows is based on interviews with people who make, influence, and implement decisions and on examination of speeches and writings of political elites. Interviews were held with Cameron James Tudor, Foreign Minister of Barbados (August 1987); Senator Harcourt Lewis, Minister of State, Office of the Prime Minister, Barbados (August 1987); Dr. Peter Laurie, Permanent Secretary, Ministry of Foreign Affairs, Barbados (July 1987; August 1988); Dr. Colin Hope, editor, *Caribbean Contact* (August 1987); Cuthbert Phillips, Commissioner of Police, St. Lucia (August 1988); Cmdr. Peter Tomlin, Staff Officer, Regional Security System (July 1988); Augustus Compton, Deputy Director-General, OECS (August 1988); Earl Huntley, Permanent Secretary, Ministry of Foreign Affairs, St. Lucia (August 1988); Lt. Cmdr. Godfrey Rolle of the Royal Bahamas Defense Force (November 1988); Thelma Ferguson, Deputy Permanent Secretary, Attorney General's Office, Bahamas (November 1988); and the Rev. Allan Kirton, Secretary General, Caribbean Conference of Churches (July 1987). Speeches and writings examined include John Compton, "Working Out a Time Table for the Future," Interview in *CARICOM Perspective* 38 (April–June 1987): 14–15; Mary Eugenia Charles, "Independence Day Message 1983"; "Isolation vs. One-ness," *Caribbean Affairs* 1 (1988): 150–54; Gary Brana-Shute, "An Eastern Caribbean Centrist: Interviewing Prime Minister James F. 'Son' Mitchell," *Caribbean Review* 14 (1985): 27–29; Cameron James Tudor, "General Statement at the 16th Regular Session of the General Assembly of the OAS, 1986," in Ministry of Foreign Affairs, Barbados, *Diplomacy and Development,* Bridgetown, 1987; Desmond Hoyte, "The Economy: The Diplomatic Effort," Address at Heads of Mission Conference, Georgetown, Guyana, July 11, 1986; "Reaching Out Boldly for Progress," Speech to the 7th Biennial Congress of the People's National Congress, Georgetown, Guyana, August 11, 1987; Rashleign Jackson, *Safeguarding the Security of Small States* (Georgetown, Guyana: Ministry of Foreign Affairs, 1982); James Mitchell, "Address at the Opening Ceremony of the 11th Meeting of the Authority of the OECS," British Virgin Islands, May 27, 1987; CARICOM Secretariat, *Communique 49/1987,* Castries, St. Lucia; Edward Seaga, "Toward Resolving the Debt Crisis," *Caribbean Review* 16 (Spring 1988): 3, 15.

15. See Linda Edwards-Romain, "Overt Racism in Trinidad and Tobago," *Caribbean Contact,* October 1987, pp. 1, 2; Lindsay Mackoon, "Trinidad and Tobago: The Fangs of Race Bared," *Caribbean Contact,* January 1988, p. 6; and Selwyn Ryan, "One Love Revisited: The Persistence of Race in the Politics of Trinidad and Tobago," *Caribbean Affairs* 1 (1988): 67–127.

16. See "A Transcript of Bush's Address on the Decision to Use Force in Panama," *New York Times,* December 21, 1989, p. A19; and Andrew Rosenthal, "U.S. Forces Gain Wide Control in Panama: New Leaders Put in but Noriega Gets Away," *New York Times,* December 21, 1989, pp. A1, A18.

17. See Chapter 2 of this volume; Tom Barry, Beth Wood, and Deb Preusch, *The Other Side of Paradise* (New York: Grove Press, 1984); and Jorge Rodriguez-Beruff, "Puerto Rico and U.S. Militarization," *Contemporary Marxism*, Issue 10, 1985, pp. 68–91.

18. For discussions of Cuban strategy and foreign policy in the Caribbean, see Anthony Maingot, "Cuba and the Commonwealth Caribbean: Playing the Cuba Card," in Barry Levine, ed., *The New Cuban Presence in the Caribbean* (Boulder: Westview Press, 1983); Jorge Dominguez, "Cuba's Relations with Caribbean and Central American Countries," in Alan Reiding and Reid Reading, eds., *Confrontation in the Caribbean Basin* (Pittsburgh, University of Pittsburgh Press, 1984); and Edward Gonzalez, "The Cuban and Soviet Challenge in the Caribbean Basin," *ORBIS*, Spring 1985, pp. 73–94.

19. See Ministry of Foreign Affairs, Guyana, *Memorandum on the Guyana/Venezuela Boundary* (Georgetown, 1981); Ivelaw L. Griffith, *On the Western Front* (Georgetown: Ministry of Information, 1981); Jacqueline Braveboy-Wagner, *The Venezuela-Guyana Border Dispute: Britain's Colonial Legacy in Latin America* (Boulder: Westview Press, 1984).

20. See Desmond Hoyte, "Good Neighbours," Address of the President to the Fourth Sitting of the First Session of the Second Supreme Congress of the People, Georgetown, Guyana, April 3, 1987.

21. See "Trinidad Rebels Threaten to Kill Premier and Other Hostages," *New York Times*, July 29, 1990, pp. L1, L14; David Pitt, "Muslim Rebels in Trinidad Free All Their Hostages and Surrender," *New York Times*, August 2, 1990, pp. A1, A8; Michael Roberts, "Terror in Trinidad," *New York Carib News*, August 7, 1990, p. 3; "Over 100 Muslimeen to Be Charged with Treason," *New York Carib News*, August 21, 1990, p. 3.

22. See Charles, "Isolationism vs. One-ness," pp. 153–54.

23. "Barbados Would Go Outside," *New York Carib News*, August 14, 1990, p. 27. The Trinidad authorities refused to invite Caribbean or other security assistance during the actual crisis but accepted military assistance from Caribbean countries afterward.

24. See Perry Mars, "Destabilization, Foreign Intervention, and Socialist Transformation in the Caribbean," *Transition*, Issue 7, 1983, pp. 33–54. Using a definition of the Caribbean to include Cuba, Mars also talks about the "Belligerent Opposition" approach used by that country.

25. See Mars, "Destabilization," p. 48.

26. See U.S. House of Representatives, *The English-Speaking Caribbean: Current Conditions and Implications for U.S. Policy*, Report by the Congressional Research Service for the Subcommittee on Western Hemisphere Affairs, Committee on Foreign Affairs, 99th Cong., 1st Sess., September 13, 1985, p. 96.

27. See "Sandiford Addresses Caribbean Coast Guards," *New York Carib News*, July 31, 1990, p. 36. Sandiford was at the time addressing participants of the Caribbean Maritime Training Assistance Program in Barbados in July 1990.

28. Frank Taylor, "Does Trinidad Have a Drug Problem?" *Caribbean Review* 15 (Spring 1987): 15.

29. *Report of Commission of Inquiry Appointed to Inquire into the Illegal Use of the Bahamas for the Transshipment of Dangerous Drugs Destined for the United States of America, November 1983–December 1984* (Nassau, Bahamas, 1984), p. 35.

30. "Statement of Explanation: The Bahamas," Appendix C of Raphael Perl, *International Narcotics Control: The President's March 1, 1989, Certification for Foreign Assistance Eligibility and Options for Congressional Action,* CRS Report for Congress 89-141F, April 7, 1989.

31. See Ron Sanders, "Narcotics, Corruption, and Development," *Caribbean Affairs* 3 (1990): 83.

32. "Text of a Statement Made at a Press Conference at Up Park Yesterday by the Minister of National Security Errol Anderson," in *The Sunday Gleaner,* January 8, 1989, p. 16B. See also "Arms Shipment: Traffickers, Terrorists Involved," *The Sunday Gleaner,* January 8, 1989, pp. 1, 13B. Another recent international incident with drug connections is the arms scandal involving Antigua, Israel, and Colombia. At the time of writing, this affair was under official investigation by Louis Blom Cooper, a British lawyer retained as a one-man Commission of Inquiry by the Antiguan government. See "Antigua Arms Scandal," *New York Carib News,* May 1, 1990, p. 4; Jeff Gerth, "Israeli Arms Diverted to Colombian Drug Traffickers," *New York Times,* May 6, 1990, pp. L1, L23; and Dennis Seon, "Arms Scandal Rocks Antigua Government," *New York Carib News,* May 22, 1990, p. 3.

33. See Oscar Ramjeet, "Concern over Drugs," *Caribbean Contact,* May 1988, p. 1; Michele Griffith, "Drug Legislation Hits Pushers Hard," *Guyana Chronicle,* May 30, 1989, pp. 4–5; and Ikael Tafari, "Barbados Draconian Drug Laws," *Caribbean Contact,* July/August 1990, p. 12.

34. See Brana-Shute, "Eastern Caribbean Centrist," p. 28.

35. See Commonwealth Study Group, *Vulnerability: Small States in the Global Society* (London: Commonwealth Secretariat, 1985), esp. pp. 16-35, 54-90; Sheila Harden, ed., *Small Is Dangerous* (New York: St. Martin's Press, 1985), pp. 7–13; Edward Azar and Chung-in Moon, "Third World National Security: Toward a New Conceptual Framework," *International Interactions* 11 (1984): 103–35.

36. See Compton Bourne, *Development Performance and Prospects in the Caribbean Community to the Year 2000,* Report prepared for CARICOM Secretariat, March 1988; William Demas, "Consolidating Our Independence: The Major Challenge for the West Indies," Distinguished Lecture, Institute of International Relations, St. Augustine, Trinidad, June 10, 1986; Carl Stone, "The Caribbean and the World Economy: Patterns of Insertion and Contemporary Options," in Jorge Heine and Leslie Manigat, eds., *The Caribbean and World Politics* (New York: Holmes and Meier, 1988).

37. See Demas, "Consolidating Our Independence," pp. 6–19.

38. Caribbean Development Bank, *Annual Report 1989* (Bridgetown, Barbados, 1990), p. 17.

39. See Lindsay Mackoon, "Strike Shuts Down T&T," *Caribbean Contact,* April 1989, p. 2; Courtney Gibson, "Guyana Devalues Dollar," *New York Carib News,* April 11, 1989, p. 3; Rickey Singh, "Guyana Strike Crippling," *New York Carib News,* April 24, 1989, p. 17; Bert Wilkinson, "Protest over Harsh Budget," *Caribbean Contact,* May 1989, p. 8.

40. See Seaga, "Toward Resolving the Debt Crisis," p. 3.

41. See Jerome McElroy and Klaus De Alburquerque, "Recent Debt and Adjustment Experiences in the OECS Countries of the Caribbean," *Caribbean Affairs* 3 (1990): 49–64; Roland Ely, "Guyana and the International Monetary Fund," Paper presented at the 15th Annual Conference of the Caribbean Studies

Association, Trinidad, May 1990; and Terrence Farrell, "Structural Adjustment and Transformation in the Caribbean: Management Strategies Based on the Lessons of Experience," in Bryan, Greene, and Shaw, *Peace, Development, and Security in the Caribbean*.

42. On this question see Robert Jervis, "Hypotheses on Misperception," in James Rosenau, *International Politics and Foreign Policy*, pp. 239–54; and the Introduction to Jervis, *The Logic of Images in International Relations* (Princeton: Princeton University Press, 1970).

43. For profiles of present leaders, see Harold Hoyte, "Erskine Sandiford: A Profile," *Caribbean Affairs* 1 (1988): 96–104; Raoul Pantin, "The Man from Castara, Tobago: A Moses Leading His People to the Promised Land?" *Caribbean Affairs* 1 (1988): 161–71; and Darrell Levi, *Michael Manley: The Making of a Leader* (London: Deutsch, 1989). Vere Bird, Sr., is profiled in "A Man for All Seasons," *The Caribbean and West Indian Chronicle*, October–November 1981, pp. 21ff. See also the relevant sections of Robert Alexander, ed., *Biographical Dictionary of Latin American and Caribbean Political Leaders* (New York: Greenwood, 1988). For biographies of other recent leaders see F. A. Hoyos, *Tom Adams: A Biography* (London: Macmillan, 1988); and Ken Boodhoo, ed., *Eric Williams: The Man and the Leader* (Lanham: University Press of America, 1986).

44. For excellent explorations of these linkages, see Leslie Manigat, "The Setting: Crisis, Ideology, and Geopolitics"; and Carl Stone, "The Caribbean and the World Economy: Patterns of Insertion," in Jorge Heine and Leslie Manigat, eds., *The Caribbean and World Politics* (New York: Holmes and Meier, 1988); Anthony Maingot, "The U.S. in the Caribbean: Geopolitics and the Bargaining Capacity of Small States"; and Anthony Bryan, "The Geopolitical Environment: Latin America," in Bryan, Greene, and Shaw, *Peace, Development, and Security in the Caribbean*.

45. Paul Johnson, "The Subordinate States and Their Strategies," in Jan Triska, ed., *Dominant Powers and Subordinate States: The United States in Latin America and the Soviet Union in Eastern Europe* (Durham: Duke University Press, 1986), p. 297.

46. These are the most prominent security concerns, but they are not the only ones. In the context of a wider redefinition of security, there is also concern about the environment. See, for example, Tony Best, Earl Bousquet, and Colin Hope, "Danger: Toxic Waste in the Caribbean," *Caribbean Contact*, May 1988, pp. 8–9; Desmond Hoyte, "Growth, Development, and the Environment in the Caribbean," *Caribbean Affairs* 4 (1989): 63–70; and *The Port-of-Spain Accord on the Management and Conservation of the Caribbean Environment*, Declaration of the First CARICOM Ministerial Conference on the Environment, Port-of-Spain, Trinidad and Tobago, May 31–June 2, 1989. For a broader conceptual redefinition of security see Azar and Moon, "Third World National Security"; and Jessica Tuchman Mathews, "Redefining Security," *Foreign Affairs* 68 (Spring 1989): 162–77.

2 Decolonization, Demilitarization, and Denuclearization in the Caribbean

Humberto García Muñiz

U.S. military presence in the insular Caribbean consists mainly of installations of varied sizes and purposes. Some installations serve several functions at the same time, linked to interlocking regional or global networks. U.S. and British imperial domination lies at the origin of this presence, which in 1989 comprised more than 50 installations in six countries — Antigua, Bahamas, Bermuda, Cuba, Puerto Rico, and the U.S. Virgin Islands — with the total of more than 5,000 military personnel.[1] In Puerto Rico, a U.S. colony with limited self-government under the Commonwealth arrangement adopted in 1952, is ensconced the most important U.S. base hub in the region (headed by the Roosevelt Roads Navy base), with half of the U.S. military personnel in the Caribbean. Guantanamo is the oldest U.S. overseas base, a vestige of Cuba's semicolonial relationship with the United States and the only country in the Western Hemisphere with both U.S. and Soviet installations.[2] The other facilities, located in Antigua, Bahamas, and Bermuda, are the legacy of British acquiescence to U.S. military control of the Anglophone Caribbean subregion since the early 1990s, leading to a presence from World War II onward.

In reviewing the literature on U.S. military and security themes in the Caribbean, one finds that no comprehensive research has been conducted on U.S. military installations in the Caribbean.[3] Moreover, as a result of the unfortunate fragmentation of the study of the Caribbean, these studies analyzed mainly isolated insular experiences, one aspect of their role — in conventional or nuclear warfare — and rarely referred to the historical regional environment and consequences of the insular communities of their establishment, transformation, and eventual disappearance.[4] Only lately has the internal security role of these installations been emphasized.[5]

The purpose of this chapter is to describe and analyze the scope of U.S. installation structure in the Caribbean, their position within the U.S. military command arrangement, and their roles in conventional and nuclear warfare as well as for internal security and intervention. A short historical overview on the origins and evolution of the installations is provided; their social, economic and political impact to individual islands is succinctly studied. Although installations in all islands are analyzed, Puerto Rico is discussed in greater detail because the U.S. military presence is deeper and more complex there than elsewhere in the Caribbean. The presence of U.S. military installations carries great weight in the current discussions on status change in Puerto Rico, and their future is of large consequence for a truly decolonized, demilitarized, and denuclearized Caribbean.

HISTORICAL BACKGROUND

The United States began to build its overseas empire late in the nineteenth century, after it completed and consolidated its land expansion to the west and the south, mainly at the expense of Mexico, and to the north with the purchase of Alaska. As a result of the Spanish American War of 1898, the United States acquired its first Caribbean colony, Puerto Rico, and established a naval base in Guantanamo, Cuba, the outcome of the Platt Amendment forced upon a very reluctant Cuban Constitutional Convention. Apprehensive of German moves, the United States purchased the Danish Virgin Islands (St. Thomas, St. Croix, and St. John) in 1917. U.S. control of the Panama Canal Zone since 1900, which in the first instance sparked the acquisitions of all these islands, enhanced their strategic-military value.[6]

In the World War II period, Guantanamo served as the winter home for maneuvers and training exercises for the Atlantic Fleet and Marine Corps and as a base for the Ninth Marines, ready for deployment to the Panama Canal Zone in the event of a crisis. Guantanamo played an important role in the militarization of Caribbean politics: "In fact, the station's most important function during those years, in terms of carrying out U.S. policy, may have been its training and sending of Marines to pacify Haiti in 1915 and the Dominican Republic the following year."[7] One result of U.S. military occupation of Haiti (1915–1934), the

Dominican Republic (1916–1924), and later in Nicaragua (1927–1932) was the same from earlier U.S. military interventions in Puerto Rico, Cuba, and Panama: local security forces, established by the U.S. military, subservient to U.S. interests. The interventionist role of U.S. military installations in the Caribbean was present from their inception.

During World War II, for all practical purposes, the Caribbean fell under the occupation of U.S. armed forces. U.S. goals were defensive: to prevent the enemy from possessing any island or territory from which the Panama Canal, the continental United States, or the sea lanes could be attacked. Old military installations in Cuba, Puerto Rico, and St. Thomas were upgraded. Of the new ones constructed, Roosevelt Roads was the most important. Under the Destroyer-Base Agreement of September 2, 1940, Great Britain gave the United States the right to lease naval and air sites in Newfoundland, Antigua, Bahamas, Bermuda, British Guiana (now Guyana), Jamaica, St. Lucia, and Trinidad and Tobago for 99 years, in return for 50 old destroyers. Bermuda's legislative body, composed of the dominant white proprietary class, was able to change the original location of the bases, but in Trinidad the colonial governor was unsuccessful in his efforts. In most of these British colonies, several installations were built. U.S. military presence was felt also in Barbados (an airfield), in Tobago (a small garrison), in Anguilla (an emergency landing field), and Redonda (as bombing target).[8] In addition, U.S. military personnel were stationed in the Dutch colonies of Aruba, Curaçao, and Surinam as well as in the Dominican Republic, Haiti, and French Guiana. The Caribbean became a truly militarized "American Mediterranean."

The building of bases resulted in uprooting communities: the Culebra and Vieques Islands (both off the east coast of Puerto Rico) and in Aguadilla (in the northwestern end of Puerto Rico); in St. David's Island in the Bahamas; and Chaguaramas, in Trinidad and Tobago.[9] In 1941 the U.S. Navy expropriated 26,000 out of the 33,000 acres of land in Vieques, 76 percent of the island's land area. As the short-lived economic boom from military construction faded and the sugar-based economy finally died, Vieques was in a most desperate situation: "The richest and most fertile lands were expropriated by the Navy. . . . Families lost their houses, cows, horses and farmland and had to make good with a makeshift roof, a handful of money. . . . Those with subsistence plots or who lived in the property of others . . . lacked even air to breathe."[10] Pedro Juan Soto's novel, *Usmaíl*, dwells on the human tragedy of this uprooting whereas V. S. Naipaul's *Miguel Street* touches upon the negative influence of U.S. military presence in the lives of several street dwellers in the Trinidad capital, Port-of-Spain.

Immediately after the war, the relocation of the entire population of Vieques to St. Croix was discussed within U.S. government circles and presented to the Puerto Rican colonial government, but no official action was taken. In time, however, migration from Culebra and Vieques to St. Croix accelerated, changing the social, racial, ethnic, and linguistic configuration of this island as well as the political scenario of the U.S. Virgin Islands.[11] The U.S. military, which took over 10 percent of already land-scarce Bermuda, "tore at the very historic fiber" of the island, immediately destroying life as it was in the community of St. David's Island.[12]

Race relations were the most salient social aspect of the U.S. military presence in the Caribbean. The introduction of black soldiers from the United States caused the discontent of the white propertied classes in Trinidad and Tobago. They were still displeased when the blacks were replaced by Puerto Ricans. The U.S. brand of racism, different from the British, proved to be disturbing throughout the Anglophone Caribbean even though a preview had been shown in the Eastern Caribbean by the U.S. Navy's administration of the U.S. Virgin Islands from 1917 to 1931. Segregationist practices were imposed on U.S. Virgin Islanders as well as on Puerto Ricans in the U.S. armed forces.[13] By the end of the war, Puerto Rican soldiers constituted more than half of the U.S. military forces guarding the Caribbean.

With the end of the German submarine attacks in late 1943, the war moved away from the Caribbean. After the war the U.S. military was rapidly demobilized. Of the U.S. military installations in the Caribbean, only Guantanamo in Cuba, several bases in Puerto Rico, Chaguaramas in Trinidad, and the facilities in Bermuda remained active; all very much downgraded. Even before World War II ended, Roosevelt Roads had lost its importance. In 1945 it was on maintenance status. In the years prior to 1957 the base closed and opened several times. In 1957, due to "its crucial location and the rapid changes in naval weaponry," Roosevelt Roads became the hub for the Atlantic Fleet's guided missile operations.[14] In 1959 Camp García was officially activated in Vieques by the Marine Corps as a training base for the Atlantic Fleet Marine Force. The revival of Roosevelt Roads was part of a global expansion of the U.S. base system following the Communist attack in Korea and was given its greater impetus by that attack.

Of the 87,000 acres of land the United States leased during the war in the Anglophone Caribbean, it was using about 17,000 acres in 1950 and would eventually retain only about 10,000. In the early 1950s the emergence of new technologies led to overseas installations in the British Caribbean of a totally different character from the ones of 1941.[15] Four missile tracking stations were built in the Bahamas and one each in Turks and Caicos Islands, Antigua, St. Lucia, and Trinidad. Agreements were also signed with the Dominican Republic, but no installation was ever built. Oceanographic research stations were built in Barbados and Turks and Caicos Islands. In 1961 a new agreement superseding the previous ones with Great Britain was signed between the United States and the Federation of the West Indies. It involved Antigua, Barbados, Jamaica, St. Lucia, Trinidad and Tobago, and Turks and Caicos Islands. Termination was set for 1977.

As Guyana and Bermuda had not been part of the Federation of the West Indies, the United States was adamant in its efforts to treat them separately from the others. Of U.S. installations in Guyana, Atkinson Field (now known as Timehri Airport) became the country's major international airport; Makouria/Essequibo was evacuated in 1944. In view of the limited need for Atkinson Field, and bending to the wishes of the administration of Forbes Burnham that was taking Guyana to independence in May 1966, the United States relinquished its rights to the leased areas. But probably fearful of Cheddi Jagan's return to power, it retained a right to use Atkinson Field for at least 17 years. U.S. installations remained in Bermuda under the original 1941 lease until 1978, when an updated agreement provided for base rights until 2040.

The largest base in the Anglophone Caribbean, Chaguaramas in Trinidad and Tobago, was the only installation remaining on the originally leased lands. In the late 1950s the selection of Chaguaramas as the most suitable site for the capital of the federation was an issue that immensely complicated the fledgling integrationist movement. Suffice it to say here that the United States refused to close or relocate the base, even after a strong campaign by then Premier Eric Williams, who eventually compromised in exchange for U.S. economic assistance and the agreement by the United States to review the base status after 17 years. The immediate political effect was the division of the nationalist movement in Trinidad and Tobago and reinforcing the conflicts in the top leadership of the federation, a factor contributing to its demise in 1962.

Dr. Williams challenged the United States by criticizing the legality of the lease and of various operations in Chaguaramas, such as commercial cultivation at an agricultural plantation, importation of commodities, and sale of surplus material.[16] In the end he himself was trapped as the local conservative political opposition attacked his stance and the United States was intransigent in light of the Cuban Revolution and Cheddi Jagan's ascension to power in Guyana. Chaguaramas was dismantled in 1967, but a small facility, which turned out to be a VLF Omega station for the navigation and positioning of nuclear submarines to aid their precise targeting, remained until the late 1970s when it was quietly phased out.[17]

In the early 1960s the United States did not expand its installations structure in the Caribbean. No new installations were constructed, even though Jamaican Prime Minister Alexander Bustamante and Haitian President François Duvalier offered their territories for the establishment of installations. In both cases the United States had no interest, although a training mission comprised of men from the U.S. Marine Corps, Navy, and Coast Guard went to Haiti in January 1959 and a military assistance agreement was signed with Jamaica in 1963.[18]

The facilities in Jamaica, St. Lucia, and Turks and Caicos Islands were eventually closed because of technological obsolescence. The Turks and Caicos lost an annual lease of $800,000, some 10 percent of its budget. After bitter negotiations, the United States closed its naval facility in Barbados in early 1979; it was unwilling to pay the quid pro quo that Barbados was asking. As a result, the U.S. Navy laid cables out of St. Croix and St. Thomas to replace some of the capacity lost in its underwater activities.

In 1977 Antigua negotiated with the United States an 11-year agreement to be in force up to December 31, 1988, with an annual rent of $1.2 million. In 1980 $20,000 was added for the Voice of America relay transmitter. In 1984 Bahamas and the United States concluded a ten-year, $100-million agreement for the lease of the U.S. facilities in the island chain. Securing this agreement led the United States to downplay (even pressuring to stop the investigations) the complicity of high Bahamian government officials in the transshipment of drugs to the United States.[19] Even though "the relations of friendship" between the United States and Cuba that served as the basis for the treaty of 1934 are obviously nonexistent, the treaty did not set a date for the closing of Guantanamo, but only provided that it could not be altered or abrogated without the agreement of both parties.

In sum, with the exception of Cuba, most U.S. military installations in the Caribbean had their origin in World War II and their role was defensive. By the 1950s the facilities in the Anglophone Caribbean had been dismantled, and new ones were built in other sites, with new functions, under new agreements. U.S. installations in Cuba and Puerto Rico retained their interventionist role in the region. The emergence of nuclear and space technology added an offensive dimension to the defensive role played by most installations in the Caribbean. Their reactivation was a consequence of the Cold War.

THE BATTLE FOR THE CARIBBEAN: LANTCOM VS. SOUTHCOM

U.S. installations in the Caribbean are part of the U.S. Atlantic Command's (LANTCOM) area of responsibility. LANTCOM is a unified command established in 1947, headquartered in Norfolk, Virginia, and controlled by the U.S. Navy. It has area responsibility for all joint U.S. military actions in the Atlantic Ocean from the North Pole to the South Pole. Included in these 45 million square miles of ocean are the Caribbean Sea; the Norwegian, Greenland, and Barents Seas; the waters around Africa extending to the Cape of Good Hope; and the Pacific Ocean west of Central America (extending to 92 degrees west longitude). LANTCOM has elements assigned from all three services: Army Forces Atlantic, Air Forces Atlantic, and the Atlantic Fleet, by far the largest component with 312 active and reserve ships, 1,100 aircraft, 29 fleet ballistic missile submarines, and more than a quarter million personnel.[20]

To manage its area of responsibility, LANTCOM is organized into four subunified commands: the Iceland Defence Force; U.S. Forces, Azores; U.S. Forces, Caribbean; and the Special Operations Command, Atlantic. The last two are of direct concern to the Caribbean. U.S. Forces, Caribbean (previously known as the Antilles Defence Department), has its headquarters in Key West, Florida, and is responsible for the conduct of joint and combined exercises in the Caribbean Basin and with the implementation of the security assistance program for countries in the Caribbean area, including the Dominican Republic, Haiti, Jamaica, Trinidad and Tobago, and the states of the Regional Security System (RSS) in the Eastern Caribbean — Antigua-Barbuda, Barbados, Dominica, Grenada, St. Kitts-Nevis, St. Lucia, and St. Vincent and the Grenadines. By the end of 1989, U.S. Forces, Caribbean, was to be disestablished. LANTCOM will assume its responsibilities, with the coordination of military operations falling to headquarters in Norfolk as it was before 1980.[21]

From 1978 to 1988 navy personnel in U.S. Forces, Caribbean, averaged 80 percent of an active military force, fluctuating between 7,000 and 8,000.[22] LANTCOM, which bypassed U.S. Forces, Caribbean, in the execution of the Grenada invasion in 1983, accelerated a massive (by Caribbean standards) U.S. military assistance program to the Caribbean since that first U.S. military intervention in the English-speaking subregion:

> Essential to the defense programs of the Caribbean island nations, more than $130 million has been expended over the past five years for equipment, supplies and training for regional security forces. This relatively small investment has enabled the *military and paramilitary forces* of 12 Caribbean nations to make vast improvements in their readiness and has assisted some nations in *establishing defense programs where none existed before.*[23]

LANTCOM's military strategy — a forward strategy to support NATO northern flank and to ensure the Atlantic sea lines of communication (SLOCs) — views the Caribbean as extremely important to the flow of supplies and military equipment for the reinforcement and resupply of forces in Europe. U.S. military literature is particularly sensitive to the role of Cuba, because of its strategic position and alleged military capabilities, in interdicting U.S. shipping lines of supply.[24]

With headquarters at Quarry Heights, Panama, the Southern Command (SOUTHCOM) is responsible for the defense of the Panama Canal and for coordinating military activities in South and Central American countries (U.S. troops are concentrated in Panama and Honduras). Under the terms of the Panama Canal Treaties of 1977, Army-dominated SOUTHCOM will be leaving its facilities in 1999 as the responsibility for the operation and security of the canal are turned over to the Panamanian government. Because of the unpopularity of SOUTHCOM, a new agreement for maintaining U.S. facilities in Panama is not probable but within the realm of the possible, depending on the political outcome of the present crisis. In the early 1970s, recognizing the singularity of the "political military nature" of SOUTHCOM's mission, it was stated that "UNCINCSOUTH encompasses a military posture *unlike* those of other unified Commanders. In administering the Military Assistance Programs, USSOUTHCOM helps to safeguard the *internal security* of the Latin American countries."[25]

Over the last years a discussion within U.S. politico-military circles on an adequate military command structure has been very much alive. Unsuccessful calls have been made to include the whole Caribbean Basin within SOUTHCOM.[26] At present it seems that the potential for conflict in Europe is receding, and there is less concern for the Caribbean SLOCs needed to resupply that theater. The strategic value of the Panama Canal has diminished because of its vulnerability to missile attacks.[27] U.S. military (mainly the army) interest is centered in the Caribbean Basin, and Cuba is perceived as being the "lion's share of the threat." However, in view of the predominance of the navy within the U.S. armed services, it is difficult to see the army winning the "battle" for the Caribbean.[28]

INTERNAL SECURITY IN THE CARIBBEAN

The division between LANTCOM's Caribbean and SOUTHCOM's Central America is not watertight. In 1984, Alvaro Magaña, interim president of El Salvador, casually revealed that in Roosevelt Roads a police school established by the Federal Bureau of Investigation (FBI) had, for two years, been offering monthly courses to attendees from El Salvador, the Dominican Republic, Costa Rica, Honduras, and Puerto Rico.[29] It can be expected that installations in the Caribbean will have a wider internal security role in any joint Central American and Caribbean military command arrangement.

Examples of cooperation between the internal security apparatus and military installations in Puerto Rico abound. The FBI's most notorious activity has been its failure to aggressively investigate before, during, and after (still not accounted for) the murder by Puerto Rican intelligence police of two *independentistas* in Cerro Maravilla in 1978. The FBI worked with one of the protagonists of that crime, Alejandro González Malavé, together with the Naval Investigative Services of Roosevelt Roads, in several task forces between 1978 and 1983.[30] An FBI-Roosevelt Roads link was again in evidence when 11 alleged members of the pro-independence group, *Macheteros,* were taken in 1985 to the base on U.S. Navy helicopters for their extradition flight to Connecticut. It was unusual, but not unexpected in view of this link, that one of the accused, Filiberto Ojeda, was imprisoned at the base in September 1988 for new charges related to his arrest in 1985.[31]

FBI operations in the Caribbean are not restricted to Puerto Rico. For example, in April 1966, an FBI report from the Dominican Republic disclosed that Juan Bosch was thinking of declining the presidential candidacy of his party to support Francisco Caamaño, the rebel military leader of the *constitucionalista* forces during the 1965 crisis. Bosch was reported as saying at that time that "neither the United States Government nor the Dominican Armed Forces . . . will ever accept him as President."[32]

Following the 1979 New Jewel coup in Grenada, annual exercises in the Camp Santiago training base have been held between the U.S. National Guard in Puerto Rico and military forces from the Dominican Republic, Jamaica, and Barbados.[33] The role of Camp Santiago as a training facility seems to have expanded since 1985 when the School of the Americas in Panama was moved to Fort Benning in Georgia. Even though there was a tripartite call against sending the National Guard to Central America, Governor Rafael Hernandez Colon displayed his accustomed subservience toward U.S. foreign policy initiatives, particularly its military and defense manifestations, by offering spiritless criticisms at the last minute.

Internal security in the Anglophone Caribbean has been a top priority of the United States in recent years. The dismantling of the naval facility in Antigua was imminent, but in June 1983 the Secretary of Defense directed the U.S. Navy to continue leasing the base from Antigua pending the result of a study into the potential military value of the base to the United States. In 1985 it was announced that a training center for the security forces of the Eastern Caribbean was to be established at this naval installation at a cost of $11 million.[34] The recently U.S. promoted Special Service Units (SSU) are the core of the RSS in the Eastern Caribbean, and its "training scheme puts more emphasis than ever on internal security."[35] The creation of the SSU was a subterfuge to circumvent the congressional prohibition of training foreign police while simultaneously continuing its bilateral relations with the force of each island, making the security component of the Organization of Eastern Caribbean States (OECS) a dead letter.

Together with the RSS, the Jamaican Defence Force under the Seaga administration was reared to act as surrogates for the United States in the subregion. Most of the training of these security forces has been conducted by the Special Operations Command, Atlantic, with headquarters in Fort Bragg, North Carolina. The training takes place regularly. Exercise "Tradewinds," held for nearly 40 days during May and June 1989, for the third straight year, involved the defense forces of Jamaica, the Bahamas, and Trinidad and Tobago, the RSS members, the United States, and Great Britain in a combined military training operation allegedly aimed at promoting drug interdiction capability. Playing an active part in the exercise were two U.S. installations in Puerto Rico: Roosevelt Roads and Camp Santiago.[36]

CONVENTIONAL/NUCLEAR SCENARIOS

U.S. installations in the Caribbean have assigned roles in U.S. conventional/nuclear warfare plans as well as in internal security functions. In this regard, the value of Roosevelt Roads is multidimensional. In 1984 Naval Forces, Caribbean (NFC), which has authority over all naval activities in the Caribbean, was the major command at

Roosevelt Roads. NFC, a naval command of LANTCOM, is under the operational command of the Atlantic Fleet (with headquarters in Norfolk, Virginia). Fleet Air Caribbean (FAIR), headquartered at Roosevelt Roads, is a subordinate command of Naval Air Forces, U.S. Atlantic Fleet, with its headquarters at Naval Air Station, Cecil Field, Florida, which exercises command over aircraft and aircraft operations in the Caribbean. FAIR also exercises command over the Atlantic Fleet Weapons Training Facility (AFWTF), which has its control center in Roosevelt Roads and embraces Vieques and the U.S. Virgin Islands. AFWTF has been described as "irreplaceable" by the U.S. Navy as it provides for the evaluation of new weapons systems, personnel training, and integrated training operations so necessary for fleet readiness.[37] Also Roosevelt Roads is the coordinating center for four annual exercises, of which Operation Springboard (the U.S. Navy's Caribbean wartime maneuver) and Operation Readex (an exercise to train and test participating units in weapons systems) are the most important.[38]

To complete the picture on Roosevelt Roads, the deployment of nuclear weapons to the base must be considered. In a detailed 1984 study, William Arkin, noting that the United States does not store nuclear weapons in Puerto Rico, concluded that "(t)here is evidence of the U.S. intention to bring nuclear weapons into Puerto Rico in a crisis or during wartime."[39] In case of the destruction of U.S. bases in the mainland, Roosevelt Roads has been designated as an alternate command center for missile submarines in the Atlantic. In his analysis of the nuclear infrastructure established in Roosevelt Roads and other areas of the island, Arkin indicates that U.S. military policy violated the proscription of nuclear weapons in Latin America and the Caribbean by the Treaty of Tlatelolco, to which the United States is a signatory.

The violation is in four areas: in preparations and plans for the command and control of nuclear missile carrying submarines from Roosevelt Roads; in plans to activate a base for nuclear antisubmarine weapons at Roosevelt Roads (and at Key West, Florida) to carry out nuclear antisubmarine warfare (ASW) operations in the Caribbean; in training with and testing nuclear weapon systems within Puerto Rico and elsewhere in the Caribbean; and in command and communications of nuclear weapons from facilities in Puerto Rico and the Caribbean. In 1985 Arkin also made public a document, "Nuclear Weapons Deployment Plans," that delineated U.S. contingency plans to deploy nuclear weapons in Canada, Iceland, Bermuda, and Puerto Rico.[40]

Five communications facilities in Puerto Rico have a function related to a nuclear weapons program, in some cases in addition to their normal role. The U.S. military has three main long-range communications stations in Puerto Rico: the low frequency (LF) transmitter at Aguada, the high frequency (HF) transmitter at Isabela, and the HF receiver at Sabana Seca (used also for intelligence collection). The transmitter in Aguada, one of about 20 communication facilities in the world that back up six major very low frequency (VLF) transmitters, is a primary means of communication from land to submerged submarines and, with the transmitters at Isabela, would be the principal means in Puerto Rico to communicate with submarines and ships.[41] The Arkin report identified two previously unknown facilities, the "Mystic Star" transmitter at Fort Allen and receiver at Salinas, which, as part of the U.S. president's special communications network, is used for communications with airborne command posts, including the National Emergency Command Post and the LANTCOM's airborne center, both of which would send orders to launch nuclear weapons. This nuclear infrastructure, comprising various installations with different functions, is placed in Puerto Rico as a result of one of the basic tenets of the Commonwealth arrangement, "common defense." In the words of Raymond Carr, the result is "the *possibility* of nuclear attack on Puerto Rico."[42]

In conventional terms, Roosevelt Roads is seen as crucial in providing necessary port, airfield, and logistics facilities for supporting fleet and naval operations in Atlantic area contingencies, in the protection of the SLOCs from the United States to Latin America, and in facilitating force projection to South America and Africa. It has played an important role in U.S. interventions in Central America and the Caribbean, such as in Guatemala in 1954, in the Dominican Republic in 1965, and in the final rehearsal of the invasion of Grenada, which took place in Vieques (code named Universal Trek I-83) just four months before that poorly executed military operation.[43] During the Grenada invasion, Tactical Air Command F-15s were positioned in Roosevelt Roads "to provide surveillance and defense against possible interference by Cuban Forces."[44]

As in other Caribbean communities, the U.S. Army presence in Puerto Rico is extremely modest. In addition to Camp Santiago (which falls under the U.S. National Guard), its only other installation is Fort Buchanan, located in the south shore of San Juan Bay and today almost entirely surrounded by the San Juan metropolitan area. Its role is purely internal in that it provides some administrative, logistical, and training support and supervision to the U.S. National Guard in Puerto Rico, the Reserve, and the ROTC; conducts some Army intelligence activities; provides commissary and exchange benefits to retired personnel and their dependents as well as to veterans; and coordinates the recruitment program of the U.S. armed forces in Puerto Rico. The necessity for this installation is evaluated from time to time, and its retention is partly due to the large outcry in its favor by the Puerto Rican military-related community (about 100,000). The U.S. military itself is reluctant to close it because its strategic location in the metropolitan area of San Juan is seen as a deterrent "to any aggressive action or civil disorder from the enemies of government" and perfect for mobilization purposes "in case of sabotage, subversive actions, and open aggressions by anti-government groups in the San Juan area."[45]

Located in the southeast tip of Cuba and recognized as the best deep-water port in the Caribbean, Guantanamo naval base dominates the Windward Passage, the principal channel for traffic between the Panama Canal, the posts of South America, and the U.S. east coast. The base, operated by the U.S. Navy, has port and logistics facilities to support recurring naval operations and for naval task force deployments during contingencies. There are two operational airstrips used primarily for training naval and marine pilots. These are capable of supporting additional fleet and ASW patrol aircraft during a contingency. In sum, Guantanamo can serve to give protection to the SLOCs and as a support base for training, sea surveillance, and regional contingency operations.

Guantanamo never really expanded as an important base because of its proximity to the United States. After the Cuban Revolution it declined further until the 1980s when it underwent some upgrading and expansion, but its vulnerability has hindered its development. From Cuba's side, Guantanamo is seen as a very real threat to national security as well as a "permanent center of irritation and provocation."[46]

The remaining facilities in Antigua, Bahamas, and Bermuda are smaller, mainly linked to the U.S. nuclear infrastructure, with functions related to ASW, surveillance, communications, and testing. Antigua is the only place in the Anglophone subregion with U.S. installations with an internal security role. These are the naval facility — now transformed training center — and a relay transmitter of the Voice of America (VOA) to broadcast in medium wave or AM to the Eastern Caribbean. It is said to be the hub of the CIA communications network for the Eastern Caribbean. Regarding its role in U.S. nuclear infrastructure, Antigua plays a key role in strategic submarine missile testing programs. The United States operates an AN-FPQ-15 tracking radar that doubles as satellite tracking station, an optional station, a telemetry collection station, and timing and weather system supporting missile testing from the Eastern Space and Missile Center (ESMC), with headquarters in Air

Force Base, Patrick, Florida. Also supporting missile tests from ESMC is Missile Impact Location System (MILS), an underwater hydrophone target array, located northeast of the island. The facility also has a satellite communications link to Cape Canaveral in Florida.

Andros Island in the Bahamas is the major shore facility for a complex of deep underwater facilities known as the Atlantic Underwater Test and Evaluation Center (AUTEC). AUTEC is the only permanent underwater noise measuring facility on the U.S. east coast. It is used for Trident submarine certification trials, for ASW training, and certification of mobile targets. AUTEC is one of a global network of installations for submarine detection and tracking of the Sound Surveillance System (SOSUS).[47] Data from these facilities are first transmitted to associated shore facilities, known as Naval Facilities (NavFacs), and then by satellite to the Acoustic Research Center at Moffett Field, California. SOSUS was described by one U.S. admiral as "the backbone of ASW detection capability."[48] Its value has since declined with the introduction of very long-range missiles in the Soviet submarines that now operate in the seas near the Asian continent. Most installations in the Bahamas are located in Grand Bahama Island. They are a tracking radar, a telemetry collection station, a command and control station, and timing and weather systems supporting missile tests from ESCM. In sum, the Bahamas host valuable U.S. facilities, which play a key role in submarine training, testing, and certification, as well as supporting strategic missile testing from ESMC.

Described as "strategically sensitive and classified," U.S. naval activities in Bermuda are seen as "a strong thread in NATO's defense fabric."[49] To protect the North Atlantic sea route, the United States operates three naval facilities in Bermuda: U.S. Naval Air Station (NAS), Kindley, Bermuda; a smaller NAS Annex; and Tudor Hill Laboratory. The navy uses the NAS as a regular deployment airfield for nuclear-capable P-3 Orion ASW operations. Its command facilities include an ASW Operations Center, and it has a NASA tracking radar and command and control station supporting missile testing from ESMC. It has been designated deployment base for nuclear depths-bombs in Advanced Underwater Weapons Detachment in wartime and its marine barracks has a nuclear weapons security role. During peace-time no nuclear weapons are stored in Bermuda, but for advanced readiness of ASW operations, authorization has been given for the deployment of 32 nuclear depths-bombs. The NAS Annex is a processing station for SOSUS, and Tudor Hill laboratory is part of the acoustic research programs under the Naval Underwater Systems (with headquarters in Newport, Rhode Island, a major laboratory in New London, Connecticut, and other major detachments in West Palm Beach, Florida, and the Bahamas).[50]

In sum, the multidimensional role of Roosevelt Roads, together with the other installations on the island, make Puerto Rico the center of U.S. military presence in the Caribbean. Puerto Rico is the major naval staging base for conducting training, fleet deployments to the region, and testing weapons systems as well as providing port, airfield, and logistics facilities for supporting fleet naval operations during contingencies. It also has a nuclear weapons related infrastructure ready to be activated in time of crisis, including a number of communications facilities in different parts of the island. Roosevelt Roads has been used for internal security purposes in Puerto Rico and as a training ground of security forces from Central America and the Caribbean as well as for intervention in these same regions.

At present U.S. military installations in the independent states of Antigua, Bahamas, and the self-governing colony of Bermuda deal mainly with training, research and development, intelligence, surveillance and detection systems, long-range communications, submarine monitoring, and missile-testing technology related to nuclear functions or to regional and world networks. With the exception of Bermuda, all other U.S. installations in the Anglophone Caribbean are in member states of the Caribbean Community and Common Market (CARICOM). Considering the value of these installations for the U.S. nuclear weapons program, it is surprising that the Bahamas receive such a low monetary return— worse still, gratis, as in the case of Bermuda — particularly when they will likely be targets during a nuclear confrontation. "The technical facilities of the nuclear infrastructure do not at first appear to be provocative, *but they are as deadly as the nuclear arsenal. They tie these countries into nuclear plans in such a way that they not only become nuclear targets, but nuclear catapults on the front lines of the next war.*"[51]

Given CARICOM's poor record in one of its aims — the coordination of foreign policies — it is not unexpected that Antigua and Bahamas deal directly with the United States on these matters, or even worse, never refer to it, as was the case with Trinidad and Tobago. Indeed, the most recent scholarly writings on security issues focusing on CARICOM and OECS ignore the issue.[52] Its significance can be gauged by the fact that the discussion of a CARICOM declaration of the Caribbean as a Zone of Peace was a casualty of the presence of military installations in its midst.

A sharp conflict of views erupted with the then radical regimes of the Region alone favouring the idea (of the Caribbean as a Zone of Peace) while other Member States indicated that their lack of enthusiasm took account of the existence of bases or installations within their territories from which the host State derived economic and other advantages.[53]

Clearly the denuclearization of the Caribbean must go much further than the absence of nuclear weapons as envisaged by the Treaty of Tlatelolco: a nuclear free zone must exclude installations related to the nuclear infrastructure. The presence of these installations means the unilateral imposition of U.S. security interests. Independence is a mere formality when regional security is controlled and endangered by an external power. Complete denuclearization is a necessary requirement for the true decolonization of the Caribbean.

PUERTO RICO: THE CRUCIBLE OF CARIBBEAN DECOLONIZATION

U.S. military installations in Puerto Rico have been established without consulting the people of Puerto Rico. "Common defense" with the United States has meant in reality that Puerto Ricans share the consequences of a unilaterally imposed U.S. defense policy. Puerto Rican elected colonial administrators can only rely on informal means to express their positions. For example, in the early 1960s, as one of the military responses to the Cuban Revolution, the secretary of defense wrote to the then governor of Puerto Rico, Luis Muñoz Marín, on:

a) The need for the remainder of Vieques Island, including the necessity to relocate all 7500 residents to provide for a secure location for overt and covert training and/or staging of U.S. and foreign forces.
b) The need for the remainder of Culebra Island, including the necessity to relocate all 570 residents to provide a suitable impact area for the rapidly increasing missile training of our fleet and naval air units.[54]

The documentation on these plans is still classified, although clearly Muñoz Marín killed the proposal without making it public.

At present Puerto Rico is immersed in preparation for a referendum on status whose parameters are to be determined by the U.S. Congress. The leader of the Commonwealth Party, Governor Hernández Colón, together with the pro-statehood and independence parties are engaged in negotiations with the U.S. Congress leading to a change in Puerto Rico's status. But such a change will not necessarily end in the decolonization of the island. Following historical precedents and the weakness of the decolonizing forces in Puerto Rico, it is difficult to imagine the U.S. Congress relinquishing its final say in any decision regarding Puerto Rico. Also, adequate weight on any decision of a status change must be given to the value assigned by the U.S. Navy to its interests in Puerto Rico.

In congressional hearings held in June and July 1989, the continuation of several U.S. military installations in Puerto Rico was one of the key issues. The pro-Commonwealth side continued its support for common defense, even though it connotes the "lack of any effective participation of Puerto Ricans in the shaping of defense policies for the United States, *crucial as they are for their own survival.*"[55] Statehooders, known for their strong defense posture, have more pressing matters in their agenda, such as the issues of language, culture, and federal taxes, but their stance is not necessarily consistent with retaining the "suppurating sore" of Vieques or even the mobilization of the U.S. National Guard in Puerto Rico to Central America.[56] These two parties presented no new positions; instead, the pro-Commonwealth side recanted on some as it has distanced itself more and more from previous claims of self-government.

For reasons of *realpolitik,* the Puerto Rican Independence Party said it would agree to a transition period for the "transfer of properties presently under the control of the United States for military purposes." The PIP's call for Puerto Rico to be "a nuclear free zone" and for "total demilitarization," in order to devote all efforts and resources to social and economic development, was not well received. Senator Bennett Johnson was blunt, saying that Roosevelt Roads will be needed for "a long period of years" (with an adequate quid pro quo, of course) and that it might be used "in case of regional conflict."[57]

As expected, the DOD spokesperson noted that "the independence option would have the most significant implications . . . but under any option we would need to retain and use" the entire Roosevelt Roads complex, the Vieques islands facilities, the Naval Security Group at Sabana Seca, the Punta Borinquen and Punta Salinas radar sites, access to the Muñoz Marín International Airport/Muñoz Air National Guard Base, and Borinquen International Airport, and the Camp Santiago training area.[58] The retention of these installations is based on their alleged importance in the event of regional and/or global conflict, for a U.S. presence and support (including training) of friends and allies in the Eastern Caribbean (specifically the RSS) and the Caribbean Basin as a whole, and for the drug eradication campaign.

The ongoing discussion on status change in Puerto Rico shows how the United States manipulates the situation to its advantage and how unfortunate it is that broad and exhaustive studies have not been carried out on the socioeconomic, political, and security consequences of U.S. defense and military policy in the Caribbean when it is obvious that three aspects — U.S. military installations, the development of client security forces, and military-related industries — are pressing issues calling for detailed examination.[59]

The Vieques controversy is a case in point.[60] In 1975 President Nixon ordered the U.S. Navy to leave Culebra as a result of a united front of the island community against its presence, led by its mayor Ramon Feliciano, and the lukewarm support of the Ferré and Hernández Colón administrations to Richard Copaken's campaign against the Navy. The immediate and predictable result was the navy's increased shelling, bombardment, and practice landings on nearby Vieques.[61]

The Vieques issue has several important contrasts with the Culebra controversy: the larger Vieques community was politically divided; at the initiative of then Governor Carlos Romero Barceló, the case was diverted to the district federal courts (controlled by judges who are pro-U.S. zealots) concentrating on important yet secondary environment issues; and the change in the regional and international scenario (due mainly to the coup by the New Jewel Movement in Grenada, the Sandinista victory in Nicaragua, and the fall of the Shah in Iran) strengthened the U.S. militaristic approach toward the region, reinforcing the already intransigent position of the navy. This led in turn to an official change in the Commonwealth's stand, and the navy's attitude (at least publicly) became less arrogant and more understanding. Finally, the U.S. Navy versus Vieques conflict became a highly politicized issue because of the alleged murder of Angel Rodríguez Cristóbal (one of numerous trespassers onto land claimed by the navy) in the Tallahassee Federal Correctional Institution; the reprisal killing of two navy men in a bus coming from the Sabana Seca facility; the charging of the navy public relations specialist, Lt. Alex de la Zerda, with the bombing of the Bar Association; and the destruction of nine U.S. Air National Guard planes in early 1981 while stationed at the Muñiz base, adjacent to Muñoz Marín International Airport.

All pending litigation was brought to an end in October 1983 when the U.S. Navy and the Commonwealth signed an accord that placed a limit on the live-shelling area on Vieques island and included environmental conservation concessions. The agreement, however, gave the navy "the right to conduct prompt and sustaining operations as a result of the events in the Caribbean and Central America."[62] The navy also pledged to seek the creation of more jobs in Vieques by trying to attract new industries.

A few days after signing the accord, top executives of nine of the largest U.S. corporations and an important contingent of DOD procurement officers visited Vieques and said they would seek means to generate enough new jobs in defense subcontracts to eliminate the island's high unemployment. After some initial success, it was clear by mid-1988 that the Vieques development program had failed. Dandie Corporation, manufacturer of military shirts and the island's biggest employer, suddenly closed its operations in the summer of 1988.[63] The situation reached a critical stage. In February 1989 the conservative, pro-U.S., most widely read dailies *El Vocero* and *El Nuevo Día* criticized the neglect of Vieques ("the major consequence of the annual artillery volleys of the Navy is deafness . . . the official deafness that ignores the just claims of the *viequenses*") and noted that navy relations with the community had fallen to a new low ("It seems that the relations between the Navy and the *viequenses* have deteriorated to the point of disintegration").[64]

As in Culebra, it is a matter of time for the *viequenses* to agree among themselves that the presence of the U.S. Navy, a military force of an alien culture, is responsible for truncating the life of their community, for the depopulation of the island (in 1920, 11,651; in 1940, 10,362; and in 1980, 7,662), and for its underdevelopment.[65] In April 1989, navy men and U.S. federal marshals attempted to evict Carmelo Félix Matta from land that allegedly belonged to Camp García. This led to the burning of two navy vehicles by about 100 angry *viequenses* in Lope de Vega's *Fuenteovejuna's* fashion. By late May 300 families had expropriated 880 acres of U.S. Navy land.

Notwithstanding the power of the navy and the futile attempts of the colonial government on duty to defuse the issue, opposition to the U.S. Navy in Vieques will be steadfast in years to come — not necessarily for political reasons, but for reasons of survival. Antonio Figueroa, one of the leaders, says, "My big fear is that the Navy will think this is an act of aggression against them. It's not. It's an act of self-defense, of survival for the people of Vieques."[66]

Except to note his concern for the strained relations in Vieques due to the navy's action, Governor Hernández Colón did not intervene in any way in the defense of the *viequense* community. At a time when government's official policy is strengthening relations with the Eastern Caribbean (exemplified by the recent agreement for the promotion of industries signed between the Economic Development Administration of

Puerto Rico and the Eastern Caribbean Investment Promotion Services), Vieques, Puerto Rico's closest link to the Eastern Caribbean, is left to fend for itself.[67]

It is worth highlighting here that the panel appointed by the House Committee on the Armed Services to evaluate the controversy remained unconvinced of Vieques' indispensability for the navy and urged finding an alternate site.[68] Moreover, the limited role played by Roosevelt Roads in the Grenada invasion, in contrast to the major one of the southern mainland installations (particularly Norfolk), indicates that the proximity as well as the increased ranges of ships make fewer installations in the Caribbean necessary. The Strategic Homeporting Plan, which entails placing ships in different ports, is a step in this direction. "Homeporting in the Gulf is needed to protect our SLOCs . . . to the European Theater and will also enhance our responsiveness to potential Caribbean/Central American conflicts."[69] Also, technological advances should continue to render some facilities redundant. Still, the reduction or closure of U.S. military installations will be difficult because the U.S. armed services (especially the navy) are very powerful in the bureaucratic politics of Washington. It is significant that in the recent exercise of base realignments and closures, naval installations, including those in Puerto Rico, were not even considered because the U.S. Navy "stonewalled and got away with it."[70]

The neglect of Vieques by the Puerto Rican government is the repetition of a Caribbean phenomenon. The larger islands disregarded the smaller ones, as in the cases of Antigua with Barbuda, St. Kitts with Nevis, and Trinidad with Tobago. In Vieques the condition is aggravated by the U.S. Navy's occupation of two-thirds of the island, making its viability an issue in itself. Certainly Vieques, as well as Culebra, because of its *sui generis* situation, must have a special relationship with Puerto Rico and not be a colony of a colony.

Vieques' economic plight has been part of an even bleaker picture as the wider project of boosting Puerto Rico's participation in Pentagon procurement contracts derailed, because of the fallout of the Wedtech and Amertech scandals, discrimination, and lack of the necessary capabilities that led to low-quality production. In 1986 a ten-year dramatic increase in defense procurement contracts awarded to Puerto Rico stopped.[71] From the $496 million totaled in the peak FY 1985, they fell to $414 million in FY 1986, $323 million in FY 1987, and $213 million as of November 1988.[72]

It should be noted that most defense contracts were awarded to U.S. firms based in Puerto Rico. The share — not more than 15 percent — of

Puerto Rican-owned companies was mainly limited to construction and security work in the U.S. installations. Commonwealth officials promoted the shaky apparel industry, and by 1988 textile products accounted for almost half of the sales to the Pentagon. A consultant of the Puerto Rico Federal Affairs Administration says, "Much of the money for the contracts goes to the cost of import materials or for profit of non-resident owners."[73] In 1987, Mayagüez was the leading municipality; nine companies had defense contracts totaling nearly $62 million. Ceiba, where Roosevelt Roads is located, was in second place: 60 companies shared $51 million in contracts. Vieques was in twentieth place, one company with one project for $1.2 million.

The plan to increase Puerto Rico's share during the Reagan administration's unprecedented peacetime military buildup came as a response to the island's critical economic situation, dating back to the mid-1970s recession. The immediate impact of the 1970s crisis was offset by massive transfers of federal funds to the Puerto Rican population (from $455 million in 1970 to $2,906 million in 1979).[74] However, the Reagan administration's policy to reduce social spending promptly put an end to this solution.

In 1985 Rear Admiral William O'Connor, Commander of U.S. Naval Forces, Caribbean, played a vital role in the Commonwealth's effort to prevent congressional action against Section 936 of the U.S. Internal Revenue Code, which provides a tax shelter for U.S. corporations operating in Puerto Rico. According to O'Connor, Congress finally abstained from removing Section 936 because of national security considerations. The Commonwealth's 936 attorney in Washington, Richard Copaken, cloaked his defense with this mantle also, arguing, "With Guantanamo, there's always uncertainty in the long term, it could always be subject to some discounting. Even in Panama there's an agreement that at some time has to be renegotiated. But the one unqualified American military presence in the Caribbean is Puerto Rico, the one certain place."[75]

U.S. military spending and defense-related industries have been useful in saving the Puerto Rican economy from total collapse. However, one item — the wages earned for their service by 128,000 veterans (4 percent of the population) of the U.S. armed forces in Puerto Rico — is not accounted for in the DOD figures. From 1976 to 1985 the Veterans Administration averaged an annual budget of nearly $238 million. Since World War I, as a direct consequence of the imposition of U.S. citizenship in 1917, Puerto Ricans have enrolled in the U.S. armed forces. In proportion to Puerto Rico's population (at least in the Korean War), casualties have been higher than the U.S. average: Puerto Rico had one soldier killed for every 660 inhabitants whereas the United States had one for every 1,225 inhabitants. In the Vietnam War 1,300 Puerto Ricans were killed, and today 56 percent of the 20,000 veterans suffer different types of mental illness.[76] A large number is also undergoing treatment associated with their exposure to Agent Orange, one of several pesticides tested in Puerto Rico during the 1960s for their effects on tropical flora and fauna. Commonwealth authorities claimed ignorance of these experiments. However, they did admit that, because of the lack of funds, the affected tropical forests were neither cleaned up nor reforested.[77] The fact that the largest single category of veterans' benefits is disability compensation has been explained only by saying "that a disproportionate percentage of Puerto Ricans served in the combat arms in Viet Nam."[78]

CONCLUSION

Puerto Rico has paid high human, social, economic, and political costs for the strategic-military role played by the island within the framework of U.S. national security interests. Some of these costs are the loss of Puerto Rican lives; the dispossession, removal, stunting, and truncation of communities (particularly Vieques with its impact on the U.S. Virgin Islands); the contamination of tropical flora and fauna and damage to the ecology; and the intervention of U.S. armed and internal security forces in the political life of the island.

Some of these costs have also been paid by other Caribbean islands, particularly establishing and strengthening security forces with the concomitant danger they pose to formal democracy. U.S. installations in Puerto Rico have been used for training these surrogate forces and others of Central America, as well as for military interventions in these regions. The demilitarization of Puerto Rico is necessary for its own decolonization and for decolonizing the rest of the Caribbean.

Last but not least, because of the nuclear infrastructure present in the Caribbean, there is the ever present danger of nuclear accidents or of a nuclear attack in case of war. This affects not only the communities where nuclear capabilities are installed, but also the surrounding ones. The presence of U.S. military installations is a unilateral imposition of its security interests, putting the survival of the Caribbean at risk. The linkage of the three D's — decolonization, demilitarization, and denuclearization — is indispensable for the creation of a truly regional security system. The process to attain real decolonization requires the demilitarization as well as the complete denuclearization of the Caribbean.

NOTES

1. I am using Hagerty's definition of "base" and "facility," where the main distinction relates to both size and tenancy. A base is usually a larger complex, including both operating and supporting assigned personnel; a facility tends to be smaller, with a more limited function and few operating personnel regularly resident. An "installation" is a generic term, applicable to both. H. G. Hagerty, *Forward Deployment in the 1970's and 1980's*, National Security Affairs Monograph 77-2 (Washington, D.C.: Research Directorate, National Defense University, 1977), p. 32.

2. Soviet installations in Cuba are studied in L. Schoultz, *National Security and United States Policy toward Latin America* (Princeton: Princeton University Press, 1987), pp. 249–67.

3. See the relevant sections in R. Crassweller, *The Caribbean Community* (New York: Praeger, 1972); A. J. Cottrell and T. H. Moorer, *U.S. Overseas Bases: Problems of Projecting American Military Power Abroad* (Washington, D.C.: Center for Strategic and International Studies, Georgetown University, 1977); and Schoultz, *National Security*.

4. An evaluation, with emphasis on the conventional side, of the U.S. base network in the Caribbean for the late 1970s is presented in U.S. Congress, Senate, Committee on Foreign Relations, *United States Foreign Policy Objectives and Overseas Military Installations*, 96th Cong., 1st Sess. (Washington, D.C.: U.S. Government Printing Office, 1979). For information concerning nuclear installations in the Caribbean, this work draws heavily on W. A. Arkin and R. W. Fieldhouse, *Nuclear Battlefields: Global Links in the Arms Race* (Cambridge, Mass.: Ballinger, 1985). The most comprehensive work on military installations is R. Harkavy, *Bases Abroad: The Global Foreign Military Presence* (New York: Oxford, 1989).

5. The first analytical works with this approach were carried out by Jorge Rodríguez Beruff. Some of his essays have been recently published in his *Política militar y Dominacion: Puerto Rico en el contexto latinoamericano* (Río Piedras: Huracán, 1988).

6. See. F. David, *The Atlantic System* (New York: Reynal & Hitchcock, 1941), pp. 68–74.

7. B. Reynolds, "Guantanamo Bay, Cuba, U.S. Naval Base, 1988–," in P. Coletta and K. J. Dauer, eds., *United States Navy and Marine Corps Bases, Overseas* (Westport, Conn.: Greenwood, 1985), p. 149.

8. See A. C. Palmer, "The United States and the Commonwealth Caribbean: 1940–45," Ph.D. dissertation, Howard University, 1979, pp. 139–44.

9. No information has been found on the dispossession and removal of any community in Guantanamo. For a moving account of the Culebra experience in 1903–1904, see C. C. Feliciano, *Apuntes y comentarios de la colonización y liberación de la isla de Culebra* (Culebra, 1981); for the military context, see M. E. Estades Font, *La presencia militar de Estados Unidos en Puerto Rico, 1898–1918* (Río Piedras: Huracán, 1988).

10. J. Pastor Ruiz, *Vieques antiguo y moderno* (Yauco: Tip. Rodríguez Lugo, 1947), p. 206.

11. In the congressional hearings of 1980, the mayor of Vieques told the U.S. Virgin Islands congressional delegate: "Congressman Evans . . . knows very well that there are many people of Vieques residing in the neighboring islands of St. Croix and

St. Thomas that have had to abandon this island because of the economic conditions
... that do not permit the people of Vieques, after they finish high school, to stay on
the island because there are no economic opportunities here for those who have
graduated or for our people." U.S. Congress, House, Committee of the Armed
Services, *Hearing before the Panel to Review the Status of Navy Training Activities
on the Island of Vieques* (Washington, D.C.: U.S. Government Printing Office, 1980),
p. 216. See also C. Senior, *The Puerto Rican Migrant in St. Croix* (Río Piedras:
Social Science Research Center, University of Puerto Rico, 1947).

12. See D. L. Woods, "Bermuda, U.S. Naval Bases, 1918–1919, 1941–," in
Coletta and Dauer, *United States,* p. 31. For a description of St. David's before its
destruction, see E. A. McCallan, *Life on Old St. David's Bermuda* (Hamilton:
Bermuda Historical Monument Trust, 1948); for a contemporary, favorable view of
U.S. military presence, see H. Stroude, *The Story of Bermuda,* rev. ed. (New York:
Harcourt, Brace, 1946), pp. 369–80, 434–56.

13. D. D. Creque states, "Puerto Ricans were also segregated on the basis of how
white they looked to the classifying officer. This often resulted in ridiculously
segregating two brothers of the same parents." *The U.S. Virgins and the Eastern
Caribbean* (Philadelphia: Whitmore, 1968), p. 116.

14. L. D. Langley, "Roosevelt Roads, Puerto Rico, U.S. Naval Base, 1941," in
Coletta and Dauer, *United States,* p. 273.

15. For an analysis of the establishment of U.S. installations in the British colonies in the Caribbean, see N. Burn, "United States Base Rights in the British West
Indies, 1940–1962," Ph.D. dissertation, Fletcher School of Law and Diplomacy, 1964.

16. For further elaboration, see C. A. P. St. Hill, "The Chaguaramas Question:
The Origin and Consequences of the United States—United Kingdom Leased Bases
Agreement, 1941," M.Sc. thesis, University of the West Indies, Mona, Jamaica, 1970.

17. Harkavy, *Bases Abroad,* p. 161.

18. See R. D. Heinl, Jr., and N. G. Heinl, *Written in Blood, The Story of the
Haitian People* (Boston: Houghton Mifflin, 1978), pp. 618–25; and H. García-Muñiz,
"Defense Policy and Planning in the Caribbean: An Assessment of Jamaica on Its 25th
Independence Anniversary," *Journal of Commonwealth and Comparative Politics* 27
(1988): 75. In its reply to Haiti, the United States noted that "it would be useful to
have access to sites suitable for international amphibious training." *Declassified
Document Quarterly Catalog* (hereafter *DDQC*) 9 (1983), 001791, "Department of
State Cable, Secretary of State to American Embassy, Port-au-Prince, Subject: U.S.
Views on President Duvalier's Offer of Submarine Bases and Training Camps, 22
September 1959."

19. See A. Maingot, "Laundering Drug Profits: Miami and Caribbean Tax
Havens," *Journal of Inter-American Studies and World Affairs* 30 (1988): 172.

20. Adm. L. Baggett, Jr., USN, Commander in Chief, U.S. Atlantic Command,
"U.S. Atlantic Command: Strengthening for Forward Strategy," *Defense*
(November/December 1987): 30.

21. The phasing out of U.S. Forces, Caribbean, was the result of a cost-cutting
study, headed by the Pentagon Deputy Inspector General, D. J. Vander Schaaf, which
said, "[I]n all the important contingencies imaginable it appears the command will
either get in the way or be ignored." D. J. Vander Schaff, Chairman, Study Team,
*Report: Review of Unified and Specified Command Headquarters Prepared at the
Request of the Secretary of Defense,* February, 1988, p. 42.

22. Estimates based on Department of Defense (DOD), *Active Military Personnel Strengths by Regional Area and Country*, June 30, 1978–June 30, 1988.

23. Baggett, "U.S. Atlantic Command," p. 33. (My emphasis.)

24. For an excellent analysis of this issue, see M. C. Desch, "Turning the Caribbean Flank: Sea Lane Vulnerability during an European War," *Survival* 29 (November/December 1987): 528–51.

25. "Unified, Specified Commands Protect Nation's Security," *Commanders' Digest* 13 (June 28, 1973): 8. (My emphasis.)

26. The Caribbean Basin is a geostrategic region that comprises the insular Caribbean, all Central American countries, Mexico, Venezuela, Guyana, and Surinam. For further elaboration see García Muñiz, *La estrategia de Estados Unidos y la militarizacion del Caribe* (Río Piedras: Instituto de Estudios del Caribe, Universidad de Puerto Rico, 1988), Chap. 8.

27. For a discussion of these issues see Schoultz, *National Security*, pp. 191–222; and P. Sutton, "The Caribbean as a Focus for Strategic and Resource Rivalry," in P. Calvert, ed., *The Central American Security System: North-South or East-West?* (Cambridge: Cambridge University Press, 1988), pp. 18–44.

28. It must be noted that two previous presidential commissions appointed to study the DOD recommended the abolition of SOUTHCOM and the integration of its functions to LANTCOM. See *Report to the President and the Secretary of Defense on the Department of Defense by the Blue Ribbon Defense Panel*, July 1, 1970 (Washington, D.C.: U.S. Government Printing Office, 1970), p. 57; and *The National Military Command Structure. Report of a Study Requested by the President and Conducted in the Department of Defense* (Washington, D.C.: U.S. Government Printing Office, 1978), p. 13.

29. L. Chavez, "Salvador Leader Says the F.B.I. Is Training Investigation Squad," *New York Times*, May 30, 1984, pp. A1, 13.

30. See A. Nelson, *Murder under Two Flags: The U.S., Puerto Rico, and the Cerro Maravilla Cover-up* (New York: Ticknor & Fields, 1986), p. 245, and the foreword to the book by Samuel Dash).

31. Ojeda's lawyer refused to visit him at the base unless he was recognized as a prisoner of war. See "Pone peros la defensa de Ojeda," *El Mundo* (Puerto Rico), September 3, 1988, p. 7.

32. *DDQC* 13 (1987), 001609, "FBI Report on the Dominican Situation — Received April 4, 1966 — 1:13 p.m.," p. 1.

33. "Guardsmen, Caribbean Soldiers Train," *San Juan Star*, June 6, 1988, p. 13. For more information on the internal role of the U.S. National Guard in Puerto Rico, see J. Enders, *La presencia militar de Estados Unidos en Puerto Rico*, Serie Militarismo 1 (Río Piedras: Proyuecto Caribeño de Justicia y Paz, 1980), pp. 26–32.

34. See "Crearan escuela militar caribeña en Antigua," *Claridad* (Puerto Rico), November 22–28, 1985, p. 32.

35. A. Walker, "Security of the Eastern Caribbean," *Jane's Defense Weekly*, January 17, 1987, p. 61. It is worth noting that a loan service team of British servicemen, based in Barbados, undertakes the SSU's basic training, while the U.S. Green Berets from Fort Bragg, North Carolina, concentrates on NCO and leadership training. See E. Fursdon, "The British, the Caribbean, and Belize," *Journal of Defense & Diplomacy* 6 (1988): 40.

36. "Military Exercises Aimed at Bettering Drug Interdiction," *San Juan Star*, June 2, 1989, p. 14.

37. R. Carr, *Puerto Rico: A Colonial Experiment* (New York: Vintage Books, 1984), p. 311.

38. Other exercises are also held, such as Fleetex-7 in which the United States, Great Britain, Canada, Brazil, and Venezuela "invaded" and shelled Vieques. For further details see Langley, "Roosevelt," pp. 273–75; and L. A. Andreu, "Siete países 'invaden' Vieques," *El Mundo*, February 19, 1987, p. 89.

39. Añejo 1: W. M. Arkin, "The Treaty of Tlatelolco, Nuclear Weapons, and Puerto Rico. Findings for the Bar Association of Puerto Rico Special Commissions on the Nuclear Weapons Threat," in *Informe de Comisión Especial sobre Armamentos Nucleares y el Tratado para la Proscripción de las Armas Nucleares en América Latina* (San Juan, Colegio de Abogados de Puerto Rico, August 17, 1985), p. 1.

40. See L. H. Gelb, "U.S. Has Contingency Plan to Put A-Arms in 4 Countries, Aides Say," *New York Times*, February 13, 1985, p. 1.

41. The transmitter in Aguada was reconditioned after the dismantling of a signal tower in the Panama Canal Zone. See "Navy's Signal Tower for Carib Upgraded," *San Juan Star*, May 6, 1983, p. 1.

42. Carr, *Puerto Rico*, p. 314. (Author's emphasis.)

43. See Rodríguez Beruff, "Puerto Rico y la militarizacion del Caribe: 1979–1985," *Política*, pp. 227–28.

44. W. L. McDonald, Commander-in-Chief, U.S. Atlantic Command, *Operation Urgent Fury*, October 25–November 2, 1983, p. 2.

45. "Case Study and Justification Folder and Environmental Impact for Retaining Fort Buchanan at Minimum Essential," FORSCOM, Ft. McPherson, Georgia, Revised October 26, 1976, Section 1, p. 6. Quoted in: Enders, *Presencia*, p. 10.

46. R. Hernandez, *La seguridad nacional de Cuba y la cuestión de la base naval de Guantánamo*, Cuaderno 2 (La Habana: Centro de Estudios sobre América, 1988), p. 10.

47. SOSUS is a global network of hydrophones laid out on the sea floor that passively detect sounds generated by submarines. For more detailed treatment of SOSUS, see Richelson, *The U.S. Intelligence Community* (Cambridge, Mass.: Ballinger, 1985), pp. 146–50.

48. Ibid., p. 146.

49. U.S. Congress, House of Representatives, Committee on Armed Services, *Report on Inspection of Military Facilities in Panama and Bermuda*, 97th Cong. 1st Sess., September 15, 1981 (Washington, D.C.: U.S. Government Printing Office, 1981), p. 18.

50. Woods, "Bermuda," pp. 37–38.

51. Arkin and Fieldhouse, *Nuclear Battlefields*, p. 150. (My emphasis.) A Commonwealth Secretariat-sponsored study notes that "there is the possibility in normal times of subversive activities by domestic groups hostile to the presence of such facilities." *Vulnerability: Small States in a Global Society* (London, 1985), p. 24.

52. See, for example, W. A. Axline, "Regional Cooperation and National Security: External Forces in Caribbean Integration," *Journal of Common Market Studies* 27 (1988): 1–25; and A. Serbín, *El Caribe: ¿Zona de Paz?* (Caracas: Nueva Sociedad, 1988). Only safety regarding nuclear reactors has been discussed in a

CARICOM publication. See "Nuclear Safety: An Interview with Professor Gerald Lalor," *CARICOM Perspective* (July–December 1986): 2, 19.

53. L. Searwar, "The Small State in the Caribbean — Policy Options for Survival," Paper prepared for the Conference on Peace and Development in the Caribbean, Kingston, Jamaica, May 16–18, 1988, p. 14.

54. In return the U.S. Navy was to relocate all naval activities (except communications) from the San Juan area to Roosevelt Roads. *DDQC* 8 (1982), 002394, "Memorandum for the Naval Aide to the President, 14 December 1961. Subject: Puerto Rico Real Estate Negotiations. Enclosed: (1) Status of Commonwealth of Puerto Rico-Department of Defense Discussions Relative to Military Installations in Puerto Rico."

55. C. J. Friedrich, *Puerto Rico: Middle Road to Freedom* (New York: Rinehart, 1959), p. 72. (My emphasis.)

56. "Enérgico Repudio," *El Nuevo Día,* March 28, 1988, p. 15.

57. H. Turner, "Johnson Conditions Accepted by Berríos," *San Juan Star,* June 3, 1989, p. 12.

58. "Prepared Statement of Brigadier General M. J. Byron, Acting Deputy Assistant Secretary of Defense (Inter-American Affairs), Department of Defense before the Committee of Energy and Natural Resources, U.S. Senate, July 11, 1989," p. 10.

59. On military-related industries, a preliminary study has been carried out by H. A. Watson, "Coalition Security Development: Defense Industrial Restructuring and Defense Electronics Production in the Caribbean," Paper presented at the Second Conference of the Association of Caribbean Economists, Christ Church, Barbados, May 28–30, 1989. Watson criticizes strongly what is perhaps the first work on this topic: Col. J. R. Bremer et al., "Mobilization Studies Program Report: Electronic Industry and the Caribbean Basin" (Washington, D.C.: Industrial College of the Armed Forces, National Defense University, April 1985). See also S. Grusky, "The Changing Role of the U.S. Military in Puerto Rico," *Social and Economic Studies* 36 (1987): 37–76. For a bibliographical essay dealing with client armies in the Hispanic Caribbean and Central America, see L. A. Pérez, Jr., "Armies of the Caribbean: Historical Perspectives, Historical Trends," *Latin American Perspectives* 14 (1987): 490–507. For the development of client security forces in the English-speaking Caribbean, see García Muñiz , *Estrategia,* Chaps. 3–11.

60. For summaries presenting the anti- and pro-Navy positions, respectively, see L. L. Cripps, *Human Rights in a United States Colony* (Cambridge, Mass.: Schenkman, 1982), pp. 115–38; and E. Langhorne, *Vieques: History of a Small Island* (Vieques: The Vieques Conservation and Historical Trust, 1987), pp. 62–68.

61. In accordance with the Culebra agreement, the Commonwealth offered the navy the use of the two smaller uninhabited off-shore islands Desecheo and Monito, but they were rejected because they did not comply with the navy's requisites. For the hearings on Culebra, see U.S. Congress, Subcommittee on Real Estate, *Subcommittee on Real Estate Consideration of and Hearings on the Acquisition Report No. 192 and Disposal Report No. 300* (Washington, D.C.: U.S. Government Printing Office, 1970).

62. "Pact Limits Live Shelling in Vieques," *San Juan Star,* October 22, 1983, p. 1.

63. Dandie Corporation was apparently linked to the Amertech scandal. See "Desempleo y fracaso se cultivan en Vieques," *El Nuevo Día,* August 28, 1988, p. 16.

The *Vieques Times* estimated unemployment at about 62 percent out of a total work force of 3,100. See "Vieques Development Survey, Unemployment Breaks 50% Mark," *Vieques Times*, August 1988, pp. 1, 3.

64. "Editorial: Vieques quiere empleos," *El Vocero* (Puerto Rico), February 3, 1989, p. 14; and "Entrelineas: Vieques," *El Nuevo Día*, February 27, 1989, p. 2.

65. See M. Capó, "Youth of Vieques: Seeking Better Future," *Caribbean Business*, May 18, 1989, p. 14. For demographic and economic data on Vieques, see J. S. Bonnet Benítez, *Vieques en la historia de Puerto Rico*, 2d ed. (San Juan: F. Ortiz Nieves, 1977).

66. D. Hemlock, "Vieques Squatters Dig on Navy Land," *San Juan Star*, May 30, 1989, p. 1.

67. See D. Hemlock, "PR-Eastern Carib Accord Set," *San Juan Star*, June 9, 1989, p. 2.

68. See *Naval Training Activities on the Island of Vieques, Puerto Rico. Report of the Panel to Review the Status of Navy Training Activities on the Island of Vieques of the Committee on Armed Services*, House of Representatives, 96th Cong., 2d Sess. (Washington, D.C.: U.S. Government Printing Office, 1981).

69. U.S. DOD, Office of the Assistant Secretary of Defense, *Base Structure Report for FY 1988*, pp. 56–57.

70. "Additional View of Thomas F. Eagleton," *Base Realignments and Closures. Report of the Defense Secretary's Commission*, December 1988, p. 88. U.S. military installations in Puerto Rico and the Virgin Islands, unlike all others studied in this chapter, were considered as being "inside the United States" (p. 39).

71. See Grusky, "The Changing Role," p. 46. It is not correct to refer, as Grusky does, to U.S. military expenditures in Puerto Rico as "military aid" or to compare them to U.S. military assistance appropriations to other Caribbean or Central American countries because these funds go to the U.S. military infrastructure and personnel (including the National Guard) in Puerto Rico whereas in the other countries it is assigned to national security forces (pp. 48, 61).

72. See L. Luxner, "Pentagon Spending Shrinks Here 4th Year in a Row," *Caribbean Business*, November 17, 1988, p. 4.

73. G. Martin, "The United States Armed Services and the Puerto Rican Economy," *Puerto Rico Business Review* 9 (August 1984): 11, and "Apparel Industry Eyes High Fashion with High Hopes," *San Juan Star*, June 29, 1986, p. 2.

74. F. López, "La militarización de la economía de Puerto Rico," *Pensamiento Crítico* (Puerto Rico) 8 (January/February 1985): 5.

75. B. De la Torre, "Navy Builds up Base," *Caribbean Business*, July 23, 1986, p. 18.

76. Ibid.

77. See "Exigen Mayores Beneficios," *El Mundo*, March 5, 1989, p. 3; "Ensayo con el Agente Naranja en la Floresta," *El Nuevo Día*, June 12, 1983, p. 4; and "Están contaminados los bosques en Puerto Rico," *El Reportero*, May 25, 1983, p. 1.

78. Martin, "The United States," p. 11.

3   Political Violence in the Caribbean

Neville C. Duncan

Violence and conflict are pervasive aspects of all societies. Trinidad and Tobago, Guyana, Jamaica, St. Lucia, Grenada, Dominica, and St. Vincent and the Grenadines, with a history of conquest, slavery, colonialism, and petty capitalism have not been free from this persistent threat to orderly society. The manifest instances of overt violence have been few throughout their history, but this does not infer an absence of continuous conflict in these societies.

It has now become self-evident that violence and bloodshed represent only the extremes of conflict and that structures of conflict exist in the ordering of these societies. Challenges to the established order have been met with appeals for law and order and by increased coercion. Jails are full, but the level of violence and crime does not diminish. More and more repression simply begins to undermine the very values it was intended to protect, and a sense of failure is promoted. How the problem of violence is treated depends upon the diagnosis experts act on.

One response is "law and order," involving greater repression. It is a response that seeks to label and thereby treat and suppress what is defined as deviant behavior. In this perspective, people become "criminals," "preachers of violence," "outcasts," "terrorists," "mad people," "drug addicts and pushers," "wildcat strikers," "guerrillas," and "rebels." They are so categorized in order to be dealt with using exceptional measures. These have been the normal responses of elites throughout history. Governments, whether black or white, have always acted as though they have the right to pursue such policies, even in the face of widespread and strong public opinion against such.

Governments see force as the legitimate use of state power to prevent, restrain, or punish breaches of the law. And they see violence that lacks the legitimation of constitutional and legal sanction as essentially arbitrary.[1] This use of force by governments is referred to as "structural violence" in circumstances when "a person is prevented by social deprivation or political repression from fulfilling his or her aspirations."[2] Violence, seen as "the illegitimate use or threatened use of coercion resulting, or intended to result in, the death, injury, restraint or intimidation of persons or the destruction or seizure of property" is deemed particularly unacceptable and frightening in liberal democracies.[3]

The political systems under examination are modeled on the Westminister variety of liberal democracy and have a particularly sound record of liberal democratic practices. Such models of government have been lauded for their capacity "to tolerate, respond to and harness the forces of popular protest and discontent." Indeed, some scholars see the process as one of managing political conflict and deem the liberal democratic mode peculiarly suited for this. In this view, it would be normal to expect modes of conflict that are "essentially non-violent, un-institutionalized and spontaneous," and one may find tolerable conscientious objection and/or persuasive (as opposed to coercive) civil disobedience. There is an implied right to break the law provided that a group is prepared to accept the punishment after due process of the law and provided that it does not attempt to coerce or intimidate others. The line is crossed, Wilkinson argues, when a group resorts to political violence, blackmail, and intimidation because this is incompatible with the rule of law and liberal democratic theory.

The relationships among violence, liberal democracy, and change in the Caribbean constitute the main concerns of this chapter. This involves assessing the effects of the violence and considering when and if the particular conflict ended. Mitchell identifies conflict as originating in individual and group reactions to situations of scarce resources; divisions of functions within society; and differentiation of power and resultant competition for limited resources, status, valued roles, and power as an end in itself.[4] Use of this approach will facilitate an appreciation of Caribbean circumstances. This is followed by a discussion on "correct" responses and future safeguards.

SYSTEMIC AND ANTISYSTEMIC VIOLENCE IN THE LARGER STATES

Jamaica

In spite of the aftermath of Jamaica's labor revolts of the 1930s, it was not until the 1960s that the country's leadership and the middle classes were shaken to the very core by flashpoint activities of antisystemic violence. These included the Henry Revolt of 1960, the Chinese Riots of 1965, the Rodney Riots and downtown Kingston events of 1968, Political Warfare and states of emergency in 1966–1967, 1972, 1976, and 1981 (all inclusive of polling day in the various general elections), and the Gas Strikes of 1979. These took place within a larger subculture of violence and change-oriented activities further manifested in the Abeng Movement and left-wing political movements and parties, the growing combativeness and violence between trade unions, and the rise and success of new and more aggressive trade unions. Overall, too, the economy had begun its downward slide, hastened after 1973–1974 at a ruinous pace. Today no sustained recovery is underway.

In April and May, 1960, following the arrest of the Reverend Claudius Henry and some 30 of his followers in a preemptive raid mounted by the Jamaican police force on suspected guerrilla training camps, a "series of civil disturbances and extensive arson in rural areas" commenced. The Reverend Henry was said to be collaborating with a group of New York-based First Africa Corps (FAC) armed militants who were planning to take over Jamaica by force. With the help of certain segments of Rastafarians, Reynold Henry, son of Claudius, and members of the FAC mounted their assault on the Jamaican society. The resistance ended on June 27, 1960, when 500 British and Jamaican soldiers and policemen combined to hunt down the marauding band. Over 100 Rastafarians were arrested, two British soldiers were killed, and several other persons were critically wounded.[5]

The 1963 Coral Garden incident and the 1965 anti-Chinese riots were not politically motivated, but, along with the Henry Revolt, set the scene for "political warfare" especially in Kingston and St. Andrew up until 1981. In the 1963 incident an attack upon a Shell gas station led to a shoot-out between the group and police and civilians in which eight persons were killed and four others seriously injured. In the week dating from August 25, 1965, numerous Chinese business places were looted and set afire by marauding mobs of up to 300 persons in downtown

Kingston. Two policemen and 6 civilians were shot, and 90 persons were arrested.[6]

Policemen and soldiers are obvious symbols of authority. When they start getting killed in incidents such as those described above, an atmosphere that emboldens lawless activities is engendered. Their vulnerability and limited citizen support are further increased when they are asked to carry out government policies that hurt the poor and dispossessed. One such incident occurred on June 20, 1966, when 300 police, supported by Jamaica Defense Force helicopters and launches, raided the Industrial Terrace and Foreshore Road squatter areas, enabling the Land Department to serve "quit notices" and announce when the areas would be bulldozed. The government had intended to build low-income houses on the cleared areas, to be made available to some of the squatters. But the action generated unintended consequences. No real alternative sites were provided for the squatters, and a particularly virulent and nasty "rude-boy" subculture was spawned. The violence unleashed was especially mindless and vicious. Protesters were openly defiant of legally constituted authority and enjoyed a vicarious infamy lyricized in ghetto music, song, and dance (Ska, Rock Steady, and early Reggae).[7]

Very soon some of this violence became converted into partisan political violence, which reached a climax in which PNP and JLP supporters were shot, a cinema bombed, power to Western Kingston cut off, buses attacked, and, after an incredible delay, the police cordoned off the JLP and PNP headquarters in Western Kingston. Three months yielded at least five politically related killings, and hundreds of persons were injured and hospitalized. During the joint military and police operations, 50 guns, 800 rounds of ammunition, 66 sticks of dynamite and some Molotov cocktails were found. Through January and February 1967, partisan violence continued, including the polling day and a few more days following. As Lacey noted, partisan violence diminished and was transformed into general violence by March 1967. The level of violence, however, never slackened. Holdups, arson, and gang warfare shootings became frequent occurrences. The subculture of violence resumed its own underlying dynamic.

This pattern of general violence changing to partisan political violence about the time of general elections and then dissipating into sustained criminal activity was repeated for the 1972, 1976, and 1980 general elections. Indeed, the six-month period leading to the 1980 general elections constituted an unbridled orgy of partisan violence in which over 800 persons were killed, including a PNP candidate. This was virtually a civil war in all the important urban centers in Jamaica, but especially in

Kingston, St. Andrew, and Spanish Town. The utmost depravity was practiced by partisans on both sides. Babies and children were cast back into the fires of their burning homes from which they were fleeing as a result of political feuds between rival and contiguous housing areas.

Yet, the political system of liberal democracy was not under direct assault. The elections were held, and, in spite of election-day violence at a few polling booths, the election results were generally accepted as legitimate. It brought about a change in government from PNP to JLP in which the latter obtained a resounding proportion of the seats in the House of Representatives. This consistent pattern of violence did not presage a revolution. Nevertheless, it does raise the specter that if a revolution were to eventuate in Jamaica, it would be characterized by deliberate terrorism and extensive loss of life.[8]

In between the political violence came the violence in the wake of the Rodney Demonstration in 1968. University of the West Indies students were marching in front of the downtown government offices to demonstrate against the banning of Dr. Walter Rodney from Jamaica when police physically sought to stop the march. Very swiftly and unexpectedly, while the police were engaged with the students, youth gangs from the lumpenproletariat began an orgy of looting and rioting. The government did not like the fact that Rodney and other university persons were lecturing on African history to ghetto people and raising the level of black consciousness among them. An embryonic political consciousness, already existing among Rastafarians, was spread, mainly to youth gang leaders. Thus when the government tried to preempt a revolution, it triggered civil disturbances distinguishable from other riots in the 1960s by their scale, duration, and the large numbers of foreign-owned, particularly North American, properties attacked, looted, and burned.

Lacey described the significance of the riots in this way:

> The Rodney riots were frightening because they manifested a reservoir of antagonism against the Jamaican government and the national bourgeoisie, and because they pointed to a source of political strength, and, in a wider than party sense, of political violence, which was largely outside of and beyond the control of the conventional political system and whose main relationship with the political system in 1966 and 1967 had been to provide mercenary warriors serving the ends of Jamaican politicians.[9]

The actions of the mobs, however, were not politically motivated in any great way. Looting provided them with access to much needed and desired material goods granting them for a brief moment "instant integration into the dominant material culture."

The following January, another flashpoint incident occurred in Jamaica. Thousands of citizens took to the streets of Kingston and St. Andrew, blocking most major roadways in response to an increase in the price of petroleum products.[10] It was initially led by the National Patriotic Movement, an affiliate of the JLP. It was a burgeoning crisis in which a small protest by a handful of persons catalyzed into a mass civil protest. As Dennis Forsyte recorded, "It was the 'little people' (the unorganized mass) who spontaneously provided the movement with energy, determination, manual labor and vigilance."[11] This type of protest activity quickly spread to Montego Bay and to rural parishes such as Hanover and Westmoreland. The protesters were said to be "disciplined, restrained and self-directed."

There was no abatement in Jamaica's violence as the 1980s gave way to the 1990s. According to police statistics, 156 of the 270 murders in the first six months of 1990 were committed in the corporate areas of Kingston and St. Andrew. In June 1990 alone, 64 murders were recorded. And by the end of August the number of deaths for the year had jumped to 450. In some cases the brutality of criminals has been unbelievable. For example, on June 29, 1990, armed bandits used high-powered guns to help murder Hopetown Ward, a 30-year-old resident of De-la-Vega City on the outskirts of Jamaica's old capital, Spanish Town. When they ran out of bullets, they stabbed him 35 times, ripping apart many of his internal organs, including his heart.

Some observers attribute the upsurge in violence to U.S., Canadian, and British crackdowns on the crime networks called the "posses." Many posse members were deported from Europe and North America, and some returned home voluntarily. They have resumed their criminal activity in Jamaica, creating nightmares in many places. Many posse members were allegedly political thugs who migrated from Jamaica with the complicity of local politicians. With the present narrowing of the philosophical divide between the ruling People's National Party and the Jamaica Labor Party, the former thugs are now operating independently.

National Security Minister K. D. Knight links the violence to several factors. The proliferation of guns used to ensure the electoral victory of some candidates is one. In addition, the economic deprivation in Jamaica has aggravated the poverty, creating greater incentives for people to become involved in the already significant drug-related crimes. Moreover, greed is said to contribute to the problem. Many people who commit crimes live comfortably and use their crime proceeds for conspicuous consumption.[12]

Guyana

Guyana is a society of repressed violence. Although the society exists in an atmosphere of calm, it is one in which citizens live in fear. Unlike in Jamaica, the violence of its underclass or subcultural movements does not generate this atmosphere. It stems from the institutionalized violence of its state apparatus and parastatal gangs, in the context of an executive president who is above the law, and the doctrine of Paramountcy of the ruling People's National Party (PNC). This violence was, initially, unrelentingly directed against the majority Indo-Guyanese population, but now it is also used against all Afro-Guyanese movements and groups that dare criticize and oppose the government.

In recent times, flashpoint incidents related to riots associated with the 1962 (Kaldor) budget, the riots resulting from the 1963 Labor Relations Bill, the Guyana Agricultural Workers Union strike of 1964, and state action against the Working Peoples' Alliance (WPA) leading to the murder of Dr. Walter Rodney in 1980. Perry Mars noted that the most important causes of major acts of violence in Guyana were basically political in nature but recognized that "ethnic cleavage can at times contribute to the escalation of violence."[13] Robert Manley noted that the 1961–1964 period was one of considerable ethnic and ideological conflict. The three riots of that period certainly manifested racial polarization and bitter conflict and suggest that the primary political reasons merely provided the opportunity for deeply felt primordial resentments to emerge fully.[14]

In February 1962, following the presentation of the government budget and a proposal for a constitutional committee, a protest demonstration led by Forbes Burnham and Peter D'Aguiar was held in Georgetown. They charged that the budget contained policies biased toward the Indian population. The demonstration grew into a massive crowd. Extensive arson and rioting caused significant damage to the city. Five persons were killed, and 80 were injured.

In April 1963, the introduction of a Labor Relations Bill by the government became the occasion for a general strike. It included civil servants who were mainly Afro-Guyanese. According to Robert Manley the strike became "a test of strength between competing ideological and ethnic factions, played out against a cold-war background." It lasted for 80 days. The strikers reportedly received approximately US$80,000 a week from the American Institute for Free Labor Development (AIFLD). The bill was withdrawn but not without the accompanying widespread racially inspired terror.

In early 1964, the Guyana Agricultural Workers Union (GAWU), a sugar workers union affiliated with the People's Progressive Party (PPP), engaged in a power struggle to replace the Man Power Citizens Association (MPCA) as the major sugar union. In the resulting strikes and acts of violence, 176 persons were killed, 920 were injured, 1,400 homes were destroyed by fire, and almost 15,000 people were forced to migrate to more racially homogeneous communities.[15] An incident on the west coast of Demerara proved decisive in converting the struggle into a full-scale racial war. East Indian supporters attacked and shot several strikebreakers. Fourteen persons were killed. Nine were Indo-Guyanese and five were Afro-Guyanese. Of the 176 injured, 99 were Indo-Guyanese and 77 were Afro-Guyanese. After that it was racial mayhem. Later, part of the Amerindian population, the original occupants of Guyana, insulted, ignored, and exploited, rose up in rebellion. Called the 1968 Rupununi Uprising, the movement was quickly suppressed by government forces.

The Working Peoples' Alliance was founded in 1976. The group brought together the Indian Political Association headed by Moses Bhagwan, the Working Peoples Vanguard Party, the Ratoon Group of scholars, and the Association for Social and Cultural Relations with Independent Africa. The rapid progress and acceptability of this multi-racial movement by the Guyanese people, and the emergence of Walter Rodney as its main spokesperson, offered a serious threat to the Jagan/Burnham (Indo-Guyanese/Afro-Guyanese) competition. It also appeared to be genuinely interracial and offered the real prospect of a unified Guyana. It was physically and psychologically harassed by government forces and by the pro-PNC House of Israel, a religious group led by Rabbi Washington, an American fugitive. WPA meetings were violently smashed, members were severely beaten, houses were arbitrarily searched, passports withdrawn, jobs were taken away, and finally, Rodney was killed by a planted bomb in June 1980. Since then the movement has been transformed into a political party. However, it has not appeared to grow and has not been the force it once was.

Trinidad and Tobago

Among the several flashpoint incidents of political violence in contemporary Trinidad, two stand out — the failed revolution/coup of

February 1970, and the July 26, 1990, Muslimeen coup attempt. Contemporary Trinidad is marked by sporadic outbreaks of arson and a forlorn and unsuccessful guerrilla effort in the hills above Port-of-Spain (after a series of bank robberies). The events of 1970 and 1990 were cataclysmic and, perhaps, cathartic. Were it not for the massive and unanticipated oil wealth that was generated through OPEC petroleum price increases, the "peace" might not have held until 1990. That wealth was used in part to keep the poor, frustrated, and angry Trinidadians at bay.

On the day of the "February 22 Revolution," 200 students from the University of the West Indies and their supporters went to Port-of-Spain to hold a solidarity march with students involved in the crisis at Sir George Williams University in Montreal.[16] There was a confrontation with the police. The following day, 12 persons were arrested for assembling in a place of worship (The Cathedral, Woodford Square) and on other charges. At the trial, the leaders of the demonstration organized a solidarity march that attracted a crowd of nearly 10,000 supporters. Geddes Granger, the student leader, then took the crowd into Shanty Town. A spate of arson followed. Another demonstration in early March from Port-of-Spain to San Juan attracted a crowd of 10,000 people. Organizations of all sorts began to mushroom overnight. A major department store, Kirpalani, was burned down, raising the cry that black power was anti-Indian. The response was a march for Afro-Asian solidarity. The march to Caroni, 28 miles long, attracted 10,000 marchers and proved a tremendous success.

The government's initial response on March 23 was to raise TT$10 million by increased taxation to create work for the population. Marches with massive crowds proclaiming Black Power emerged in every part of the twin-island state. Stokely Carmichael, Trinidad-born American Black Power leader, was banned from entering Trinidad. The deputy leader of the ruling party (PNM) resigned from the Cabinet on April 13. All these events took place against a background of violence and arson. A work stoppage at the Water and Sewage Authority on April 15 of 600 workers at Brechin Castle and a series of solidarity marches organized by the National Joint Action Committee (NJAC) kept the political situation at a boiling point.

On April 21, the prime minister declared a state of emergency in the country and asked for the support of the U.S. government in the form of warships and troops. He also arrested 15 key Black Power leaders. A mutiny by a section of the 750-member Trinidad and Tobago Defense Force was contained with the help of a U.S. Coast Guard patrol boat at Chaguaramas. After several days of negotiations, its leader, Lieutenant

Raffique Shah surrendered the hostages, and the mutineers were arrested. By this act, the government also forestalled a planned general strike, which was to include the powerful Oilfield Workers' Trade Union led by George Weekes. A revolution may very well have occurred if the government finally had not moved decisively with U.S. assistance against the burgeoning popular forces aided by a section of the military.

The July 1990 Jamaat-al-Muslimeen revolt and hostage taking was unanticipated by the government although the group had been under observation by the police force. On the late afternoon of July 26, black Muslim leader Iman Yasin Abu Bakr appeared on Trinidad and Tobago Television to announce that he had taken the Trinidad and Tobago Cabinet hostage and was in charge of the country. Red House — the parliament building — and the Trinidad and Tobago Television station were occupied by the Muslimeens, and the St. Clair police station was bombed and set on fire. An indeterminate number of persons were killed in that attack, and many were injured.

Negotiations commenced the following day among the Muslimeen and government ministers and officials, Roman Catholic Archbishop Anthony Patin, and Anglican Bishop Clive Abdulah. During all this there were widespread shooting and looting in which at least 22 persons were killed and scores more wounded. Robinson spoke on short-wave radio requesting the chief of the defense force to cease firing weapons in the vicinity of the Red House. And on Monday both he and Minister of National Security Selwyn Richardson announced that an agreement had been reached with the Jamaat-al-Muslimeen.

Prime Minister Robinson was released on Tuesday, after 1:00 p.m. During Wednesday, all the hostages were released, and at 2:15 p.m. the Muslimeen surrender began, first from the Red House and then from the television station. Then it was all over. The report was that the group had surrendered unconditionally and were taken to Camp Ogden for detention.

The Muslimeen action took place against a background of severe difficulties in the economy, a growing hostility toward the government and its policies since attaining power in 1986, and the emergence of new political and social groupings. Specifically, the Muslimeen were annoyed that the High Court had ruled against them the previous April. They were declared to have illegally constructed buildings on a plot of land at Mucurapo Road. The group was actually demonstrating outside the Red House while Parliament was in session to bring attention to their complaint. Ironically, this made it easy for the group to amass its forces without arousing much suspicion of their damaging, illegal, and terroristic intentions.

MANIFESTATIONS IN THE EASTERN ISLANDS

Grenada

Grenada is the only country in the Anglophone Caribbean where violence consolidated into a revolution. The relatively bloodless coup of March 13, 1979, was transformed into one of noncapitalist development aiming toward socialism. That "revolution" was excoriated a few days after a combined military force of U.S. Marines (up to 6,000), and, later, 300 soldiers from Jamaica, Barbados, and four members of the Organization of Eastern Caribbean States (OECS) invaded the country on October 25, 1983. Starting with a brief look at the Eric Matthew Gairy movement, which awakened the Grenadian masses, an examination is made of the New Jewel Movement (NJM) and the role played by the Committee of Twenty-Two. These activities led into the coup of March 13, 1979, and the bloody coup by the military on October 19, 1983.

Grenada was one of the four Anglophone Eastern Caribbean states where social and labor movements did not develop during the labor disturbances of the 1930s. Grenada did, however, have a revolutionary tradition in the famous Fedon Revolt.[17] Although many Caribbean countries had already generated their popular and charismatic leaders who personified the movement for constitutional change, independence, and justice in the 1940s, in Grenada it was not until 1949, when Eric Gairy was deported from Aruba for participation in labor agitation there that the underlying forces for protest and change found a champion. Manifestations of unrest started before his arrival, but once there he directed the course of events.

Arson, strikes, marches, and political harangue became the order of the day. When the first general elections under Universal Adult Suffrage came in 1951, Gairy's Grenada United Labor Party (GULP) won resoundingly. His party subsequently won seven electoral contests. These victories were based upon his strong support among the peasantry and rural-based population who had their lot markedly improved under Gairy's leadership. The middle strata were always implacably opposed to his rule.

The year 1973 was a watershed in Grenadian politics. It was set against the background of the Caribbean Black Power movements, especially around 1970, and against the background of the nurses' strike of November and December 1970. This strike led to a massive demonstration and sit-in, and many new movements and organizations emerged in Grenada. Gairy's government had become mercilessly brutal. In a 1970 speech on Black Power, he announced that he had assembled some of the "toughest and roughest roughnecks" to maintain law and order and that "it takes steel to cut steel." This marked the turning point in real harassment, intimidation, and violence by police and parastatal groups on members of the new movements.

A committee of concerned citizens gave way to the formation of a Joint Effort for Welfare, Education, and Liberation (JEWEL). Later, Maurice Bishop and Kenrick Radix formed the Movement for the Assemblies of People in November 1972.[18] These two groups were merged in March 1973 and became the New Jewel Movement (NJM). The NJM became the nucleus of the group that later mounted a successful coup on March 13, 1979. It was to become honed in battles with the government, on its own and sometimes in collaboration with a wide cross section of other groups.

It was Gairy's determination to proceed rapidly to formal independence from Great Britain. The manner in which he sought to do this created massive opposition to his regime, especially among organized groups, both traditional and nontraditional. In a secret meeting with the British minister responsible for Commonwealth affairs, Britain would move to terminate the associated statehood status with Grenada under certain conditions, thus obviating the necessity to hold a referendum and secure a two-thirds majority in favor of independence. The Chamber of Commerce and the Employers' Federation insisted upon a referendum.

On Gairy's return from London in October 1972, he invited various interest groups to hold discussions with him on the independence issue. This led to a round of protests, walkouts, and a signature campaign against independence under Gairy's leadership. There was a two-day general strike on April 5 and 6, 1973. The police slaying of a young man in Grenville occasioned a mob action and mass demonstration. The police were forced to close the Grenville police station, the Pearl's Airport was closed for two days, Radio Grenada was fire bombed, and other acts of arson occurred in St. Georges and in Grenville. Grenada businessmen closed their stores in protest to Gairy's independence moves on May 14, 1973. Three hundred dockworkers joined in the protest. The following day the Chamber of Commerce, secondary school teachers, secondary and primary school children, bank clerks, electricity, telephone, and water authority workers, and a wide variety of other workers joined action, bringing the country to a complete standstill by May 16, 1973.[19] After May 20, the country began to return to normalcy.

Another dramatic occurrence took place on November 4, 1973. The NJM held a "Peoples Congress" at Seamoon, St. Andrew's, which attracted over 10,000 people. Twenty-seven charges were laid against the Gairy regime, ranging from corruption to incompetence. They demanded that he resign or face a general strike. On the day appointed for the strike, November 18, six NJM members, who had gone to Grenville to hold discussions with some businessmen regarding the planned strike, were beaten, arrested, and jailed by the police and their "Police Aids."

A general strike was held, this time as the Chamber of Commerce, the Employers' Federation, the churches, the schools and anti-Gairy trade unions came together to protest police brutality. Twenty-two organizations came together and passed a resolution demanding the arrest of those police responsible for acts of brutality, the disbandment of the "Police Aids," and the end of arbitrary searches and arrests by the police. Thus the Committee of Twenty-Two was born. The strike was called off after one week when Gairy agreed to a commission to inquire into the operation of the system of justice in Grenada. Gairy, nevertheless, continued his intimidatory pressure on the various social groupings.

This pressure was maintained continuously through to the 1976 general elections in which Gairy's GULP won 9 of the 15 seats — a result which the tri-party alliance group, including Herbert Blaize's Grenada National Party (GNP) and the NJM, never accepted as legitimate. When the coup of March 13, 1979, came, it was merely the culmination of growing popular alienation of the Gairy regime, which, in its final years, had reduced Grenada to be "the laughing stock" of the Caribbean. It explains why, until internal party disputes led to the bloody military takeover on October 19, 1983, there was no opposition to the Bishop regime — the various groups quietly welcomed the regime.

Dominica and St. Lucia

Dominica and St. Lucia were the remaining Anglophone Caribbean states by-passed by the 1930s labor disturbances. As in Grenada, broad-based trade unions arose only in the late 1940s and early 1950s, and "they constituted the mass base for the parties which were later to hold the reigns of government authority. Movements, using some violence, and rooted in broad-based groupings, including the Civil Service Association, churches, trade unions, political groupings and opposition political parties, the Chamber of Commerce, and civic bodies, came together to bring about change. The initial action was to put in an interim leadership, which then prepared the country for general elections within a few months. This was done on the basis of a presumed constitutionality because elected representatives were involved and because the groups were acting together in the "national interest." The very low level of accompanying violence also served to offer some legitimacy for this method. Unlike the Grenada coup, efforts were made to return immediately to the existing constitutional order.

Persistent manifestations of a high degree of political instability in terms of constant changes in or problems associated with state personnel, and an unresolved authority structure, led to the rise of coalition movements, which quickly evaporated after achieving their immediate objectives. In both countries there was a background of frequent strikes, political struggles, public servants' political activities through their associations, and governmental efforts to control them through legislation.[20]

In Dominica, the immediate precipitants were, first, the implication of the Patrick John administration in secret relations with the government of South Africa and in a planned invasion of Barbados by 350 mercenaries and, second, in response to severe political and economic pressures, John's attempt to introduce new and oppressive bills in Parliament.[21] In response, a crowd of 13,000 demonstrators gathered in front of the parliament building. The Dominica Defense Force fired on them, killing two persons and seriously injuring nine more. The demonstrators were protesting against an amendment to the Industrial Relations Act and the strengthening of the Slander and Libel Act. Further pressures came from a protracted dispute over wages with the Civil Service Association, from the Dominica's Farmers Union, and from a Committee for National Salvation, which was subsequently formed and dedicated to bringing down the regime.[22] The government was brought to a standstill, and a "constitutional dethronement" of Patrick John and his government was effected. The committee also had to be reconstituted later to force the interim government to stop dawdling and call early elections.

Patrick John and the army, not satisfied with the outcome of events, sought to overthrow the government. Prime Minister Eugenia Charles had to deal with two attempted coups and a disloyal army, subsequently disbanded, in 1981. In the March 1981 plot, Patrick John and others were arrested and charged with conspiracy to overthrow the government. Upon conviction the army chief was hanged, and John served a prison sentence.

In St. Lucia, a leadership crisis within the ruling St. Lucia Labor Party (SLP) precipitated the events leading to premature general elections. The SLP, in its drive for electoral victory, had incorporated the left-leaning St. Lucia Action Movement and other left-leaning persons in its ranks. Apparently, after the July 2, 1979, general elections, a party caucus agreed that Allan Louisy would become prime minister for six months after which he would be appointed to the governor generalship. George Odlum was then to become the next prime minister. This agreement was never carried out, and this led to severe intraparty and extraparty struggles.

St. Kitts-Nevis and St. Vincent

St. Kitts-Nevis-Anguilla experienced a secessionist movement in the 1960s. Anguilla forcibly broke away from the union. Reacting to its double "colony status" (as a colony of Britain and the secondary colonialism within the Union) and to being forced into a new constitutional arrangement for the creation of the Associated State of St. Kitts, Nevis, and Anguilla, the Anguilla islanders revolted. On March 8, 1967, the Government House in Anguilla was burnt down and the warden fled to St. Kitts the following day.[23] During the following weeks the police headquarters and the homes and business places of prominent supporters of the St. Kitts government were fired on. Petty captures the major events of the struggle very well:

At a meeting called by Peter Adams on May 29, the crowd voted by a show of hands to expel the St. Kitts policemen from the Island. The crowd left the park in procession and marched to the Police Headquarters, where they ordered the police to leave Anguilla by 10 a.m. the following day. Early in the morning of May 30, a large and hostile crowd surrounded the Police Headquarters. In the meantime, the Wallblake Airport was blocked by oil drums, trucks, bulldozers, cars and barbed wire so as to prevent the landing of any police re-inforcements which may have been sent from St. Kitts. As the 10 o'clock deadline approached, the policemen were advised that a plane was ready to take some of them to St. Kitts, and by noon all the policemen were disarmed and expelled from Anguilla. The Anguillans had taken control of their own destiny.[24]

On the morning of June 10, 1967, a party of Anguillans invaded St. Kitts and attacked the police headquarters, the defense force head-quarters, and the power station. It was a failure but was based on the notion that offense was the best form of defense. Efforts at finding a peaceful solution failed because the Anguillans were determined to have no relations at all with St. Kitts-Nevis. Indeed, by popular vote independence was unilaterally declared. Britain's emissary, William Witlock, was expelled after discussions broke down. The British government invaded Anguilla on March 19, 1969. Some 300 to 400 British paratroopers (Red Devils), marines, and policemen landed from two battleships and crushed the rebellion without a shot being fired on either side. Anguilla reverted to being a colony of Great Britain.

St. Vincent and the Grenadines experienced a revolt in the sparsely populated Union Island on the day following the December 9, 1979, elections. It was quickly put down with the assistance of troops from Barbados. They were restricted to policing duties in St. Vincent itself while the state's policemen looked after control in Union Island. It is interesting to note that the leader of the revolt had fled to revolutionary Grenada but the Bishop government returned him in chains to the Vincentian authorities.

DEMOCRACY AND CONFLICT MANAGEMENT

Flashpoints of violence have occurred in several parts of the Anglophone Caribbean. Three occurrences (in Grenada, Dominica, and St. Lucia) have led to changes of government, and there were failed coup attempts against the Eugenia Charles government in Dominica. One of these — in Grenada — led to an actual revolution. Three countries have experienced failed coups/revolutions (Trinidad and Tobago — twice; Jamaica, and Dominica). In all these cases, the system of government still in place is the liberal democratic system of Westminister democracy. Under the People's Revolutionary Government in Grenada, this form was suspended as the regime, using the existing constitution and common law practice as the base, ruled by decrees and was supported by a large army and police force. However, the country, effortlessly, after the U.S. invasion, returned to the modal political form of competitive democracy.

In the other situations of violence, the characteristics were those of civil, partisan, and ethnic strife where contestations were not so much about the inappropriateness of the liberal democratic framework as about the achievement of justice within it. Methods contrary to the law such as coercion, intimidation, arson, and murder were used, but overall there was little explicit contradiction with liberal democratic principle.

Some of the violence originated in human greed and envy and thus can be said to be a product of social deviance. This was, perhaps, the major factor involved in the downtown Kingston Rodney Riots and the Chinese Riots in Jamaica. To be sure, the significance of these riots exceed this dimension and had wider political implications, but the primary objective was in the looting of shops for material goods. Although the law-and-order response was foremost, it was also evident that material deprivation provided the easy excuse for the looters.

The partisan political violence that characterized the Jamaican situation, its pervasiveness and its viciousness, and then the reconversion by its paid practitioners to general criminal violence and activities suggest that conflict is endemic in the Jamaican society because of inherent aggressive drives. If this is the case, rather than emphasis being placed merely on suppression and elimination of violence, more attention ought to be placed on managing political violence and conflict and channeling such energies into safe activities. Jamaicans are famous for their aggressiveness, producing not only negative consequences, such as violence, but also dynamic achievements in the fine arts, theatre, dance, architecture, and sports. This indicates that an alternative or correlative approach accentuating that which is positive can be successful.

For some groups involved in the conflicts, violence became an acceptable although regrettable way to rationally pursue goals in conditions of scarce resources. The Muslimeen violence in Trinidad and Tobago, the Committee of Twenty-Two in Grenada, the Committee for National Reconstruction in St. Lucia, the antigovernment demonstrations and the Committee for National Salvation in Dominica, the 1962 (Kaldor) budget riots, the 1963 disturbances and the GAWU strike in 1964 in Guyana, and the secessionist violence by Anguillans could be so characterized. From this perspective an appropriate response would be to manage the problems through "resource distribution, or the inculcation of different sets of values, such as frugality and asceticism."[25]

In Trinidad and Tobago, after the failed coup/revolution of 1970, this was the response of the government. The massive increase in earnings from the petroleum industry enabled the government to carry out a substantial welfare-oriented redistributive policy. However, it was not sustainable when the return to protracted low oil prices threw the economy out of kilter and the resources to sustain the policy were depleted. Indeed, many of the commitments to general welfare had to be severely cut. It was against this background of retreat from welfare in which the land-hunger problem of the Jamaat-al-Muslimeen led to the 1990 violence. Presumably, the deep national embarrassment could have been avoided if the institutions of government had been prepared to find solutions other than eviction of the groups from the landed property on which it had squatted. History may not absolve the government.

In St. Lucia and Dominica the purpose was to have fresh elections as the way to resolve the extant crisis of government. Having accomplished the objective, the groups disbanded and ceased being a political force in the country. This was the situation also in Grenada with the Committee of Twenty-Two. The group disbanded permanently after Gairy met certain demands concerning the move to independence. The response in Guyana to the 1962 (Kaldor) budget was a contestation about resource allocation, which was perceived to be made on an ethnically biased basis. The 1963 80-day strike by civil servants and others in Guyana followed a similar pattern as, too, was the violent GAWU strike, played out along racial lines.

If analysts were to start from "a notion of legitimacy based, not on legality, but upon the view that legitimacy is measured by the degree to which authorities and institutions serve those over whom the authority is exercised, and in particular, by the degree to which they promote the identity and fulfillment of the people,"[26] then there would be the obligation to rethink our notions of force and violence. If certain human needs are concerned with development as well as survival, they are thereby ontological and universal, and it must be understood that individuals or groups will use all means at their disposal, legal or illegal, to pursue these, constrained only by the values they attach to relationships with others in society. Much of the violence in Anglophone Caribbean societies occurs because of systemic failures to meet the needs and wants of people. This means that a predominantly law-and-order response may only settle for a while but not resolve the underlying causes of conflict that lead to violence.

The underlying factors in all these cases of violence seem to be based upon the fact that these societies have developed to a greater degree than others beyond mere decolonization and formal independence. There are now inescapable demands for increased participation, increased assertion of human rights and needs, and a recognition of the lessened abilities of central authorities to control behavior of greater and more complex population groups with means of violence readily at hand. Merely exercising the franchise periodically is not enough. Exercising the franchise is often unhappily to renounce it. The representative principle steals from individuals the ultimate responsibility for their values, beliefs, and actions. If we were pragmatically to seek a democratic form of government in which all the people govern themselves in at least some public matters at least some of the time, then we might go some way toward achieving this sense of salience in the citizenry.[27]

To achieve this requires political education. It is most effective on a level that challenges individuals to engage cooperatively in the solution of concrete problems affecting themselves and their immediate communities. Facilitating conditions include civic education, leadership, religion, and patriotism. Limiting conditions include the problem of scale, structural inequality, rights and the ultimate uncertainty of all human vision — and of public vision in particular — in a world where no knowledge is certain, no grounds absolute, and no political decision irrevocable. Strong democratic practice requires a political program and a political strategy. Neither ideas nor institutions are self-implementing. They demand a base — a political movement comprised of committed democrats who understand themselves and have an interest in the realization of a strong democracy.

Notwithstanding all this, the immediate situation of violence and rebellion must be addressed. The Anglophone Caribbean's responses to violence and rebellion have been mainly to establish draconian laws and to seek to strengthen the region militarily. Some tougher laws are necessary, and so is some degree of militarization. Nonetheless, both responses may cause, and have been causing, more problems than those they have settled. The military has often proven to be the quickest way to state power, as the experiences of countries in Latin America and elsewhere have shown. It was not a mere coincidence that the military in Dominica and in Grenada sought government power in its own name.

Moreover, strengthening and arming the police to better cope with civil violence is also fraught with danger. The experience with police and military behavior under states of emergency in Caribbean countries cries out for an adequate protocol of acceptable conduct, dress, and stated purpose when civilians and their personal property are accosted. The experience of police behavior in Trinidad following the July 1990 coup attempt contained unnecessary hostility meted out to citizens stopped at roadblocks by nonuniformed officers carelessly wielding rifles. During states of emergency in areas of western Kingston, Jamaicans experienced similar problems.

For both the police and the military, the uppermost consideration should be to find and establish mechanisms of civilian control. Assuredly, the ideal requirements for civilian control include the presence of widely supported political institutions such as parliament or political party, coupled with a self-imposed and maintained sense of restraint by officers and politicians alike where the military is not actively solicited for resolving domestic political conflicts but is assigned to conduct relatively restricted activities.[28]

Both the police and the military in the Caribbean need to accept their subordination to the legally established civilian authorities and their duty to serve the people. The appropriate sets of behavior constituting professionalism should be carefully instilled in members of the armed forces. Institutional means to ensure compliance with these approaches and standards must be established, preferably with majority and broad-based civilian membership.

Although political violence has occurred in the Anglophone Caribbean, the liberal democratic system has withstood its test. This does not mean that all is well with the extent of democratic functioning within the region. Nor does it mean that a law-and-order response is sufficient to contain violence. Violence has indicated the need for substantial changes in the political economy and sociology of the Caribbean, and in Caribbean political history, violence has led to all the significant changes. It should be possible to develop institutions of change that can deal with problems of transformation of these societies before change is wrought by calamitous violence.

NOTES

1. See Paul Wilkinson, *Terrorism and the Liberal State* (London: Macmillan, 1977).

2. C. R. Mitchell, *The Structure of International Conflict* (London: Macmillan, 1982), p. 318. On the question of structural violence, see Johann Galtung, "A Structural Theory of Integration," *Journal of Peace Research* 5 (1968).

3. Wilkinson, *Terrorism and the Liberal State*, p. 23.

4. Mitchell, *Structure of International Conflict*, p. 7.

5. Terry Lacey, *Violence and Politics in Jamaica: 1960–1970* (Manchester: Manchester University Press, 1977), pp. 83–84.

6. Ibid., p. 85.

7. Rex Nettleford, *Identity, Race, and Protest in Jamaica* (New York: Morrow Publishers, 1972), pp. 95–97.

8. See Carl Leiden and Karl Schmitt, *The Politics of Violence: Revolution in the Modern World* (Englewood Cliffs, N.J.: Prentice Hall, 1968), pp. 25–35.

9. Lacey, p. 98.

10. Carl Stone, *Democracy and Clientilism in Jamaica* (New Brunswick, N.J.: Transaction Books, 1980), pp. 4–6.

11. Cited in Stone, ibid., p. 5.

12. See "Crime Wave Hits Jamaica," *The Weekend* (St. Lucia), July 1990, p. 4; and "Curfew in Kingston," *New York Carib News*, September 4, 1990, p. 3.

13. Perry Mars, "Political Violence and Ethnic Polarization in Guyana, 1947–1960," in Harold Lutchman, Perry Mars, and Herb Addo, eds., *Selected Issues in Guyanese Politics* (Georgetown: University of Guyana, 1976).

14. Robert Manley, *Guyana Emergent: Post Independence Struggle for Non-Dependent Development* (Cambridge, Mass.: Schenkman, 1979), p. 7.

15. Vere T. Daley, *A Short History of the Guyanese People* (London: Macmillan, 1975), pp. 306–7.

16. See Lloyd Best, "'The February Revolution' in Trinidad and Tobago," in Trevor Munroe and Rupert Lewis, eds., *Government and Politics of the West Indies* (Kingston, Jamaica: Herald Press, 1971); and Ivor Oxaal, *Race and Revolutionary Consciousness* (Cambridge, Mass.: Schenkman, 1971).

17. See George Brizan, *Grenada: Island of Conflict* (London: Zed Press, 1984).

18. See R. Jacobs, "The Movement towards Grenadian Independence," in *Independence for Grenada: Myth or Reality* (Port-of-Spain, Trinidad: University of the West Indies, 1974).

19. Ibid., pp. 28–29.

20. Neville C. Duncan, *Aspects of Statehood in the Peripheral Societies of the Anglophone Caribbean* (Mimeo, Institute of International Relations, Trinidad, 1980), p. 10.

21. Ibid., p. 15.

22. Ibid., p. 94.

23. Colville Petty, *Anguilla: Where There Is a Will There Is a Way* (Anguilla: Colville Petty, 1983), p. 21.

24. Ibid., p. 22.

25. Mitchell, *Structure of International Conflict*, p. 33.

26. See John Burton, *Global Conflict* (College Park, Md.: University of Maryland, 1984).

27. See Benjamin Barber, *Strong Democracy: Political Participation for a New Age* (Berkeley: University of California Press, 1984).

28. See Claude Welch, *Civilian Control of the Military* (Albany: State University of New York Press, 1976).

4 Postinvasion Political Security in the Eastern Caribbean

Clifford E. Griffin

Geography, history, culture, and politics are among the characteristics shared by the English-speaking Caribbean.[1] Close economic, social, political, and historical ties have shaped and continue to influence the nature of relations within this group. Consequently, political developments in one country often affect events elsewhere in the region. All Caribbean countries have been penetrated by British political culture, which has contributed greatly to their remarkable political stability. This stability, however, comes under challenge from time to time because of the lag between economic growth and political development. The resulting crisis of rising and falling expectations often plunges large segments of the population into a state of misery. Charismatic and other strategically placed individuals often emerge to orchestrate mobilization against the incumbent regime. There is much evidence of this: the secession of Anguilla from St. Kitts-Nevis-Anguilla in 1967; the Trinidad and Tobago army mutiny in 1970; coup attempts in Dominica in April and December 1981; and the bloody coup attempt in Trinidad and Tobago in July–August 1990.

In the Eastern Caribbean the problems in Grenada precipitated by this dysfunction developed to their extreme. The inability of the Eric Gairy regime in Grenada to reconcile the dilemmas created by this lag led to a severe political crisis there. This has had profound implications for the rest of the region. Given their historical, political, and other similarities, any analysis of political security in postinvasion Grenada must entail an examination of political security in the rest of the English-speaking

Caribbean in general and in the Organization of Eastern Caribbean States (OECS) — Antigua and Barbuda, Dominica, Grenada, Montserrat, St. Kitts and Nevis, St. Lucia, and St. Vincent and the Grenadines — in particular. This chapter, therefore, focuses on the OECS and analyzes the implications for political security in the aftermath of the U.S. intervention in Grenada. It is argued that a military solution to a fundamentally economic problem that arose in Grenada serves to undermine the political and social bases of stability, not only in Grenada itself, but also in the subregion generally. In addition, Grenada and other states in the region risk being placed under the economic tutelage of the United States because of the U.S. policy of "intervention by invitation." Moreover, the militarization of the region now has the potential to exacerbate the original security problem that it was intended to remedy.

SECURITY ISSUES

A secure nation is relatively invulnerable to threats to its development and national sovereignty. These threats may be territorial, political, and/or economic and may take on a military character. By this definition, no nation is really secure, and certainly not Grenada or any in the OECS group. These countries have a combined population of 570,000, an average per capita gross national product of $1,000, and none of these countries exceeds 300 square miles in area. Their small size and limited wealth reflect immediate security issues. Alone, the Eastern Caribbean is incapable of resisting an attack by any external power that has significant naval and air forces at its disposal. The 1985 report of the Commonwealth Consultative Group indicates that security concerns in Grenada and the rest of the Commonwealth Caribbean entail threats to territorial integrity that might stem from external aggression, the establishment of foreign bases, secession, or the use of territory for unauthorized or illegal purposes.

Political security threats involve foreign pressures for policy change, destabilization and subversion, extraterritorial jurisdiction, and the undermining of social and cultural identity. Economic security threats reflect a country's ability or inability to take actions and responsibility for improving its economic conditions.[2] Military threats may be a derivative of all of these factors.

The Caribbean Community and Common Market (CARICOM), which include all OECS member countries, outline the following set of security concerns for the region:

internal stresses due to the high expectations of their people, unacceptable levels of unemployment, and the assertion of identity;

incursion or threats of incursions by mercenaries, a situation to which several of these island-states, irrespective of their position on the political spectrum, have been exposed;

the need to isolate the area from the effects of conflicts from outside.[3]

Although it might be difficult, at best, to control events that might impinge on the third concern, the first two are clearly within the security portfolio of the OECS. An armed insurgency by a small group of adherents to an opposition party might conceivably overthrow a government that is incapable of effectively managing the conditions that might result in scenario one. This might also result from scenario two. With previous attempts having been made in St. Kitts and Nevis and in the Grenadines (Union Island), the events in Grenada in 1979 suggest that, at best, a coup d'état is the most likely manifestation of political security threats to the OECS.

Another dimension of security relates to the preferred system of government. Political security entails establishing and maintaining the political structures, institutions, and processes that give the citizens opportunities for participation and a sense of political efficacy. When these institutions and procedures are abused, the potential for political instability increases. This was the case in Grenada that led to mobilizing popular opposition to Eric Gairy's rule and the subsequent Grenada Revolution. As small, extremely dependent, economically open and, therefore, highly vulnerable microstates, Eastern Caribbean states must effectively address these political security concerns. Because threats to the security (autonomy) of small nations emerge not only from superpowers but also from middle powers, large organizations with legal or illegal motives, and even from opportunistic individuals and/or mercenaries, security concerns for this region are now more complex, real, and pressing.[4] These security issues have political, military, and economic dimensions and inherent in the pursuit of political security objectives is the danger of selecting ineffective or inappropriate mechanisms.

Developed as a consequence of their lengthy period of exposure to British political, social, and cultural norms, symbols, and procedures, the political culture of the English-speaking Caribbean has important implications for their future political security. Three hypotheses are posited in this analysis: one, the political culture of Grenada — and the rest of the OECS — will play a vital role in political security matters; two, the economic realities of Grenada — and the rest of the region — are directly related to its security; and three, the militarization of the Eastern Caribbean microstates undermines their political culture — the traditional basis of their political stability — and, therefore, threatens their political security.

A rather uneasy calm surrounds the island of Grenada and the rest of the Eastern Caribbean since the counterrevolution and subsequent U.S. invasion of Grenada in October 1983. Known for their luxurious climate, sandy beaches, and their special attraction to tourists, these islands have been referred to variously as peaceful, tranquil, quiescent, Westministers-in-the-Sun — terms that immediately conjure up a strong sense of political stability. This has been so since decolonization. Like the rest of the English-speaking Caribbean, the OECS is predisposed to democratic norms, structures and processes adopted and institutionalized after a lengthy period of exposure to British political culture and political socialization.

Before March 1979, political participation for most citizens centered on the selection of the political directorate through competitive elections, secret balloting, and full suffrage. Constitutional provisions, legal systems based on the principles of English common law, plus norms and conventions all combine to guarantee and protect political rights and civil liberties for citizens and to provide protection from the arbitrary exercise of state power. Voluntarism, rather than state coercion, induces the growth and development of independent organizations that compete for political power and influence. Regular elections, interest group politics orchestrated largely through labor unions and political parties, and a conspicuous absence of an institutionalized military have been characteristic of these societies. They pride themselves on strong democratic principles and are predisposed to using the ballot rather than the bullet as the main vehicle to attain political power. Previously, therefore, political security was not a critical issue.

Citizens of the OECS have become habituated to democracy. This is a special case of political socialization in which a political community legitimizes a political system by providing continuous support for it. Legitimacy is maintained not merely because of the process of politicization entailing a network of rewards and punishments, as David Easton contends in *Systems Analysis of Political Life*. It is maintained precisely because the political system continues to provide a consistent output of norms to which the political community habituates itself. Their output, in turn, is fed back into the political system as an input in a dynamic process that secures the system's legitimacy and reinforces its stability.[5]

In the OECS, like the rest of the former British Caribbean colonies, democratic attitudes, institutions, and processes resulted largely from the lengthy period of British political socialization, beginning in the eighteenth century. British political tutelage emphasized a tendency toward creating strong bureaucratic structures that included the civil service, a judiciary, a police force, and "an ideology that stressed the legitimate role of state authority in the preservation of order."[6] With an emphasis on political stability, order was to be preserved through specified procedures and strict adherence to the rule of law, not through the use of arbitrary force or through the abuse of state power. The court system would operate in ways that were virtually consistent with those in England — with allowances for peculiarities of the given country.

British political culture also created a system of representation through election and the principle of power sharing. It was through this system that local politicians became socialized to the process of engaging, not only the British, but each other as well in an open political arena. This consolidated the procedure for transferring political power to elected officials. The legitimacy of governments in Grenada — and in the rest of the English-speaking Caribbean — was thus based on their establishment through representative elections. Although this system allowed for disagreement on policy-related issues, there was general agreement on procedural norms, such as for choosing candidates for election, the actual conduct of elections, and for the way that the elected officials must conduct themselves.

As Weiner and Ozbudun point out:

> Not that these procedures are always followed or that democratic norms of behavior are always observed; but there is agreement about what is appropriate and what is not, and leaders and parties are often criticized by their opponents and by a free press for failing to act in accordance with accepted rules.[7]

Imposing limits on government, establishing norms of conduct for those in positions of power, and creating procedures, such as the Commission of Inquiry, for managing conflict have been part of the legacy of British political culture in these countries. Continued observation and adherence to these traditions have contributed to their political stability.

A particular feature of politics in these countries is the manifestation of a low level of tolerance for political extremism. As in other pluralist democracies, political parties reflecting different ideological positions are allowed to operate. Left-leaning parties, however, are consistently rejected at the polls, and the dominant parties consistently pursue middle-of-the-road politics. Leftist parties have the option to, and do, field candidates for political offices in the general elections. The People's Progressive Party (PPP) of Guyana has the dubious distinction of being the only Marxist party that has consistently contested general elections in that country. No victory has been secured by this party in more than 25 years. Although it seems highly unlikely (at least in the near future) to see a leftist party coming into political prominence in Grenada as did the NJM, the years of exposure to a new consciousness between 1979 and 1983 have laid the foundations for access to political participation upon demand. A reluctance or inability to minimize the social and economic conditions that give rise to these movements could result in renewed instability and political insecurity in the OECS.

DEMOCRACY IN GRENADA

Was Grenada ever democratically stable? Did democracy ever exist in Grenada? If so, did it exist in both form and substance? Why has security become a matter of concern in Grenada and the OECS? According to Western democratic theory, a number of indicators reflect the institutionalization of democracy in a given country.[8] The record in Grenada under Gairy demonstrates convincingly that a number of these principles were grossly violated, delegitimizing Gairy's rule and creating and exacerbating the problem of democratic instability and political insecurity among the OECS. Critical to the events to 1979 were Gairy's abuse of political power and violation of the established norms of the political process.

The constitution bequeathed to Grenada caters for cabinet government formed on the basis of the single-member plurality system of voting. The party winning the most seats, based on a simple majority tally of the votes, forms the government. The head of the wining party invariably becomes the head of the government and has the last word on legislation and policy. The party is personified in the maximum leader. In a small country like Grenada, a political boss wields tremendous power and influence. Unlike in advanced industrial countries where politicians are the brokers or clients for big business, business looks to politicians for favors. While cleavages tend to develop around class, color, and ethnicity, a special form of political clientelism facilitates the preservation of institutional unity. Institutions like the ombudsman, parliamentary committees, the civil service, and Commissions of Inquiry exist to serve as checks and balances in these countries. Support for established institutions of power and process, therefore, tends to transcend narrower, parochial interests. Still, these are often subject to abuse and misuse by unscrupulous political leaders. The result is the undermining of the integrity and, hence, stability of the political system.

Under the regime of Eric Gairy, the political process in Grenada typified such abuse and misuse and consequent political instability. Gairy relieved the civil service of its decision-making powers to the extent that every matter, from the hiring of janitorial staff to a major public works project, became subject to a Cabinet decision — one in which he had the last word. As a result, he could reward his supporters and punish his opponents. Several violations were recorded in the report of the "Commission of Inquiry into the Control of Public Expenditures in Grenada during 1961." These included financial irregularities, such as using public funds to purchase luxury items for personal use, and weakening the morale of a key institution — the civil service.

Gairy's abuses grew worse after independence in 1974 through his intimidation of public employees by arbitrarily transferring and/or terminating their employment, political favoritism and nepotism, harassment, police brutality, summary arrest and imprisonment without trial, political assassinations, and forcing officials to be personally beholden to him as he tried to effectively stamp out opposition and dissent. Political rights and civil liberties were severely curtailed, and draconian laws were passed to muzzle discontent. The rights of free speech, assembly, and free press were abrogated, and the parliamentary process was effectively subverted as a virtual reign of terror was unleashed. In 1975, legislation was passed to harass and control the media through the Newspaper Amendment Act; public address systems were banned in 1976; limitations were placed on the ability of unions to strike through the Essential Services Amendment Act of 1978. The farcical nature of the parliamentary process based on Gairy's cult of personalismo made the fledgling democracy in Grenada quite insecure.

In 1979 Grenada underwent a collective reaction to this state of affairs. Having had enough of rigged elections, the employment of a secret police force (the Mongoose Gang), corruption, economic depression, and financial mismanagement, Grenada erupted in widespread mass political disorder. This volatile situation eventually culminated in a successful military coup d'état that ultimately transformed itself into the very popular but short-lived Grenada Revolution. This event brought security concerns among the OECS into saliency.

Political stability and political security do not mean the absence of political conflict. Conflict is consistent with democracy, and a democratic nation must have the mechanisms to contain conflict without destroying its most basic institutions. Political conflict in Grenada emerged largely from gross violations of political norms. Political conflict will emerge in the rest of the OECS for similar reasons. Once political norms are violated, left-leaning parties (like the NJM) tend to emerge and question the "democraticness" of national politics. As contenders and, quite often, challengers for control of the political space, these parties are generally highly critical of the elite base of democracy. They call into question the reluctance, inability, and/or failure of the regime to meet the rising levels of expectations of the citizens.

These expectations are conditioned by the gap between socioeconomic development and political development and are generally reflective of the regime's failure to expand the democratic process to provide for the meaningful participation of all citizens. Criticisms often become interpreted in terms of East-West politics, and Cuba is often charged with responsibility for undermining the security of these countries. The 1970 army mutiny in Trinidad and Tobago, the attempted coups in Dominica, the Grenada Revolution, the election of known left-wing politicians in St. Lucia and St. Vincent, and the rebellion on Union Island have all been painted with the brush of Soviet-Cuban aggression.

ECONOMIC SECURITY

The lack of economic growth may not necessarily lead to political instability in developed countries; however, it is relatively easy to make the argument that the political security concerns of small, economically dependent countries are closely linked to their economic realities. In countries like Grenada and the OECS, political security issues become salient when a government is reluctant to or unable to provide the opportunities for social and political mobilization and economic development.

When the incumbents respond with force and fraud to the demands of citizens for increased political, economic, and social opportunities rather than relinquish the reins of leadership to the opposition, political instability is likely to result. Political instability in Grenada under Eric Gairy was occasioned by these factors, which gave rise to strong challenges from the NJM. With the democratic process having been reestablished following the U.S. invasion, the test for political stability lies in the capability of the Grenadian government to provide the economic opportunities to facilitate that process. This, of course, depends greatly on the amount and type of aid that the United States, in particular, is prepared to provide on an ongoing basis.

The United States invaded Grenada in October, 1983, partly to "restore democracy." Seven years later, Grenada has not turned into the showcase of the "magic of the market" envisaged by the Reagan administration. President Reagan reasoned that the Caribbean Basin Initiative (CBI) was necessary because worldwide recession had severely hampered opportunities for economic development in the Caribbean and that, consequently, leftist movements were gaining fertile ground upon which to undermine democratically elected governments. By its own admission, the U.S. government noted that political security in the region was being compromised because of economic reasons. This failure was evident one year after the invasion. Despite the infusion of $57.2 million in U.S. aid to Grenada, the regime installed by the United States had failed to deliver on its promises, especially that of attracting foreign investment to revitalize the economy. There was widespread deterioration in the infrastructure. The *Guardian* noted that long-neglected public services such as electricity, water, telephones, and education and health services had broken down in some areas. The U.S. chargé d'affaires admitted that the "physical infrastructure had deteriorated badly."

In keeping with President Reagan's "magic of the market" strategy for economic development, one of the first policy actions of the first postinvasion government was to cut the 1984–1985 budget by 18 percent, from EC$254.5 million in 1983–1984 to EC$211 million for 1984–1985.[9] At the urging of the United States, radical attempts were made to streamline the civil service, and the 1,000-man army was disbanded. These actions were taken in order to reorient the society from the statist program of the Peoples Revolutionary Government (PRG) to a market-oriented economy — the system highly desired by the United States. This strategy is based on conventional monetarist and modernization theories. Essentially, the argument is that economic development is impeded whenever the role of the state in these matters is a large and active one. That is, increase in state size, state expansion, and state consumption will result in strongly negative impacts on economic growth and physical quality of life.[10] This was the evaluation of the socio-economic situation in Grenada after the invasion.

Consequently, whereas 40 percent of the economy was run by the government in 1983 — 38 farms, 6 hotels, 2 banks, and several industrial projects — by July 1984, 8 farms had been returned to their original owners. Meanwhile, the chief economist of the Caribbean Development Bank, Marius St. Rose, noted that there was great pressure on the bank not to lend the Grenadian government money to rehabilitate state-owned enterprises. According to an Agency for International Development (AID) report, state farms, which employed 700 people — twice as many as were needed — lost about $250,000 in 1983.[11] These policy changes entailed severe austerity measures and caused unemployment to rise from about 14 percent to 33 percent, officially. Unofficially, it was much closer to 60 percent.[12]

The *New York Times,* on the one hand, noted that "there was a growing resistance to the concept of a free-enterprise economy on Grenada." St. Rose, on the other hand, pointed out that an unregulated business environment was "alien and impractical." But this is true not only of Grenada, but also of the rest of the English-speaking Caribbean and most of the Third World. Economic security is contingent upon the government's being able to "pick up the slack" for an otherwise extremely weak private sector. Government spending is critical to the stability and economic viability of these countries. The "free market mechanism" conflicts with the economic and political reality of countries like Grenada. It was no surprise then that the proposed budget for 1986 reflected a 20 percent increase in government spending. Structural deficiencies militate against the private sector being the engine of growth in these countries and necessitate a substantial amount of government intervention in the economy.

TABLE 4.1
Economic Support Funds/Development Assistance to
OECS States 1980–1990
(in $ millions)

Year	Amount
1980	46.0
1981	27.0
1982	50.0
1983	58.1
1984	104.6*
1985	58.9
1986	49.3
1987	50.8
1988	32.7
1989	29.1
1990	18.6**

*Increase due to aid given to Grenada.
**Projected for FY 1990 USAID, 1990.

The nature of economics and politics in countries like the OECS is that the state is a central and increasingly large and active player in the development process. The relative stability of these countries is reflected by this prominent role of the state, particularly in its capacity to implement programs and policies conducive to economic development and improvement in the physical quality of life. This was not merely typical of Grenada under the NJM; it is characteristic of the OECS, the English-speaking Caribbean, and the Third World. Economic strategies that overlook these realities are bound to create security concerns in these countries.

Since 1984, the United States has established an assistance relationship with Grenada that has affected virtually every sector of is economy. Operated largely through USAID, this relationship obligates the United States to provide approximately $125 million for Grenada from regional and bilateral sources through 1990 (see Table 4.2). This amounts to about $250 per inhabitant per year and is by far the highest assistance per capita for any country in the Western Hemisphere. The basic strategy of this program has been "to assist the public and private sectors to promote sustainable economic growth through development of a strong market-oriented economic foundation — thus establishing the base necessary for stable democratic development." Four objectives are at the core of this strategy:

expansion and improvement of productive infrastructure;
expansion and improvement of social infrastructure;
stabilizing of the economy and financial structure
strengthening of the private sector and improvement of the investment climate.[13]

TABLE 4.2
Economic Assistance to OECS
(in $ millions)

Country	FY 1988*	FY 1989	FY 1990	FY 1991
Antigua	33.489	2.526	1.640	2.386
Dominica	35.535	5.261	2.765	4.349
Grenada	116.350	5.088	3.719	6.595
St. Kitts	34.993	3.780	1.893	2.158
St. Lucia	47.505	3.870	2.791	3.696
St. Vincent	34.689	4.364	2.494	3.920

*Up to and including FY 1988.

The theory driving this policy is that economic growth produces economic development, which in turn leads to democracy. Arguably, in the minds of the policy makers, economic growth equals economic development, which still leads to democracy. This thinking is flawed, of course. On this premise, however, stable democratic development was expected to result from the 2 percent growth achieved in 1984, 3.7 percent in 1985, 5.6 percent in 1986, and 6.2 percent in 1987. These figures, especially those for 1986 and 1987, are extremely impressive, by any standards. If these are the rates of growth achieved, why has the economy not improved as expected? One answer is that economic growth, that is, the impressive growth rate of the gross national product, does not imply a correlatively impressive growth in the level of economic development. Economic development is evaluated by its redistributive character. Redistribution is a role played principally by government.

The reality is that nature of growth in Grenada (and the OECS) reflects a perpetuation of the traditional pattern of dependent capitalism following which there has been no effective redistribution of resources since the invasion. The policy of focusing on the private sector as the basis for economic development does not conform to the social, economic, and political reality. This dilemma is captured by Nelson who notes, "Many I.M.F.-supported programs and all World Bank structural adjustment loans stress reduced direct government intervention in the economy and greater reliance on market incentives for public corporations and services."[14]

The reasoning for this is that government is too large and intrusive. This is reflected in its tendency, among other things, to allocate too large a percentage of its budget to social programs and subsidies and to allow all workers to earn very high wages. Consequently, austerity measures must be introduced via "shock treatment" policy. This "simple" solution of reducing government's involvement in the economy will facilitate economic growth by means of a "trickle-down" process. This entails, among other things, a curtailment and/or elimination of many social welfare programs as well as a reduction of wages.

Although it was stated that both the private and public sectors in Grenada were to be assisted, "the restoration of economic stability" is expected to be achieved through emphasis on the private sector as opposed to the "statist economic policies prevalent before October, 1983." Five Economic Support Fund (ESF) grants totaling $22.2 million, plus technical assistance in fiscal management and tax reform reflected the principal mode of assistance. This, however, was conditional upon Grenada's resolving certain economic problems, particularly "excessive public spending," a result, in large measure, of the excessive size of the government's payroll.[15] The implementation of the $5 million ESF programs for 1987, for example, was conditional upon the government's agreement to retrench 1,800 of Grenada's 7,000 civil service employees by June 1988 and on participation in an approved structural adjustment program.

These conditions conflicted with Grenada's political reality. Like all politicians, then Prime Minister Herbert Blaize realized that his primary objective was to stay in power by putting himself and his party in a position to be reelected. One way to achieve this was by doing nothing to alienate the electorate. Although desperately in need of development assistance, Blaize realized that retrenching the civil service was an act destined to be politically damaging. In fact, this pressure by the United States for policy change created instability within the Blaize Cabinet in April 1987 and led to the resignation of Ministers George Brizan and Francis Alexis from the four-party New National Party (NNP) coalition.[16] Following these resignations, further restructuring occurred within the NNP. Keith Mitchell made history in West Indian politics when he was elected as head of the NNP. Blaize became the first prime minister of an English-speaking Caribbean country who was not simultaneously head of the governing party. Immediately thereafter, great pressure was put on Blaize to hold new elections, and when a vote of no confidence against him was tabled, he requested the governor-general to prorogue Parliament.

It was no surprise then that by May 1988, only 437 civil servants had been terminated, and estimates were that by the end of the new year, there would be no net retrenchment. As many as 944 new civil service positions were expected to be created, and of the 200 who were actually retrenched, many had been scheduled for retirement. The initial $1.2 million of the $5 million ESF grant was used for severance pay. These issues clearly impacted on the 1990 general elections in which the NNP won only two seats and Blaize's TNP won two seats. Blaize had died in December 1989. The party was later led by his deputy, Ben Jones. The NDC of Brizan and Alexis won seven seats and eventually formed the government because someone from another party defected.

The expected outcome of changes in fiscal management and the implementation of the structural adjustment program were to be cushioned by revenues from tax reform and a grant of $1.8 million in ESF assistance. Under pressure from USAID, the Grenada government implemented a sweeping tax reform program designed to increase incentives for savings, investment, and production. According to a

USAID report, the government yielded to political pressure from special interests and undermined its revenue collection capacity. In 1988, the government attempted to improve its fiscal situation by raising revenues through a combination of import duties and sales taxes. This effectively dismantled the value added tax program of 1986. This action did not sit well with USAID officials who impressed upon the government that tax measures that reduce revenues require compensation revenue increases and spending reduction measures, together with improved tax administration. The structural adjustment program required certain revenue and expenditure measures perceived by Blaize to be politically dangerous. He, therefore, rejected them.

Blaize's unwillingness to follow the line dictated by USAID resulted in the loss of approximately $25 million over a three-year period in which the International Bank for Reconstruction and Development (IBRD) and the International Monetary Fund (IMF) were willing to provide support. This also caused USAID to continue to withhold the disbursement of $1.8 million from the 1987 ESF funding. In addition, eliminating ESF for the Caribbean in 1988 negatively affected USAID's assistance to Grenada to the extent that only $6.8 million was available for development assistance during that year.

The net result of Blaize's unwillingness to overlook Grenada's realities and completely transform the economy to one that is essentially dependent on private sector initiatives is a private sector that has not spearheaded any economic recovery or economic development projects. The *Washington Report on Latin America and the Caribbean* noted that businessmen on a tourism mission to Grenada in 1989 pointed to "a lack of industrial and agricultural development and a 'lazy private sector,' and a lack of tax incentives as stumbling blocks [to development]."[17] They noted as well that a number of potential investors lost interest because of the absence of daily, nonstop flights to the United States. Nonstop flights were introduced in 1990. This obvious struggle based on policy preferences of the donor country and the political reality of the recipient nation reflects the dilemma that microstates like Grenada face in maintaining their sovereignty and ensuring their security.

Another dimension of economic insecurity stems from the fact that the OECS possesses limited resources. Because of Grenada's high degree of dependence on agriculture, it must export in order to survive. Its export concentration index for 1980 was .498, and the export concentration ratios for 1970, 1982, and 1983 were .610, .500, and .431, respectively.[18] The character of agriculturally based economies is such that the exporting country must be a price taker on the world market. Economic and, therefore, political stability can be maintained only if the government can provide the material benefits through economic development opportunities, especially through economic diversification. The government's ability to do this is highly dependent on events taking place within the world economic system, events over which Grenada has no control. In fact, there seems to be very little that Grenada can do to minimize its external dependence and insecurity. Consequently, if the United States continues to focus exclusively on private sector initiatives that are inconsistent with Grenada's social and political reality, the current rate of unemployment of 30 percent strongly suggests that political instability will inevitably continue.

One specific policy change has severely affected the principal export crop, nutmegs. Sales dropped precipitously following the cancellation of the Soviet contract under which 500 tons per year were purchased. Strapped still with low international nutmeg and cocoa prices, the vital agricultural sector has not delivered its share of economic growth. Although the Grenada Cooperative Nutmeg Association (GCNA) considered the output successful, it was still forced to cut prices on some of its products. For example, the price per pound of green nutmegs was lowered by one-third to EC$1.50, and the price per pound of top quality mace was reduced from EC$6.00 to EC$4.00. These price reductions were attributable in part to decreases in world demand.

A similar situation faces the cocoa industry. Output in 1989 decreased by 18 percent, to 3.113 million pounds. This was caused by the onset of black pod disease. The industry, nevertheless, faced a world market for which demand had dropped as well. To add insult to injury, the sugar workers threatened to strike, an action that was averted only at the last minute. In addition, the tourist industry has not grown as was expected. A 4.3 percent decline in visitor arrivals was registered during the first nine months of 1989. This was attributed to a 12 percent decline in cruise ship calls; during the first seven months 142,708 visitors arrived on the island compared with 149,231 the previous year. U.S. tourist arrivals increased a mere 3 percent while British and Canadian visitors increased by 30 percent and 38 percent, respectively.

Disappointment and frustration manifested in the unemployment of about one-third of the labor force reflects the elusive promised well-being of Grenadians. But this all demonstrates that external imperatives and internal realities will come into continual conflict. IMF-directed government austerity programs have come under constant pressure from citizens in a number of Third World countries, and their potential impact on economic development, quality of life, and political instability is serious. The fact remains, however, that the OECS needs foreign economic assistance. With the redirection of development assistance to the reforming countries of the Eastern bloc coupled with budget constraints in the United States, the reduction of assistance to Grenada and the OECS has recreated some of the preconditions for political instability that originally led to concerns about political insecurity.

REGIONAL SECURITY

Although states are constrained by domestic economic conditions and are partly influenced by class forces, state structures are also connected to the dynamics of international military rivalries, international economic trends, and spheres of influence. Geopolitics is critical to all of this, and from this perspective security considerations for Grenada and the OECS are multifaceted. There is the superpower dimension, and there are the dynamics of the regional dimension. At both levels, security interests of the OECS are interrelated with those of the United States, which, from the beginning of this century, has demonstrated a willingness to intervene militarily in the Caribbean whenever there are perceptions of threats to its national security. The 1983 invasion represented a conflict of security interest between the United States and Grenada, and as a result Grenada's national sovereignty suffered. The implication of this is quite clear: Grenada's national sovereignty and national security interests — and indeed those of the OECS — must be consistent with or subordinate to those of the United States.

At a second level, the similarity of the historical, political, and other traditions of Grenada, the OECS, and the rest of the English-speaking Caribbean and the general consensus of this group on a number of security issues cause the security concerns of Grenada to be inextricably linked with those of this entire group. Having undergone a similar process of political decolonization from Britain, and having participated in the now defunct West Indies Federation (1958–1962) and the West Indies Associated States (WISA), Grenada is now part of the OECS. This organization has been created "to promote unity and solidarity among the member states and to defend their sovereignty, territorial integrity, and independence."

Because of the very small size of all OECS member states, and because a number of them are multi-island nations, all share common national security concerns. They all recognize that their territorial integrity is highly vulnerable to secession and economic factors, as well as to external forces. The Anguilla secession from the state of St.

Kitts-Nevis-Anguilla in 1967, the rumblings of discontentment from Barbuda against the central government in Antigua, the revolt and attempted secession of Union Island from St. Vincent, and recent threats of secession on Nevis from the federation of St. Kitts and Nevis are all reflective of one dimension of the security problem.

The OECS therefore instituted mechanisms for developing close security relationships and joint diplomatic representation precisely because insularity and small size make each country highly vulnerable to security threats of one form or another. In attempting to facilitate these objectives, this organization has brought under its direction a number of functional agencies such as the East Caribbean Tourist Association (ECTA), the Caribbean Civil Aviation Authority (CCAA), and the Eastern Caribbean Central Bank, which issues the Eastern Caribbean Dollar, the common currency used by all OECS member states.

At a third level, Grenada is a member of CARICOM. This organization has three basic objectives: economic integration through the Caribbean common market, functional cooperation, and coordination of foreign policies. CARICOM has not achieved the expected successes in the area of economic integration, but the area of functional cooperation has demonstrated positive movement, particularly in health and education. The University of the West Indies and the Caribbean Examination Council (CXC) are notable in the latter area. There has been a substantial amount of technical assistance as well. This has been achieved through the Caribbean Development Bank (CDB), cooperation in the collection and dissemination of information through the Caribbean News Agency (CANA), and in culture through the biennial Caribbean Festival of Arts (CARIFESTA). Despite strong nationalist sentiments, foreign policy objectives have produced their own successes. Consensus is strong on issues such as apartheid, the law of the sea, and the territorial claims on Guyana and Belize. Although consensus broke down on the question of the U.S. invasion of Grenada, there is, nevertheless, a sense of community that is driven by common historic, ethnic, cultural, and constitutional experiences. This can be traced to the Treaty of Chaguaramas where the sentiments of the member governments are "to consolidate and strengthen the bonds which have historically existed among their people."

Among the stated objectives of the U.S. invasion of Grenada in 1983 was the restoration of the democratic process in that country. The broader goals incorporated mechanisms purported to minimize, if not eliminate, the security threats that the OECS felt exposed to as a result of the perceived direction in which the People's Revolutionary Government

(PRG) was taking Grenada. The perception of vulnerability within the OECS to events similar to those that culminated in the Grenada Revolution of 1979 were viewed as part of a broader threat to the hemispheric security of the United States, particularly in light of the close alliance that was formed between the Maurice Bishop's PRG, Fidel Castro's Cuba, and Daniel Ortega's Sandinista regime in Nicaragua. In response to this development, and in an attempt to forestall the emergence of another group of the same ilk as the NJM, the United States encouraged and supported the signing of the "Memorandum of Understanding" in 1982 to establish a Regional Security System (RSS).[19] This has turned out to be one of the most controversial events affecting the OECS and the English-speaking Caribbean in recent times.

Opposition political parties in the region have become alarmed over the possible uses to which the RSS might be redirected. One area of concern centers on the possibility that national governments might use such a regional defense force to entrench themselves in power by interpreting popular opposition as being the result of Marxist or Communist inspired activity. The traditionally conservative political directorates in these countries have become even more so since the Grenada Revolution and subsequent U.S. invasion. They appear ready and willing to paint left-leaning opponents with the brush of Marxism and characterize them as threats to national security. The RSS might be used, therefore, to suppress political rights and civil liberties under the guise of countering attempts at destabilization and preserving political security. The logical and potential outcome of all this would be a fundamental change in the political culture of these societies.

Except for Guyana, and Grenada during 1979–1983, the inherited British tradition reflects the absence of involvement of the military in politics. The United States has contributed to the break with tradition by aiding and abetting Commonwealth Caribbean governments in developing and strengthening their paramilitary capacity. In this regard, in 1984 the United States deployed military advisers to Antigua and Barbuda, St. Kitts and Nevis, Dominica, St. Lucia, and St. Vincent and the Grenadines to train members of the police force to consolidate the RSS through Special Service Units (SSUs). These were created by bringing together 40 men from each island for special six-week training programs with the objective of creating units totaling 100 per island at full strength. They were trained to use automatic weapons, riot control equipment, and armed patrol boats and were incorporated into the local police forces.

Among the stipulations of the memorandum was the agreement that in the event of a crisis, the RSS would be made available on a voluntary basis. Its most vocal supporter, the late Prime Minister Tom Adams, of Barbados, claimed that the RSS would serve to protect the member countries from "mercenary adventure, other external aggression, domestic revolution, and other violent episodes."[20] One U.S. military official in the Caribbean stated, however, that the role of the RSS would be to handle minor developments — "small situations" — but would serve as a trigger mechanism — a "tripwire" — for U.S. involvement if the unrest assumed more dangerous proportions.[21] The potential for abuse and misuse of power, meanwhile, has been increased as a result of this militia. Toward the end of 1985, several RSS units were alleged to be involved in cases of police brutality. This was based on the unexplained deaths of a number of prisoners in Dominica, St. Lucia, and St. Vincent. In fact, critics have contended that since 1982, some elite RSS forces have operated at the whim of ruling parties as "proxy armies."[22]

This militarization has developed largely on the direction of the United States. Through the Military Assistance Program (MAP) and the International Military Education and Training Program (IMET), U.S. contribution increased by $6 million in 1984 from $1.2 million two years earlier. By the end of 1984, U.S. military assistance to the Eastern Caribbean totaled $40 million.[23] Meanwhile Britain has contributed to the militarization of the region by providing £1.5 million for upgrading the coast guard and financing police and military training in the United Kingdom by lending military trainers and advisers to the region, and by increasing the frequency of visits by warships of the Royal Navy. This increased assistance is geared clearly toward preventing another Grenadian-type crisis in the OECS (and the rest of the English-speaking Caribbean) and toward creating a strong deterrent against the emergence of "hostile influences" in the region.

The stated objective of this regional force comprising units from Antigua and Barbuda, Barbados, Dominica, Grenada, St. Kitts and Nevis, St. Lucia, and St. Vincent is partly to consolidate the democratic process in the Eastern Caribbean by providing the capability to diffuse any domestic attempts to undermine legitimate political institutions and governments. Political security concerns must focus, therefore, on the change in political culture that is being undergone through the "Latinization" of these countries. With the introduction of military apparatus into countries whose political culture has developed on the basis of negotiation and compromise, the militarization of the OECS represents a clear and present threat to political stability in the entire region.

The policy geared to counteract coups is, in effect, creating a brand new problem for the area, one for which the lessons from Latin America should be heeded. Military coups are not always ideologically determined; the failure of economic policies can and does lead to these developments. General political instability is often created by austerity measures imposed by international lending agencies like the IMF. Both Jamaica and Trinidad and Tobago are cases in point. Grenada's restructuring programs entailed, among other things, retrenchment of workers and the removal of government subsidies and other government-sponsored/run programs. The implementation of some of these measures may produce, in the absence of a well-developed capitalist class structure or a powerful working class, elite instability. This was the case with the resignation of George Brizan and Francis Alexis from Blaize's Cabinet. Additionally, increasing numbers of these financially strapped governments that cannot abide by the conditions of international financing have created off-shore banking opportunities through which international drug traders launder money. These countries are being used as transshipment points for drugs as well. Resorting to these opportunities for generating much needed revenues means that the economic and social realities have now become redefined.

The size of these countries is another significant variable affecting their political security. Small size has implications not only for preventing and/or controlling or suppressing internal challenges for state power but also for the ability (or inability) to ward off external challenges. The national integrity (security) of these countries is threatened by individual regional powers and regional groupings, as well as by superpower intervention. Difficulties are continuously experienced by these small states in preserving their national integrity and enhancing the territorial security.

Eastern Caribbean nations are unable to negotiate effectively with the larger countries of the hemisphere in order to exploit fully the potentials of their maritime space. They are therefore vulnerable to the dangers inherent in the dumping of hazardous waste products of bigger, more powerful nations in their national space. Under these precarious conditions — a changing political culture, militarization, and economic development strategies that are inconsistent with social and political realities — political insecurity in the aftermath of the Grenada invasion will most likely proceed either from elite instability because of the absence of a fully developed capitalist class or from a large, organized, and discontented working class. This will be manifested in the form of plots, coups d'état, and assassinations, which will create new security problems.

NOTES

1. These countries comprise Anguilla, Antigua and Barbuda, the Bahamas, Barbados, Belize, Bermuda, the British Virgin Islands, the Cayman Islands, Dominica, Grenada, Guyana, Jamaica, Montserrat, St. Kitts and Nevis, St. Lucia, St. Vincent and the Grenadines, Trinidad and Tobago, and the Turks and Caicos Islands.

2. Andrew Axline, "Regional Cooperation and National Security: External Forces in Caribbean Integration," *Journal of Common Market Studies* 27 (1988): 10–11.

3. Anthony Payne, *The International Crisis in the Caribbean* (Baltimore: The Johns Hopkins University Press, 1984), p. 146.

4. "Dialogue on Economic Reality and Policy Options," in *Latin America, the Caribbean and the O.E.C.D.* (Paris: Center for the Organization of Economic Cooperation and Development, 1986), p. 112.

5. See my *Democracy in the English-Speaking Caribbean: A Deviant Case of Democracy?* Ph.D. dissertation, University of Rochester, 1989.

6. Myron Weiner and Ergun Ozbudun, *Competitive Elections in Developing Countries* (Durham: Duke University Press, 1987), p. 19.

7. Ibid., p. 20.

8. See Robert Dahl, *Polyarchy* (New Haven: Yale University Press, 1971).

9. *Latin American Monitor*, August 1984.

10. On this question see York W. Bradshaw and Zwelakhe Tshandu, "Foreign Capital Penetration, State Intervention, and Development in Subsaharan Africa," *International Studies Quarterly* 34 (1990): 229–51.

11. *Latin American Monitor*, July 1984.

12. *Latin American Monitor*, August 1984.

13. USAID records on Grenada, November 1988.

14. J. N. Nelson, "The Political Economy of Stabilization: Commitment, Capacity, and Public Response," in Robert Bates, ed., *Towards a Political Economy of Development: A Rational Choice Perspective* (Berkeley: University of California Press, 1988).

15. USAID records on Grenada, November 1988.

16. In a joint press release by George Brizan and Francis Alexis in April 1987, Brizan argued that "although certain ministries were overstaffed, people should not be thrown out like that. A program of training and redevelopment of the workers into special projects should be drawn up. So the objective of reducing the size of the public service will be achieved and at the same time, the retrenched workers would be given alternative jobs." Alexis argued that "retrenchment should never be undertaken until such time as the private sector was in a position to employ the retrenched workers."

17. *Latin American Monitor*, October 1989.

18. The export concentration index discriminates more finely between countries that are relatively more concentrated in their export structure. It ranges between 0 and 1, representing the most extreme forms of export concentration.

19. For assessment of the RSS, see Gary Lewis, "Prospects for Regional Security System in the Eastern Caribbean," *Millennium: Journal of International Studies* 15 (1986): 73–90; RSS Staff, "The Roles of the Regional Security System in the East Caribbean," *Bulletin of Eastern Caribbean Affairs* 11 (1986): 5–7; and Ivelaw

L. Griffith, *The Quest for Security in the Caribbean* (Armonk, N.Y.: M. E. Sharpe, forthcoming 1992).

20. See *Caribbean Contact,* October 1985, p. 2.

21. *Keesings Contemporary Archives,* December 1985, p. 34046.

22. *Caribbean Contact,* November 1985, p. 7.

23. *Latin American and Caribbean Contemporary Record,* Vol. V, 1985–86, pp. B453–54.

II NATIONAL STRATEGY AND SECURITY

5 Change and Continuity in Barbados Defense Policy

Dion E. Phillips

When Barbados became independent on November 20, 1966, the fourth English-speaking Caribbean country to do so, the government immediately assumed control of its defense affairs. However, since then no work has addressed this critical area exclusively.[1] This chapter analyzes the defense policy and planning processes in Barbados during its first 22 years of nationhood, 1966–1988, identifying the elements in the internal and external environment that have influenced it.

The period under review has been divided into three phases, each of which is roughly consonant with the three alternate periods during which time the Democratic Labor party (DLP) and the Barbados Labor Party (BLP), Barbados' two major political parties, have been in power. The first phase lasted from 1966 to 1976, the second phase from 1976 to 1986, and the third began in 1986. Although this last period is yet to be completed, these three phases permit us to identify and explain changes and continuities in the defense policy and planning of Barbados.

The twin concepts of "defense policy" and "defense planning" provide the contextual basis for the study.[2] Defense policy in general terms refers to the military objectives of a state and involves identifying perceived threats to it. It is also more directly concerned with protecting the state and its citizens from military threats and actions by other states, and/or persons. It therefore involves defense from external threats and internal security as well. Defense policy involves an implicit, if not actual, conceptual duality of deterrence along with defense.[3] Deterrence represents policies designed to protect the state by discouraging the enemy from taking harmful actions. It is meant to so raise the cost of action against the state that the calculated cost to the enemy is counter-balanced by any possible gain, thereby forestalling any likely action. Only some — sometimes none — of the decisions of a state relative to this defense are released for public consumption. In fact, it is often very difficult to know some states' defense objectives in detail.

In this chapter, the defense policy of Barbados is taken as that reflected in relevant decisions and statements by government officials, chief among them the prime minister who, in his capacity as head of government, is ultimately in charge of security matters. This is under-standable because in Barbados as elsewhere, policy is the preserve of ministers of the government. And it is all the more natural where, as in many small states, the positions of prime minister and minister of defense are combined. Moreover, where such cases do exist, because of the understandable need for secrecy and confidentiality, defense policy is often further removed from the influence of public opinion than, quite possibly, any other area of public policy. The use of prime ministerial decision and statements as a suitable guide to a country's defense policy does not, of course, rule out the fact that defense policy positions articu-lated by government officials in small states may or may not be influenced by actors and circumstances external to the state and by so doing relegate these officials to the status of mouthpieces of larger states.[4]

The second key concept, defense planning, refers to the organization, acquisition, and mobilization of military forces (persons and materials) to provide the state with the capacity to deter and confront threats and actions against the state. Typically, defense planning involves implemen-tation and is therefore a reflection of defense policy. The defense plan-ning process is divided into three subcategories. The first is employment — actions by the state to originate or not originate a military organization as well as to increase, decrease, or otherwise alter the country's force posture. Acquisition is the second. It involves actions of the state to procure military training and equipment as well as the kinds and sources of materials. Finally, there is deployment — the manner in which the state engages the military in times of peace or disorder.

PHASE ONE: 1966–1976

After some 339 years of British rule, independence came to Barbados on November 30, 1966, as a result of a preindependence election. With the demise of the West Indies Federation in 1962 and efforts at a "Little

Eight" having failed, the general election acted as a referendum on independence. The DLP led by Errol Barrow got 14 seats. The BLP led by Grantley Adams received eight. The remaining two seats went to what became known as "The Motley Team" headed by Ernest Deighton Motley.

Unlike the two mainland states of Guyana and Belize, which have been subjected to long-standing territorial claims by Venezuela and Guatemala, respectively, Barbados — unlike many Third World countries that became independent following World War II — did not experience any threats to its peace through overt hostility or the threat of the use of force as a prelude to independence. Undoubtedly, such a history did influence Barrow and the DLP's decision not to establish a defense force to coincide with Barbados' attainment of independence. In terms of the DLP's employment position during its first ten years of nationhood, it was argued that Barbados' inability to "maintain an Army, Navy, or Air Force cannot in any way weaken [her] people's resolve to manage their own affairs."[5] After all, reminded the Barbadian independence White Paper, "Sovereignty in the middle twentieth century is not ... a country's ability to defend itself against attack since no country on earth could so qualify in the age of nuclear warfare."[6] Curiously enough, this position was in stark contrast to that of Jamaica, Trinidad and Tobago, and Guyana, all of which preceded Barbados in independence and created defense forces.

One factor that explains this position may be that Barbados did not have the level of security importance that comes with the possession of scarce resources, like bauxite in the case of Jamaica and Guyana, and petroleum in Trinidad. This being the case, Barbados relied on the Royal Barbados Police Force as its main source of internal security for the duration of the DLP's first independence period in power, 1966–1976. The Barbados Regiment was the only military body existing in Barbados until 1974 when a coast guard service was started.[7] Even so, the designated duties of the coast guard included the policing of Barbados' 200-mile economic zone, search and rescue missions, and antismuggling exercises. By so doing, it placed emphasis on civil rather than military action. This BDS $400,000 coast guard facility, which was established at Enterprise/Scarborough, Christ Church, was severely criticized by Opposition Leader Tom Adams who called it "a colossal and ghastly waste of money." Under the command of former Assistant Commissioner of Police William Phillips, the coast guard acquired four vessels, namely the *George Ferguson, J. T. C. Ramsey, Commander Marshall,* and *T. T. Lewis.*

Moreover, unlike Trinidad and Tobago's leader Eric Williams, who asked the United States to surrender the naval base at Chaguaramas, Barrow permitted the U.S. Naval Facility set up in 1956 at Harrison's, St. Lucy, to remain in postindependent Barbados. Although an avowed Barbadian nationalist, Barrow's lack of an openly anti-U.S. attitude at the time was entirely consonant with the industrialization by invitation strategy of development. This strategy was mounted even before independence and targeted the establishment of export-oriented manufacturing enterprises as the engine for economic growth, a pattern more or less endorsed by both the DLP and the BLP during phases one, two, and three.[8]

In the 1960s, both before and during the formative independence years, the DLP led by Errol Barrow enacted laws to attract U.S. and other overseas investors through granting concessions. These bits of legislation provided the framework for the promotion of massive inflow of U.S. capital for the expansion of the tourist industry as well as the development of branch plant manufacturing. It stands to reason, therefore, that any hostility in U.S.-Barbados relations would have had repercussions for the state-sponsored growth of U.S. direct foreign investment into the Barbadian economy, coupled with Barbados' increasing pattern of trade dependence on the U.S. market for exports and hard currency earnings. This reality probably explains why Barrow and the DLP chose not to make an issue of the U.S. Naval Facility remaining on Barbados soil after independence.

Against this background, not only did the presence of the U.S. Naval Facility provide Barbados with an element of stability in the eyes of investors, but it also contributed to the employment of 80 Barbadians, an even larger number of persons than the 60 U.S. Marines stationed at the naval installation. This defense policy position, which was sustained for the duration of the DLP's first independence period in power (1966–1976), underscores the fact that, unlike his then contemporaries Michael Manley in Jamaica and Forbes Burnham in Guyana, Barrow was a political pragmatist.

In fact, in the interest of that very stability which lends itself to a favorable climate for foreign investors and the local business elite, when faced with the likelihood of explosive civil disorder associated with the Black Power repercussions throughout the Caribbean, the DLP reacted by introducing the Public Order Act in June 1970.[9] This legislation was necessitated by the atmosphere of fear and instability pervading the subregion at the time, from Jamaica in the north to Guyana in the south. Also, the crisis in Jamaica, which led to a state of emergency in 1968 following student and working class protest over the ban of University of the West Indies lecturer Walter Rodney, had repercussions in Barbados. The result was solidarity meetings and demonstrations at the Cave Hill campus of the University of the West Indies as well as political rumblings in the larger society. Similarly, the Black Power revolt in Trinidad as well as the abortive mutiny by the Trinidad and Tobago Defense Force in 1970 further contributed to an escalation of the sense of some impending upheaval in many parts of the Caribbean. This constrained even the DLP, the more working class and black-oriented of Barbados' two major parties, to act firmly by placing the Public Order Act on the statute books in the interest of maintaining stability in the new tourism-oriented Barbados.

Given the safe atmosphere for business activity which the DLP defense policy set out to engender during phase one, Barbados went on to realize a fairly impressive record of economic growth. Such growth was reflected in the tourism, manufacturing, and construction sectors as Barbados endeavored to diversify its economy away from the historical emphasis on sugar. Before too long, tourism became the leading foreign exchange earner and a significant employer of labor.

In sum, regarding Barbados' defense policy during the 1966-1976 phase, the DLP government placed a very low level of emphasis on military preparedness and more on social control legislation, as evidenced by Public Order Act, in hopes of fostering an atmosphere for local and foreign business to thrive and, thereby, boost employment. Before being voted out of office, and at a time when the Barbadian economy was in a downturn, the DLP seemingly began to contemplate the creation of a defense force of about 80 persons as reflected in the proposals that were left behind. Barrow did not request closure of the U.S. Naval Facility because it provided Barbadians with jobs and gave Barbados some semblance of security. No bona fide army existed, and so the DLP relied on the police as the sole source of internal security. The Barbados Regiment was used strictly for ceremonial purposes, and the coast guard, begun in 1974 without any U.S. military assistance, was used to strengthen Barbados' ability to patrol its territorial waters and prevent smuggling and damage to maritime life. Finally, at no time during phase one is the DLP government known to have deployed its security forces abroad, as may well have been the case during the Anguilla crisis, 1967–1971. The embattled Robert Bradshaw, then premier of St. Kitts, Nevis, and Anguilla, approached Barrow to send arms and forces to invade the recalcitrant island of Anguilla and oust its rebel leader Ronald Webster. Barrow declined the offer, as did other Anglophone Caribbean leaders.

PHASE TWO: 1976–1986

The BLP, led by Tom Adams, came to power on September 2, 1976, after having soundly defeated the DLP headed by Errol Barrow. In the first two years of BLP rule, there was no real deviation in the defense policy of Barbados from that set by DLP. At the outset, the position of Adams and the BLP as reflected in its September 1976 manifesto was that: "There is no reason why Barbados should attract foreign invasion or intervention. The party will not commit our country to any foreign defense pacts. Internally, the defense forces will be limited to such as are adequate to maintain law and order. There will be no need to maintain any standing army or other defense force."[10] Grenada, which would later be seen as an acute security problem was not yet in the picture as Maurice Bishop and the New Jewel Movement did not come to power until 1979.

However, Barbados along with Jamaica under Michael Manley, Trinidad and Tobago under Eric Williams, and Guyana under Forbes Burnham had established diplomatic relations with Cuba and together had signed an air services agreement as far back as 1972, actions not favored by the U.S. government or anti-Castro forces. As reprisals for these agreements in defiance of an Organization of American States sanction, on October 6, 1976, a Cubana Airlines civil jetliner, on a scheduled flight from Guyana to Havana via Trinidad, Barbados, and Jamaica, was blown up. It crashed into the sea approximately ten minutes after departure from the Grantley Adams International Airport (then called Seawell), the result of exploded bombs planted by two members of the Commandos of the United Revolutionary Organization (CORU), an anti-Castro terrorist group code-named El Condor.[11] This midair disaster, which left 78 people dead, 11 of them Guyanese, reintroduced Barbados and the Eastern Caribbean into cold war politics.

In the aftermath of this incident, which was previously foreign to the subregion, the BLP, then in power only one month, was loathe to place the accused, who were apprehended in Trinidad, on trial. This apprehension stemmed from the implications of possible reprisals from the organizations with which the suspects were connected. Most important though, these events brought about a change in Barbados' defense policy.

Following the Cubana sabotage, Barbados and other Eastern Caribbean countries stepped up security at their airports and proceeded to equip them with metal detectors and X-ray equipment to examine baggage. Special nonmilitary airport security personnel were also assigned to reinforce regular police officers, and restricted zones were more carefully

marked and monitored by security officers.[12] Even before the Cubana air
disaster, Prime Minister Adams surprised the Caribbean on October 1,
1976, when he declared that he had received an intelligence report stating
that Sidney Burnett-Alleyne was planning to invade Barbados. Burnett-
Alleyne, intercepted off Martinique while sailing a yacht loaded with
arms, was arrested and charged. He later served a one-year jail term on
that island.

The Burnett-Alleyne threat was unprecedented and received considerable media coverage. The BLP also emphasized this incident, with
Prime Minister Adams parading a number of checks written by Burnett-
Alleyne to high-ranking members of the then DLP administration before
the Barbadian television cameras. It was small wonder, therefore, that
when word of the presence of four Russian warships approximately 15 to
20 miles southeast of Barbados appeared in the media in July 1977, it not
only "sent cold chills down the spine" of the Barbadian civilian population, but seemingly that of the police.[13]

Another sign of the BLP's increasing emphasis on security matters
came in April 1979, weeks after Maurice Bishop and the People's
Revolutionary Government (PFG) came to power in Grenada. Adams,
admittedly no friend of the PRG, signed a Memorandum of Understanding with Prime Minister Eric Williams of Trinidad and Tobago, who
in 1970 was almost toppled by his country's security forces and who had
refused to open letters sent to him by the PRG. In the Memorandum of
Understanding, signed in Port-of-Spain, the two heads of government,
among other things, acknowledged the growing complexity of the
security problems of the Caribbean region, which they identified as
"terrorism, privacy, the use of mercenaries, and the introduction into the
region of techniques of subversion."[14] The disclosure by the media of the
details of the alleged plot to overthrow the elected government of
Barbados in 1976 by Sidney Burnett-Alleyne and his cohorts seemed to
have been taken much more seriously by Adams and the BLP than by the
Barbadian people who greeted the news with widespread incredulity.[15]
However, this reaction seemed less the case when, in 1978, two years
after the first invasion scare, there was another, again involving Sidney
Burnett-Alleyne.[16] Prime Minister Adams met with press managers for
off-the-record briefings as British, French, and Venezuelan vessels
moved to intercept Burnett-Alleyne and his band of mercenaries. This
was to no avail because, as indicated by Burnett-Alleyne later, he had
called off the operation.

Regarding this second invasion scare, which was uncovered by
British intelligence, in 1979 Prime Minister Adams indicated that:

Never mind how few the rifles were, never mind that the plans which were found on Burnett-Alleyne called for 40 or 50 men. It may not seem like much. But I say this: that they were very coherent and potentially workable plans. We have seen that these small conspiracies, organized by megalomaniacs can succeed. And Burnett-Alleyne was able to get the backing of the South-African Government for his plans. We have incontrovertible proof that he was planning to disturb the peace in Barbados.

An alert and security conscious Adams, who seemed to fear for his life, further stated that "Sidney came to me and assured me that a member of the Democratic Labor Party had paid him to assassinate me (PM Adams) in 1975. At first I ignored it. Subsequently, I told my mother and the Commissioner (of police)."

The prevailing security hypersensitivity of the Barbados Regiment and the Royal Barbados Police Force was most evident when, on June 26, 1979, the entire defense force was put on full alert and troops were sent to the northern part of the island just before daybreak. This frenzy was triggered by residents of that area who became unduly suspicious of a large ship off the Animal Flower Cave.[17]

Because of the succession of security-related events within Barbados, chief among them the invasion scares and the subsequent rise to power of the PRG in Grenada, Barbados' first standing army, the Barbados Defense Force (BPG), was created in August 1979.[18] In so doing, the BLP government retreated from its opposition to a defense force. It later took the converse view in its 1981 general election manifesto: "Events within Barbados, the Caribbean and elsewhere, have proved the need for Barbados to have a limited defense force with a capacity to withstand the immediate assault of potential marauders, terrorists and mercenaries."[19] The BDF absorbed the preexisting Barbados Regiment, which was started in 1948, although the latter retained some autonomy as a squadron with its own commander. The coast guard — created in 1974 by the DLP government — was also integrated into the BDF and subsequently upgraded.

However, the most significant and far-reaching defense policy action that was made by the BLP in phase two was its decision on October 30, 1982, along with the governments of Antigua-Barbuda, Dominica, St. Lucia, and St. Vincent and the Grenadines, to sign a Memorandum of Understanding in Roseau, Dominica.[20] The purpose of this military pact was, among other things, to better coordinate security action in the Eastern Caribbean. Grenada, under Bishop, was not an original signatory to this agreement. This new defense policy initiative for the small states of the Eastern Caribbean was, in fact, the Regional Security System in embryo. This military body constitutes the second formal attempt at collective security in the English-speaking Caribbean since the failed West Indies Federation Regiment, part of the West Indies federal experiment between 1958 and 1962. Barbados provides operational headquarters for the RSS, which houses a central liaison office where plans are coordinated. The BDF's chief of staff serves as the coordinator of the RSS.

One other act of the BLP government that stood in contrast to that of the DLP was the closure of the U.S. Naval Facility in Barbados. Called the "oceanographic research station," it was located on about 50 acres of land on the northern tip of the island. While the DLP was in power, the United States, which had maintained the naval base since 1956 and which, under the agreement, had paid no taxes, was never formally asked to vacate Barbadian soil. It was only during the final stages of the DLP's reign in power, at a time when there were strained relations between Bridgetown and Washington. Barrow not only publicly expressed the view that the United States was destabilizing his government as well as those of Guyana and Jamaica because of their socialist thrust and their links to Cuba, but stated in the Barbados House of Assembly that the U.S. naval facility would shortly be returned to "its original owners."[21] The U.S. naval facility was closed on March 31, 1979, partly because it was considered technically obsolete, but also because the United States considered the BLP's stated hope to negotiate a $20 million rental for the base totally unacceptable.[22]

Three other defense policy actions indicate that Barbados under the BLP reached an unprecedented high in security awareness during phase two. In June 1984, the government appointed Barbados' first overseas military attache. Carol Mapp, a major in the BDF, was assigned to the British High Commission in London, United Kingdom, the country where Sidney Burnett-Alleyne was known to reside.[23] In October of 1984, Minister of Energy Senator Clyde Griffith declared that the Adams government in consultation with the Division of Defense and Security would produce a security and safety plan for Barbados' recently discovered oil fields. Griffith argued that "there was no such thing as a foolproof security system since oilfields are the worse candidate for security." However, the idea behind the plan, he noted, was "to secure the wells which were on leased property against sabotage and pilferage."[24] The BLP government went further. In February 1985 it passed a law that made wearing military camouflage clothing by civilians, even in peace time, illegal.[25]

In terms of acquisition, up until 1979, Barbados and other Eastern Caribbean countries had received no military assistance from the United States. However, during phase two under the BLP administration, this acquisition position changed dramatically. Given the "winds of change" in the Caribbean, the Carter administration officials made manifest the "special role" that it envisioned for Barbados. The U.S. Congress proposed $5 million to help Barbados buy communications and navigational equipment to "strengthen the security of the entire Eastern Caribbean."[26] This thrust was sustained under the Reagan administration which, in its bid to reassert U.S. hegemony in the Caribbean more so than its predecessor, saw events in the region, Grenada in particular, as threats to the security of the United States.

As a consequence of the military assistance received during phase two, not only from the United States, the principal donor, but also from Britain and Canada, the four-year old BDF rose to a strength of 610 by 1983. Three years later when the BLP left office, the size of the BDF was alleged to have spiralled to 1,800, a statistic that was concealed from the Barbadian public and only revealed when the DLP came to power. This increase in the size of the BDF was in large measure due to the BLP's decision to originate and strengthen military-to-military ties with the United States through the International Military Education and Training Program (IMET). IMET provides technical and personal contact among military professionals with the goal of fostering security. And so from a political culture and security environment in which even the British-styled Barbadian police seldom carried guns in the course of duty, the BDF was instrumental in procuring, more so in the aftermath of the 1983 Grenada invasion, jeeps, trucks, communication equipment, and armored cars as well as M-60s and M-16s.

Regarding Barbados' deployment posture during phase two, the creation of and the increase in size of the army, coupled with the acquisition of military hardware and, most important, the use to which such was put, seemed to transform Barbados, within its Eastern Caribbean sphere of influence, into somewhat of a big military power in a small subregional geopolitical pond. This BLP defense policy was dubbed the "Adams Doctrine." Its foreign military dimension was implemented between 1979 and 1983 as a corollary of the Reagan Doctrine, in which the United States used Barbados' military apparatus as a proxy-type force to advance its interests in the Caribbean.[27]

The first use of the BDF as a proxy-type force was on Union Island. On December 7, 1979, four months after its creation, the BDF was dispatched to that island, a dependency of St. Vincent, to quell an uprising by a group of Rastafarians, even though the then BLP administration assured Barbados that soldiers were sent to relieve policemen who were being deployed to Union Island. Twice in 1981, in March and December, when Prime Minister Eugenia Charles faced coup attempts, detachments of the Barbados Defense Force went to Dominica's assistance. The very next year, in 1982, Prime Minister Adams sent the *Trident,* Barbados' Coast Guard flagship, to patrol waters just off St. Lucia where elections were being held in May. There are unconfirmed reports that BDF infantry units were actually deployed in St. Lucia during the elections.[28]

Finally, in 1983, Barbados again served the interest of its superpower patron, this time with stunning effectiveness. Members of the BDF together with soldiers and police officers from four of the OECS countries (Antigua and Barbuda, Dominica, St. Lucia, St. Vincent and the Grenadines) plus Jamaica were deployed to Grenada on October 19. They were "to restore democracy" and to dislodge the Revolutionary Military Council headed by Hutson Austin, which had assumed power there after the brutal killings of Maurice Bishop and others. As part of this undertaking, Barbados' Grantley Adams International Airport was so transformed that one BDF officer commented that the country's sole airport was "almost a military base."[29] The BLP government also permitted members of the BDF and select police officers to serve on the multinational Caribbean Peace Keeping Force in Grenada. This manifest preoccupation of the BLP with the military as compared with the DLP resulted not merely from the bidding of the Reagan administration. Tom Adams seems also to have had certain personality traits that predisposed him to favor martial values. In fact, Adams, an avid reader of war materials, is reported to have said that his greatest wish in life was to be "the general of an army," a factor that may have filtered into the formulation of Barbados' defense policy, however obtusely, during the BLP's tenure in office.[30]

Accompanying Adams's undue emphasis on "the security model," as reflected in the escalation in spending on the BDF and the police, there seemed to be a growing tendency toward authoritarianism and repression in the name of "democracy and security" never before witnessed in the postindependence political history of Barbados.[31] The first real sign of BLP intolerance toward divergent viewpoints came as early as 1977. The government denied Ralph Gonsalves, a St. Vincent-born University of the West Indies professor and author of a *Daily Nation* newspaper column, "Straight Talk," access to the state-owned media.[32] However, not until 1978 was Gonsalves's work permit with the university revoked on the grounds that he had become a "security risk."[33] This defense policy position was not an aberration. It again manifested itself in the BLP's decision in 1983 to ban from the airwaves, lyric versions of "Boots," "One Day Coming Soon," and other songs by calypsonian The Mighty Gabby that were critical of the security mindset of the last Adams administration.[34] Previously, on May 21, 1982, the Adams government had introduced into Parliament an Emergency Powers Bill to forestall possible "aberrant behavior." Only public protest stopped the proposed legislation from becoming law.[35]

Somewhat similar to the Gonsalves case was that of Guyanese-born Ricky Singh, editor of *Caribbean Contact,* a regional newspaper with headquarters in Barbados. He became a subject of "intelligence interest" because his "principled stand" on the U.S. invasion of Grenada was counter to that of the government of the day. Before Singh was deported he was not only "shadowed" by local security men, but on one occasion his home was watched by helicopter.[36] The Adams government argued that Singh's work permit was revoked because, while in Barbados, he cultivated questionable contacts with Cuban intelligence (DGI) agents whose activities were under the scrutiny of local security men. Singh did not deny having Cuban contacts, "among them a diplomat and airline representative of Cuba" who "also deal with the Barbados government and who are also known to journalists in this country (Barbados) and elsewhere." But he maintained that his work permit was revoked because he had written articles condemning the Grenada invasion to which Adams's BLP was a willing partner.[37] His work permit was later restored by Barrow's DLP government during phase three.

The wrath of the BLP was not singular to foreigners but also included noted Barbadian novelist George Lamming and the then Movement for National Liberation (MONALI) group, since transformed into the Workers Party of Barbados. It is also not unreasonable to proffer that the BLP defense policy of repression may also have been galvanized by the interpretation that Adams, as minister of defense, attached to experiences involving his own safety. During phase two Adams's security consciousness, both for himself and the country, began with the first Burnett-Alleyne invasion scare in 1976. It was heightened in May 1984, nine months after the U.S. invasion of Grenada, as a result of the bomb threat at the prime minister's residence, which had now been subject to round-the-clock surveillance by the police and the army.[38] Adams informed the public in his May 8, 1984, parliamentary debate that he was privy to information, although its source was never declared, that "Cuban President Fidel Castro may seek revenge on those responsible for

Havana's humiliation in Grenada." In fact, Adams had had the bomb squad of the Royal Barbados Police Force search the premises of Ilaro Court, the prime minister's official residence on May 7, 1984, upon his notification of an alleged planned bomb attack.

Thus, regarding the Barbados' defense policy during phase two under the leadership of Prime Minister Tom Adams and the BLP, there were considerable changes. During this period, a full-fledged army, the BDF, was started on August 9, 1979. Its size spiralled from 610 in 1983 to 1,800 in 1986. Moreover, not only were U.S. military assistance to Barbados and the Barbados-headquartered Regional Security System begun, but an increase in state budgetary expenditure for security was noticeable as well. It is also noteworthy that during phase two the BDF was deployed overseas to such places as Union Island and Grenada. And the repressive apparatus of the Barbadian state came to play a greater role in the maintenance of the status quo. Barbados' new defense policy therefore stemmed partly from invasion scares, threats to Prime Minister Adams's life, and certain martial psychological traits that he possessed. But most important and precipitous it coincided with and was emboldened by the Reagan administration's interest in reasserting U.S. hegemony in the Caribbean and the world at large.

PHASE THREE: 1986–DECEMBER 1988

In May 1986, Barrow and the DLP were returned to power having roundly defeated the BLP led by Prime Minister Bernard St. John, who had taken over the leadership of the party after Adam's death in 1985. During the political campaign and even before, Barrow vociferously objected to the creation of the BDF, the shroud of secrecy in which it was concealed, and the Regional Security System. In fact, as early as August 1983, while speaking at the annual DLP conference, he had expressed grave concern at what he termed "the growth of militarism in Barbados." He stated that officers of the BDF were being trained by the CIA at the Watergate complex in Washington, D.C., and noted that Barbados soldiers had been sent to participate in exercises with U.S. forces in Puerto Rico. "It seems to me that the government intends to go to war," said Barrow. "The only question is — with whom?"[39]

Barrow's concern over the BDF even resulted in specific preelection pronouncements. He repeatedly promised the electorate that, if and when the DLP were returned to office, the BLP would most likely dissolve the BDF and leave the Regional Security System. And he continued to make similar statements during the first four months of phase three. Among the DLP's first official policy statements in early June regarding the BDF was its criticism of the secrecy of the BLP government during phase two about the size of the BDF. Barrow said: "I had to ask a foreign government what the size of the Defense Force was and they assured me that the Barbados Defense Force has 1,800 personnel."[40]

At the time, the DLP seemed in favor of a defense force, numbering between 180 and 300 persons, as more adequate for Barbados. Concerning the then four-year-old defense pact, the DLP adopted a more cautious approach. In contrast to Prime Minister Adams and his successor, St. John, Barrow indicated that "we have to watch this regional security scheme very carefully because it was contrived in Washington and I have reservations about anybody in Washington sitting down and telling me what we should have in the Eastern Caribbean."[41] However, on September 20, 1986, four months after assuming office, there appeared to be a softening of the DLP's strident criticism of the BDF and the Regional Security System.

The idea of dismantling the BDF, and by so doing being faced with the impracticality of having sizable numbers of trained soldiers join the ranks of the unemployed, proved to be an unattractive option. This more so when over 1,000 employees of Intel, a U.S. offshore electronic equipment company in Seargants Village, Christ Church, had just been retrenched. And so, on the occasion of Barrow's first review of the BDF at its St. Ann's Forth headquarters, he stated: "I shall like to assure the members of the defense force that it is not the intention of this government to exacerbate the high level of unemployment which already exists by any wholesale retrenchment of the force itself."[42] However, he pointed out that the main source of future recruitment would come from the cadet corps. He urged parents to encourage their children, both boys and girls, to join.

Barrow further stressed that the DLP's defense policy was one in which the BDF had a vital role to play in maintaining the sovereignty of this country and in defending the country against external aggression. He further stated that: "Government saw this being achieved by way of the existence within the force of a highly trained commando unit whose purpose would primarily be one of defending Barbados against aggression and enhancing the security of our shoreline to protect the fisheries resources of out territorial waters."

The DLP defense policy, regarding the Regional Security System was also announced at this time. Barrow stated:

We appreciate that a treaty would facilitate the granting of certain types of assistance by other states to the Regional Security System. I do not consider that the absence of a treaty should be regarded as any great obstacle of the flow of the right kind of aid. The absence of a treaty does not lessen the effectiveness of the system given the will on the part of the member-states to respect their obligations.

Chief of Staff Rudyard Lewis, who also serves as the coordinator of the Regional Security System, was undoubtedly less enthusiastic about this DLP defense policy position. His staff had publicly expressed support for a treaty.[43] Suffice it to say that Barbados did not elect to withdraw from the Regional Security System. Moreover, while the DLP asked for the resignation of Courtney Blackman, governor of the Central Bank since 1972 and other politically appointed top civil servants, Chief of Staff Lewis was retained as head of the BDF and Lieutenant-Colonel Deighton Maynard was appointed Deputy Chief of Staff in October 1987.[44]

This alteration in the DLP's defense policy position was further reinforced by statements attributed to Barbados' Minister of Foreign Affairs Senator Cameron Tudor in an interview with *South Magazine* in October 1986. Tudor is quoted as having said that the DLP had "no quarrel" with the Reagan administration and that not only would Barbados remain within the Regional Security System, but that it would continue to take part in military training with the United States. In fact, the report stated "the DLP government is unlikely to take a very different stance from the previous administration."[45]

Two months later, however, in November 1986, it would appear that the DLP's defense policy had reverted to its preelection position. Prime Minister Barrow, in an interview with the British Broadcasting Corporation's *Caribbean Magazine* recorded during his visit to London again stressed his original and long-standing opposition to the militarization of the Caribbean. And he announced plans to dissolve the BDF but offered no time limit. More directly, Prime Minister Barrow stated, "We intend to demilitarize the Barbados Defense Force except for ceremonial (occasions). We're going to phase them out." Barrow also promised a hefty cut in defense spending: "From the estimates of next year (1987), we are going to cut drastically on the estimates for expenditure for the defense force."[46]

This sudden reversal in Barbados' defense policy did not go unnoticed by the opposition BLP which responded by saying:

> The Prime Minister's latest policy statement is a clear breach of faith on his part in regard to the Defense Force and represents a crisis in credibility and a crisis in leadership. . . . It raises the question as to whether the words of the Prime Minister on matters of national significance can be taken at face value, and as being reflective of the real intentions of government. . . . Mr. Barrow's recent statements strikes at the very heart of the confidence a people should be able to put in government and underscores the fact that the government is totally confused and at odds with itself on matters of national significance.[47]

By then the DLP had received its first invasion scare, in September 1986. It came from Sidney Burnett-Alleyne, who demanded a Barbadian passport under threat to "declare war." But the DLP dismissed the existence of any military threat as perceived by the BLP during phase two. The expressed defense policy position of the DLP, as articulated by Prime Minister Barrow, who seemingly made little or nothing of the Burnett-Alleyne scare, was that "apart from Belize, which had a border dispute with Guatemala, and Guyana, which has a similar one with Venezuela, the invasion threat may be from the United States itself. It was not from Japan, England or France or any country like that. So our real threat is the United States."[48]

In fact, not unlike phase two, in July 1987 Sidney Burnett-Alleyne issued his second invasion scare during phase three. He stated in an article published in the Barbados *Weekend Nation,* a month after the death of Errol Barrow that, "I am the only genuine Barbadian (that was) feared by both Tom Adams and Errol Barrow." Also, in January 1988, Burnett-Alleyne, in a telex message to Prime Minister Erskine Sandiford and other government officials, again called on Barbadian government officials to restore his Barbadian passport or else face the "dire consequences." The veiled threat of this convicted gunrunner did not, however, indicate how he would carry out his avowed intention to "work toward a government that is truly representative of the Barbadian people."[49]

In all three instances, the DLP, unlike Adams and the BLP during phase two, appeared to ignore or downplay the alleged plots to overthrow the government. This calm and measured response of the DLP seemed also to obtain when, between October 4 and October 6, 1986, Andrew Batson sent a letter to then Governor-General Sir Hugh Springer threatening to kill him. Such a defense policy position during phase three regarding threats to the state and to one of its leading political figures is in stark contrast to the security consciousness and hypersensitivity that similar threats evoked from Prime Minister Adams and the BLP during phase two. This definite change in policy may very well suggest the degree to which the BLP used extant invasion scares as a pretext to engage in an unprecedented military buildup in Barbados. But more important, it underscored the surrogate role of the Barbadian state during phase two in the United States' efforts to reassert its hegemony in the Caribbean and Central America.

Going beyond the contradictory statements from DLP officials, in the final analysis the DLP's employment posture during phase three resulted in a change of emphasis from that during phase two. In March 1987, the DLP eventually declared that although there would be no reduction in the size of the BDF, its future would be centered on the coast guard in an effort to control smuggling, combat illicit trade in narcotics, and engage in search and rescue.[50] In fact, when expressing dissatisfaction with the then existing airport security arrangement, Prime Minister Barrow announced plans for 45 soldiers from the BDF to be used to man security positions at the Grantley Adams International Airport. Barrow's rationale was that "because of their military training, the soldiers would be more equipped to stamp out smuggling and terrorism."[51] These plans were, however, never implemented. This shift in Barbados' defense policy is borne out by Barrow's decision to ground the air wing of the BDF and, by so doing, deemphasize the military use of the army. Barrow, a former pilot in the Royal Air Force during World War II, must have known that this action would constrain rapid deployment of the BDF, at least with its own planes, thus limiting its involvement in any swift operation, either with the Regional Security System or alone.

Moreover, such a reorientation in the use of the BDF may partly explain why the DLP, in spite of Prime Minister Barrow's declaration "that Barbados was rapidly becoming a complacent client of the U.S." readily accepted the offer of two Boston Wailers guardian patrol boats provided under the U.S. Military Assistance Program to the Eastern Caribbean to strengthen the existing fleet of the BDF coast guard. In fact, regarding the fight against drug smuggling and the role of the BDF in it, Attorney General Maurice King declared on March 16, 1988, that, along with accepting the two Boston Wailers, Barbados was considering the purchase of another million-dollar coast guard vessel as well as reviving the harbor police. He also alluded to the use of more combined surveillance operations by the police and the BDF. On that very occasion, Prime Minister Sandiford, Barrow's successor, restated the government's position on the retention of the BDF. He explained that it was considered necessary to have an army in order to protect the sovereignty and independence of Barbados from incursions from abroad and to come to the aid of civil powers internally.[52]

However, as was indicated as early as September 15, 1986, the DLP's acquisition position on training was similar to the BLP's in some respects. The former continued to allow the BDF to participate in exercises with the United States and Britain involving the Regional Security System. In keeping with this pattern, the DLP has also permitted Barbados to continue to host the headquarters of the Regional Security System. In December 1988, Dominica's Prime Minister Eugenia Charles made a plea to reduce the top leadership of the Regional Security System from four to two persons because, in her view, it was too top heavy and "costing too much." Curiously enough, Sandiford failed to go along with the proposal, which seemed to suggest that in his defense policy thinking the Regional Security System had become something of a sacred cow to be fed rather than deprived.[53] Also, the trend of Barbadians receiving U.S. training, begun during phase two, continued during phase three, although at a reduced rate. In January 1987, a high-level nine-man team of Barbadian security and immigration officials visited the United States for exposure to antiterrorist and other security techniques.[54]

The DLP's deployment practices during phase three, were, up to the end of 1988, very different from those under the BLP, which sent BDF troops to several fellow Caribbean countries, including to Grenada during the 1983 U.S. invasion. The American-trained Special Service Units of the Regional Security System were again deployed to Grenada in December 1988 at the request of then Prime Minister Herbert Blaize. He was concerned about potential unrest by sympathizers of the 18 defendants as the Maurice Bishop murder trial neared its end. Barbados, then led by Barrow who had criticized the 1983 invasion of Grenada, which the Regional Security System supported, was not asked to send representatives to participate in this second peace-keeping operation. Blaize said that the request for outside paramilitary assistance was made because of a spate of "late night incidents of gunfire, armed robbery and ambushing in Grenada." He claimed neither Antigua and Barbuda nor Barbados (the only two Eastern Caribbean countries with armies) was approached because "we asked for help to strengthen our Special Service Unit. We did not ask for soldiers to fight war."[55]

Thus far in phase three, the DLP government has sent the BDF overseas just once — in a humanitarian capacity. This occasion was in response to a request by the government of Jamaica in the aftermath of

Hurricane Gilbert in September 1988 when some 33 Barbadian soldiers traveled to that island to engage in the hurricane relief effort.[56] In contrast to the BLP's policy where deployment of DDF troops abroad during phase two was accompanied by incidents of repression at home, the DLP's policy regarding critics of the state appears to be somewhat more low keyed. Such a conclusion may be drawn from the DLP's decision in January 1987 to overturn the BLP's revocation of work permit of Guyanese-born journalist Ricky Singh, who was formerly asked to leave Barbados.[57]

CONCLUSION

This discussion suggests that during phase one the DLP saw the police as the only security agency necessary for the nation. It placed secondary emphasis on the coast guard. The coast guard, begun in 1974 without U.S. military assistance, was not used for military purposes, but to strengthen Barbados' ability to patrol its territorial waters as well as to prevent smuggling and damage to maritime life. During phase one, perceived threats to the state were not countered with military preparedness, but with legislation, as evidenced by the enactment of the Public Order Act in 1970. Also, at no time during this period were Barbadian security forces deployed overseas for military or political purposes.

With the coming of phase two, there were changes in the substance, style, and conduct of Barbados's defense policy. Such changes came about, in large measure, because of the transformation in the security environment of the Eastern Caribbean, triggered by various issues. There was the Cubana Airlines crash in 1976, the Sidney Burnett-Alleyne invasion scares, the Grenada revolution, and, not least of all, the reemergence of U.S. hegemony in the Caribbean. As a consequence, the BLP before long attached unprecedented importance to the role of the military in security affairs as reflected in its decision to start the Barbados Defense Force (BDF) as well as its leading involvement in the Regional Security System. Also, it was during phase two that, for the first time, Barbados became a recipient of U.S. military assistance. In fact, "the Adams Doctrine" of electing to "win in the field" through troop deployment, as was exemplified in the deployment of BDF troops to Union Island and Grenada, buttresses the argument that Adams may have placed undue emphasis on military means to treat crises rather than more fully exploring political avenues. Such means were also in the name of "security and democracy," accompanied by repression to silence and deter critics of the security mindset that prevailed during much of phase two.

Although, while in opposition, DLP officials made repeated promises to change Barbados' defense policy substantially if returned to power, despite alterations in style and emphasis, there has been a good deal of continuity. During phase three, the size of the BDF was not reduced as promised; neither was there a freeze in defense spending. Moreover, Barbados remained a member of the Regional Security System. And like the BLP during phase two, the government allowed the BDF to benefit from training offered by the United States and Britain. However, in contrast to the BLP, which before being displaced seemed to favor upgrading the Memorandum of Understanding to a formal treaty, the DLP has thus far remained unalterably opposed to such a move.

The new defense policy course launched by Prime Minister Adams and the BLP during phase two regarding the need for a full-fledged army and involvement in the Regional Security System has been retained by the DLP during phase three under Prime Ministers Barrow and Sandiford. It can, therefore, be argued that such continuity in Barbados' defense policy across successive BLP and DLP administrations, though with varying intensity of commitment, suggests that, at some level, a tacit bipartisan Barbadian defense policy may now have emerged.

NOTES

1. Thus far, the only article on defense policy in the English-speaking Caribbean is written by Humberto García Muñiz, "Defense Policy and Planning in the Caribbean: An Assessment of the Case of Jamaica on its 25th Independence Anniversary," *Caribbean Studies* 21 (1988): 67–123.

2. Stephanie G. Neuman, "Defense Planning in Less-Industrialized States: An Organizing Framework," in Stephanie G. Neuman, *Defense Planning in Less-Industrialized States* (Mass.: Lexington Books, 1984).

3. Glen H. Snyder, *Deterrence and Defense: Toward a Theory of National Security* (Princeton, N.J.: Princeton University Press, 1961), pp. 3–4.

4. Given the difficulty in ascertaining some country's defense policy, it is necessary to complement public statements with defense planning information. By studying when and how a given country organizes its military manpower (employment), the kinds of military hardware it buys or accepts as well as the training it receives (acquisitions), and when and where the military is used (deployment), a fairly accurate picture of the country's defense policy can be constructed.

5. Quoted in Government of Barbados, *The Federal Negotiations 1962–1965 and Constitutional Proposals for Barbados* (St. Michael, Barbados: Government Printing Office, 1965), p. 51.

6. Ibid., pp. 49–50.

7. Col. Trevor N. Dupuy, U.S. Army, Ret., *The Almanac of World Military Power* (San Rafael, Calif.: Presidio Press, 1980), p. 21.

8. Delisle Worrell, ed., *The Economy of Barbados 1964–80* (Barbados: Letchworth Press Ltd., 1982); Clive Y. Thomas, *The Poor and the Powerless: Economic Policy and Change in the Caribbean* (New York: Monthly Review Press, 1988), pp. 268–79.

9. Barbados Public Order Act, 1970–15, Supplement to *Official Gazette*, June 8, 1970.

10. *Barbados Labor Party Manifesto* (Barbados, September 1976), p. 22.

11. The two members of CORU who planted the bombs aboard Flight CU455 were Hernan Ricardo Lozano and Freddy Lugo, both Venezuelan. It is alleged that the two were coconspirators with Orlando Bosch, a Cuban pediatrician, and Luis Posado Carrilles, a Cuban explosives expert and former secret police officer in the right-wing dictatorship of Fulgencio Batista.

12. Yusuff Haniff, "Major Caribbean Bombing Brings Safety Changes," *The Advocate News,* October 8, 1986, p. 4.

13. Al Gilkes, a leading Barbadian journalist, was the author of the newspaper article about the appearance of the Russian ships. However, because of the security perception of the BLP at that time, Gilkes was interrogated by officials of the Royal Barbados Police Force who seemingly knew nothing of the incident before it was reported in the local news. He was also cautioned against possible contravention of the Official Secrets Act. Harold Hoyte, editor of the *Nation* newspaper, alluded to the police actions as "an attempt to unnecessarily restrain reporters in the ordinary function of their jobs." An unnamed spokesperson for the BLP stated that "on security matters, the police have a duty to investigate every lead and journalists have no right pursuing a news tip of such a delicate security nature." Al Gilkes, "The Three Who Saw," *Daily Nation,* July 31, 1977.

14. Ricky Singh, "The Williams-Adams Friendship Pact," *Caribbean Contact,* June 1979, pp. 10, 11.

15. Neville Duncan, "Mood of Barbados on 13th Birthday," *Caribbean Contact,* December 1979, p. 7. Duncan, a University of the West Indies political scientist, stated that "the planned, though aborted invasion . . . never aroused any response of sympathy among the masses."

16. "Barbados: Armed Invasion, Fact or Fiction," *Caribbean Insight,* January 1979, p. 1; "Turn Your Back on This Man," *Caribbean Contact,* January 1979, p. 1.

17. In response to the presence of the *Deltona,* which turned out to be a Cayman Island registered cargo ship whose visits to Barbados are quite normal, one truckload and one vanload of heavily armed troops were rushed to St. Lucy, taking up positions near the cave. And at army headquarters, St. Ann's Fort, troops, some armed with submachine guns and automatic rifles, patrolled the base perimeter while others stood guard on the roof. Simultaneously, two coast guard boats headed to the cave. Also, when the *Deltona* eventually berthed at the Bridgetown Port, it was immediately boarded by customs officers and police officers, some of whom were from the Special Branch, which is in charge of state security and intelligence. Yussuf Haniff, "Full Alert," *The Nation,* June 27, 1979.

18. Dion E. Phillips, "The Creation, Structure and Training of the Barbados Defense Force," *Caribbean Studies* 21 (1988): 124–57. Curiously enough, the first hint of the decision to join a defense force came from Queen Elizabeth in her speech opening the Barbadian Parliament in November 1977.

19. *Barbados Labor Party Manifesto* (Bridgetown, Barbados, 1981), p. 3.

20. "Barbados and the Regional Security and Military Pact," *Caribbean Contact,* December 1982, p. 16.

21. Faith Welcome, "Barbados to End U.S. Military Base in Barbados," *Caribbean Contact,* March 1977, p. 8.

22. "U.S. Navy to Quit Barbados," *Washington Post,* December 13, 1978, p. A29.

23. "Mapp Our Overseas Military Diplomat," *Advocate News,* June 3, 1984, p. 1.

24. "Security Plan for Wells Coming," *Daily Nation,* October 31, 1984, p. 2.

25. According to this amendment to the Defense Force Act, which applies as well to "any material which in any way resembles" military uniforms, this law does not prohibit the wearing of any dress or uniform during a stage play performance "in a place licensed or authorized for stage plays or in music halls for stage performance." "Ban on Army-type Dress," *Daily Nation,* February 21, 1985, p. 21.

26. John M. Goshko, "Caribbean Ally Confront Reagan with Early Test on Military Aid," *Washington Post,* November 26, 1980, p. 4.

27. In its most basic form, a proxy is an individual or group empowered to act for another. The involvement of proxy forces must serve the interest of some stronger power. If deployment of Barbados' security forces (for example, to Grenada) met the interest of Barbados but no greater power, such an action could not be considered proxy action.

28. "Barbados Accused of Meddling in St. Lucia," *Sunday Sun,* October 10, 1982.

29. "High Airport Bill for U.S.," *The Nation,* November 15, 1983.

30. "The Question of Militarization," *The Advocate,* January 26, 1987; F. A. Hoyos, *Tom Adams: Biography* (London: Macmillan Publishers, 1988), p. 150.

31. David Commissiong, "The Policy of Repression," *Sunday Sun,* January 31, 1988, p. 7; Hilbourne Watson, "Imperialism, National Security and the State Power in the Commonwealth Caribbean: Issues in the Development of the Authorization State," in Alma H. Young and Dion E. Phillips, *Militarization in the Non-Hispanic Caribbean* (Boulder, Colo.: Lynne Reinner Publishers, 1986), pp. 17–41.

32. Ralph E. Gonsalves, "Tom in Trouble," *The Nation,* December 7, 1977, p. 5.

33. "Support for Dr. Gonsalves," *Caribbean Contact,* February 1980, p. 20.

34. "Music on the Political Nerves," *The Nation,* October 15, 1984; Frank E. Manning, "Calypso and Politics in Barbados," *The Caribbean and West Indian Chronicle* 44 (April/May 1984): 14–15.

35. F. Walcott, "The Emergency Powers Bill," *Sunday Advocate,* October 18, 1982.

36. "Barbados Order Out Singh," *The Nation,* November 3, 1983, p. 1.

37. Robert Best, "Ricky Singh and the Cuban Connection," *Sunday Advocate,* May 20, 1984, p. 9.

38. "Adams Warns of Cuban Revenge," *Barbados Advocate,* May 9, 1984, p. 1.

39. "They Are Ready for War," *Daily Nation,* 1983, p. 1. Tom Adams agreed that the BDF participated in training with the Puerto Rican and U.S. Virgin Island National Guard. He, however, dismissed allegations that the CIA was training the BDF with the remark: "The Central Intelligence Agency is not a military organization."

40. "Barrow Is Wary of Regional Army," *Daily Nation*, June 3, 1986, p. 4.

41. Ibid.

42. "No BDF Job Cuts: But Barrow Sees Need for Emphasis," *Sunday Sun*, September 21, 1986, p. 2.

43. Staff, "The Role of the Regional Security System in the East Caribbean," *Bulletin of Eastern Caribbean Affairs* 11 (January/February 1986).

44. "Maynard — BDF's 2nd in Command," *Weekend Nation*, October 23, 1987, p. 13.

45. "Alleyne in Coup Threat," *Sunday Sun*, September 21, 1986, p. 15.

46. "Government Plans Phazing Out Barbados Defense Force," *Trinidad Guardian*, December 15, 1986, p. 5.

47. *Daily Nation*, 1986, p. 1.

48. *Trinidad Guardian*, 1986, p. 1.

49. "Restore Passport or Else," *Weekend Nation*, January 22, 1988, p. 17.

50. "Coast Guard as Key," *Daily Nation*, March 18, 1987, p. 14A.

51. "Soldiers for Airport Security," *Daily Nation*, March 18, 1987, p. 1.

52. "Three More Boats Joining the Fight Against Drugs," *Daily Nation*, March 17, 1988, p. 1.

52. "Barbados Fighting Bid to Cut RSS Top Staff," *Sunday Sun*, December 18, 1988, p. 40.

54. "Security Team for the U.S.," *Daily Nation*, January 12, 1987, p. 1.

55. "We Did Not Ask for Soldiers to Fight War," *Trinidad Express*, December 9, 1987, p. 18.

56. "Army Lads on Relief Mission," *Daily Nation*, September 26, 1988, p. 1.

57. "New Status for Singh in Barbados," *Caribbean Contact*, February 1987, p. 16.

6 The Territorial Dimension of Caribbean Security: The Case of Belize

Alma H. Young

Territorial conflicts are one of the major legacies of colonialism.[1] In their quest for sovereignty, colonial powers often erected artificial boundaries; frequently these boundaries were carelessly and arbitrarily defined. In the process, they not only incorporated incompatible groups into one territory but also separated similar ethnic peoples and hindered traditional free movement in many areas. Colonial powers often settled competing claims by arbitration, but settlements were sometimes politically rather than legally formulated. Thus, when colonial territories emerged to independence, one of the formidable tasks facing them was the need to clearly define the frontiers of their sovereign states. Another task was to fashion an identity for the new state that went beyond that of the ethnic groups that often straddled two national borders. Territorial controversies were aggravated by concerns for power and prestige and, in many cases, economic gain from the territory claimed. Border and territorial conflicts have sometimes become violent, and major wars have occurred where ethnic separation has taken place.

Territorial conflicts can be a source of insecurity not only to the countries involved, but also to the whole region. Sources of insecurity vary.[2] First, insecurity can lead to intervention by external actors, especially major powers. Major powers have used territorial disputes as opportunities to promote the creation of friendly client-states. Such efforts have long conditioned U.S. policy toward countries in the Third World. Second, the major powers often view conflict in the Third World, including territorial disputes, as having an impact on their global strategic interests. Consequently, they would attempt to influence the outcome of such conflicts by providing their respective clients with arms, training, and advice. However, when such support is provided, other parties to the dispute will often seek assistance from a competing great power. This situation then tends to increase the risk of great power entanglement in local disputes. The assistance given to client-states is often in the form of enhancing their capability. Thus the third source of instability is the increase in the local arms race.

Internally, the territorial dispute can lead to a siege mentality that keeps the populace always conscious of impending doom. This mentality can become part of the social fabric and persist long after the initial threat has dissipated. For the elite, the national security obsession expands to include internal security. Attempts by the opposition to promote social and political change are labeled counterinsurgency and are quashed in the name of national security. In countries where different alliances compete for power among ethnic, tribal, religious, and class groupings maintaining legitimate consensus is often difficult. In such cases, leaders may resort to undemocratic means to maintain power. What begins as a means to create secure borders ends as a way of maintaining power for the governing elite.

The Caribbean region has experienced its share of territorial disputes.[3] The Caribbean islands, by their very nature as islands, have largely escaped the problem of competing territorial claims and border controversies. However, on divided Hispaniola there have been disputes between Haiti and the Dominican Republic over border violations and water rights. Further south, Trinidad and Tobago and Venezuela, sharing a marine border (the Gulf of Paria), have clashed over fishing rights. Moreover, Venezuela claims an uninhabited Caribbean island, Bird (Aves) Island, off the coast of Dominica. These few Caribbean controversies have been amply matched by territorial disputes occurring in the wider Caribbean Basin region.

In the southern Caribbean there are a number of disputes. One of the most salient controversies is the claim of Venezuela to five-eighths of Guyana's territory. But Venezuela also has a dispute with Colombia over the demarcation of the oil-rich Gulf of Venezuela, and Guyana has a dispute with neighboring Surinam over areas of land (the New River Triangle) on Surinam's western border. Finally, Surinam and French Guiana disagree on their common river-based boundary. In Central America, Nicaragua in 1980 revived a claim to the islands of San Andres and Providencia and to the Serrana, Serranilla, Roncador, and Quintasueno cays, all held by Colombia under an award rendered in 1928. In

1981, Belize emerged to long-delayed independence (having been a self-governing territory for almost 20 years), but only after a temporary security agreement with Britain had been negotiated — Belize had long been claimed by Guatemala on the grounds that Britain did not comply with certain stipulations of an 1859 Anglo-Guatemala treaty. Of these disputes in the Caribbean Basin, one of the most problematic has been the Guatemala-Belize dispute, a legacy of British colonialism, dating from a period of British overwhelming strength and Latin American postindependence weakness. The remainder of this chapter details some of the impacts of this dispute on security within Belize and within the region.

THE BELIZE-GUATEMALA BORDER DISPUTE

Situated on the Central American mainland below Mexico and facing the Caribbean, Belize (known as British Honduras until 1973), shares a 140-mile border with Guatemala. The Spanish never occupied and settled the area of present-day Belize, although Spanish armies may have passed close by in Guatemala. The country developed from the pirate and smuggler settlements that grew up among the secluded bays of the uninhabited coast.[4] By 1638 the British settlement had become a major provider of logwood and mahogany. However, the country did not become a British colony until 1862. By then, the traditional basis of the settlement as an English-speaking, timber-producing enclave already was eroding as a result of the immigration of an agricultural population of Indian and Spanish-speaking refugees from neighboring Yucatan. By the time Belize became an independent nation within the Commonwealth in 1981, its population of 155,000 was ethnically diverse. The two largest ethnic groups in this culturally varied society are black Creoles (about 40 percent) of West Indian heritage and Spanish-speaking Mestizos (33 percent), who are close to Mexico culturally and geographically. Today the Maya Indians, who once had complex settlements, such as Altun Ha and Xunantunich based on intensive raised bed and milpa farming, represent only a small element in the Belizean population. Many of the Indians maintain close ties to their families across the border in Guatemala.

With a total surface area of 8,867 square miles, Belize is larger than all the former British Caribbean islands. Furthermore, there are large uninhabited areas of the country, although, like neighboring Peten in Guatemala and the Yucatan Peninsula in Mexico, they represent regions depopulated since late-Mayan times. (Estimates place the population of Belize at one-half million in the tenth century.)[5] Consequently, there is relatively little pressure of population upon available resources at present.

For example, although it is twice the area of Jamaica, Belize has only 7 percent of Jamaica's population. Nevertheless, nearly one-third of the population lives in the former capital of Belize City. About one-half the population lives in the seven largest towns. The character of the settlements in the country is clearly related to the predominance of one or another of the ethnic groups.[6] Of the six administrative districts in the country, only Belize, containing Belize City, has an English-speaking majority, although many of the coastal inhabitants are also predominantly English-speaking. In the two northern districts, Spanish-speaking Mestizos predominate; in Dangriga (formerly Stann Creek) there is a significant Garifuna element; and in Toledo, Mayan and other Indian groups are important. This multiethnic and multicultural character has been further accentuated by the recent influx of refugees from El Salvador and Guatemala.

Throughout the nineteenth and early twentieth centuries, the export of timber and timber products to Britain dominated the economy. By the 1920s timber still accounted for about 90 percent of the colony's exports. But the timber industry was beginning to slump as a result of improper management of resources. Slowly greater emphasis was beginning to be placed on agricultural production so that by 1970, sugar represented 40 percent of total exports by value.[7] The mainstay of the economy today remains sugar, although citrus, banana, and seafood have become significant economic generators. There has been relatively limited development of a manufacturing industry. Increasingly, the tourist industry is being regarded as a major potential growth area and in recent governmental plans received a priority second only to agricultural development.

History of the Dispute

The Spanish conquest of Guatemala was completed in 1524, but no Spanish settlement was ever established in Belize. By the time Guatemala became independent of Spain in 1821, the British settlement in Belize had become an accepted fact. Guatemala never exercised any authority over Belize. The origins of the Guatemala claim to Belize do not lie, therefore, in the postcolonial period.[8] It was in the attempt to establish firm boundaries between the two countries that the dispute developed to the point that Guatemala claimed the territory of Belize.

British settlement on Spanish soil was first recorded in 1638, but it was more than a century later before Spain, under considerable pressure from Britain, recognized the settlers' economic activities. The Anglo-Spanish Treaties of 1783 and 1786 gave British settlers the right to cut wood in specific areas around Belize. The territory, however, remained under Spanish sovereignty. After Central America became independent of Spain in 1821, the British government continued to take the view that sovereignty still belonged to Spain; Britain denied Central America's claim that, on attaining independence, the new federation had inherited all Spain's rights in the area.[9] In 1835 Britain asked Spain to cede the territory, which Britain now claimed on the basis of conquest, long use, and custom. Nothing came of that attempt.[10]

After failing to obtain a cession of sovereignty over Belize from Spain in 1835, Britain began to exercise its own jurisdiction more formally. By 1850 the British government felt that the Anglo-Spanish Treaty of 1786 was no longer in force and that Britain itself had now acquired rights of possession. However, not until 1862 did Britain formally proclaim its own sovereignty, by the act of conferring the status of colony on Belize. Guatemala did not formally protest this change in status.[11]

As its interests in Central America increased, Britain found it advantageous to settle its dispute with Guatemala over the territory of Belize. The timing was propitious for Guatemala, too, because it saw friendship with Britain as a way of forestalling potential filibustering from the United States. Therefore, in April 1859, British diplomats arrived in Guatemala to begin negotiation to solve the problem between the two countries. Because Britain refused to concede that Guatemala had any "sovereign rights" in the settlement and because the Clayton-Bulwer Treaty of 1850 prohibited territorial cessions in the area, Britain made it clear that the treaty was one of boundaries only.[12] The treaty was signed on April 30, 1859. The first six articles of the treaty clearly defined the boundaries of Belize. All future problems between Guatemala and Great Britain were caused by the seventh article, which provided for the construction of a road from Guatemala City to the Caribbean coast. There is no doubt that Guatemala regarded the seventh article as compensation for abandoning its sovereign rights in the settlement.[13]

It is clear that Britain and Guatemala agreed to build a road, but the phrase used in the treaty, "mutually agree on con-jointly," left unresolved whether Britain was to build the road entirely at its expense.[14] The dispute over Article Seven led to a Supplementary Convention, which was negotiated in 1863. The sole obligation undertaken by Britain was to recommend that the Parliament appropriate 50,000 pounds to be given to Guatemala to enable it to build the road. The convention was to be ratified within six months, and the work was to be completed four years after it was begun.[15]

Guatemala was at war at the time and was unable to ratify the convention within the stipulated period. When Guatemala eventually did ratify it, Britain claimed that the opportunity was lost and that Britain was now released from any obligation under Article Seven. Guatemala replied that Article Seven was compensation to Guatemala for the territory of Belize and intimated that it was willing to sign a new convention. Britain denied that the 1859 treaty involved a cession of territory and repudiated Guatemala's claim to Belize.[16]

The dispute lagged until the 1930s, when Britain seemed more willing to honor its obligation than it had been in the past. However, neither side seemed willing to accept the other's suggestions on who might mediate the dispute and under what terms or on what kind of compensation Guatemala might receive. Guatemala offered several alternatives, including cessions of territory, that would provide it broader access to the Caribbean Sea. Diplomatic attempts to mediate the dispute continued to be unsuccessful. In 1940 Guatemala stated that it was no longer a question whether Article Seven could be fulfilled. Guatemala now had the right to recover territory "ceded" in 1859. The issue to be settled was, therefore, whether Britain was legitimately occupying the territory of Belize.[17] In 1945 the Republic of Guatemala adopted a new constitution, which declared in Article I that Belize was part of its national territory and that "any efforts towards obtaining its reinstatement to the Republic are of national interest." This article was reproduced in the constitution of 1965.[18]

The Webster Proposals

In 1962 Britain agreed to meet Guatemala on neutral ground and a conference was held in Puerto Rico. The decisions, if any, taken at this conference were never made public. But it is believed that the key suggestion involved establishing a three-person tribunal, with a U.S. chairman, to look into the dispute without prejudice to the case of either Britain or Guatemala. Two years later, President Lyndon B. Johnson nominated a single mediator, Bethuel M. Webster, a New York attorney.

On April 26, 1968, Webster presented his final report in the form of a draft treaty. Known as the Webster Proposals, the draft provided for cooperation between an independent Belize and Guatemala.[19] Article I of the Webster Proposals granted independence to the nation of Belize and made the country responsible for all international obligations (including the treaty with Guatemala). However, the sovereignty was rendered nominal by various aspects of the draft treaty and the wide powers conferred on a proposed Joint Authority of Belize and Guatemala. The plan placed the defense, foreign affairs, and economy of Belize under Guatemalan control after independence. Belize was to accept a customs union with Guatemala, which would allow free access to its Caribbean ports and territorial waters. In return, Guatemala was to sponsor Belize's entry into the Central American community and into the Inter-American community, particularly the Organization of American States (OAS) and the Inter-American Development Bank. No where in the document was it stated that the Guatemalan claim was revoked. Nor was Belize explicitly given the right to seek membership in the Commonwealth, the United Nations, or other international bodies outside the Inter-American system.

When the draft treaty was made public in May 1968, rioting erupted in the streets of Belize. Opposition leaders felt the treaty denied many of the prerogatives of an independent state. On May 14, 1968, the government joined the opposition in unanimously rejecting the proposals in the House of Representatives.[20] The decision put an end to the Webster Proposals because the British government had pledged not to conclude a settlement that was unacceptable to the government of Belize.

The Internationalization

Starting in the 1970s, Belize, to facilitate its movement toward independence, began to take the initiative in resolving the dispute. This new strategy became known as "the internationalization."[21] The countries of the English-speaking Caribbean became the frontline states in waging an intense diplomatic offensive on behalf of Belize to help the country win its independence with territory intact. Belizean governmental leaders felt that neither Britain nor the United States was willing to prejudice its relationship with Latin American countries, in general, and Guatemala, in particular, in order to safeguard Belize's territorial integrity. As a result of Belize's initiatives to internationalize the issue and present its case for independence, support came not only from the countries of the Caribbean Community, but also from the Commonwealth of Nations and the Non-Aligned Movement. In 1975 the first United Nations resolution on Belize was passed by the General Assembly by a vote of 110 in favor, with 9 against and 16 abstentions. This large initial support was made possible because of the undertaking by the Non-Aligned Movement, at its Foreign Ministers' Conference in Peru that year, to commit its total support to Belize. The Belize delegation had lobbied the conference participants very hard and effectively.[22] Although the UN support was substantial, it revealed a major weakness — none of the mainland Spanish-speaking Latin American countries had voted for Belize. It became Belize's number one priority to win the support of these countries. When Premier George Price met the late General Omar Torrijos, then president of Panama, at the 1976 Summit Meeting of the Non-Aligned Movement, he convinced Torrijos of Belize's right to independence.[23] At the next UN General Assembly session, Panama voted in favor of the Belize resolution. After Panama many other Latin American countries voted for Belize in subsequent UN resolutions. When the Sandinistas came to power in Nicaragua in 1979 that country became a major supporter of Belizean independence.

By November 1980 international support for Belize was virtually unanimous. In 1981 a UN resolution called for independence for Belize with territorial integrity and security. This time the United States, which had previously abstained on all the Belize resolutions since 1975, voted in favor of the resolution, and no country voted against.[24] By an overwhelming majority, in November 1981 the Organization of American States, which had until then maintained support for the integrity of Guatemala's position, endorsed the UN resolution calling for a security independence for Belize.[25]

Because of such support the Belizean government decided, with the consent of the British government and the blessing of the international community, to proceed to independence and to continue efforts thereafter to develop diplomatic relations with the government of Guatemala. The British committed themselves to continue to defend Belize. A 1,600-man contingent of British troops was to be stationed in Belize for "an appropriate period." When after 18 years as a self-governing colony the country became independent on September 21, 1981, the territorial dispute had not been settled, nor did Guatemala recognize Belize's sovereignty.

The Heads of Agreement

A last attempt at resolving the territorial dispute before independence resulted in a document known as the "Heads of Agreement."[26] This framework for a settlement of the dispute was signed by Britain and Guatemala, with Belize signing as a witness, on March 11, 1981. According to the document, Guatemala would accept the independence of Belize in return for, among other things, free access to the sea through Belizean territorial waters, free port facilities, and the right to "use and enjoy" the seabeds around two cay chains, Sapodilla and Ranguana. Led by the then opposition United Democratic Party (UDP) and the Public Service Union (PSU), Belizeans denounced the Heads of Agreement, charging that its provisions violated the nation's territorial integrity. When the opposition's demand for a referendum on the Heads of Agreement was not forthcoming, riots occurred throughout the country, and the PSU engaged in paralyzing strikes. The British governor declared a state of emergency on April 2, 1981, and sent local and British troops to end the paralyzing strikes and riots.[27] Once calm returned, the opposition continued to campaign against the Heads of Agreement and against independence without a suitable defense guarantee.

Early in July 1981 representatives from Britain, Guatemala, and Belize met in New York in an attempt to reach agreement on the proposed treaty, but the talks again failed. Guatemala made new claims relating to land, maritime boundaries, and basing troops on the Sapodilla and Ranguana cays.[28] By late July, then Premier George Price, meeting in London with representatives of the British government, agreed to move quickly to independence — without a resolution of the territorial dispute. Britain agreed to defend the country by keeping British troops in Belize for an appropriate period and to provide more intensive training for the Belize Defense Force. Britain's decision effectively foreclosed the opposition against independence; however, the opposition refused to be party to independence negotiations with Britain. Thus, because of the territorial dispute, the country went into independence without the support of the opposition.

DEVELOPMENTS SINCE INDEPENDENCE

In June 1982 Guatemala sought a meeting with Britain to discuss the territorial dispute, but Britain refused to meet, saying Guatemala had to discuss the matter with the independent nation of Belize. Because Guatemala "does not recognize the independence unilaterally granted by the United Kingdom," it had been unwilling to negotiate directly with the Belize government. However, in July 1984, informal talks between the governments of Belize and Guatemala took place in New York City.[29] Although the issue was left unresolved, that round of talks was viewed as a positive development because Belize was now negotiating on its own behalf.

In the December 1985 general elections in Belize, the United Democratic Party (UDP) supplanted the 30-year regime of the People's United Party (PUP). Like its predecessor, the UDP government considered the security and the defense of Belize its highest foreign policy priority. In his first address to the United Nations in September 1985, then Foreign Minister Dean Barrow stated, "The independence of Belize is irreversible. . . . To seek to maintain otherwise is counter-productive and counter-historical. . . . A prelude to harmonious relations between Belize and Guatemala, then, is the recognition that two separate, sovereign entities share a common border."[30] At the first informal meeting between officials of the UDP Belize government and Guatemala in February 1986, Guatemala sought an update to the 1981 proposed Heads of Agreement. At that meeting Barrow affirmed that Belize would consider an agreement similar to the one outlined but not signed in March 1981. Under Guatemala's updated proposal Belize would grant Guatemala usufruct of the Huntington Islands off Belize's shores, duty free use of at least three Belizean ports for export of goods, and free passageway to the Caribbean from the Peten area. Commercial and technical agreements were also to be established.

Barrow's willingness to consider the Guatemalan update of the 1981 agreement was unexpected, for the UDP, then in opposition, had led the protests against the PUP government's signing the Heads of Agreement. In anticipation of further developments in talks between the two countries and eager to avoid a repeat of the widespread civil unrest that followed the release of the Heads of Agreement proposed in 1981, the Belize government announced in the House of Representatives in June 1986 the establishment of the House Advisory Committee on the Guatemalan Issue. This committee, composed of members of both the government and the opposition, was charged with achieving a national consensus on the ways of settling the problem and "to provide for consultation and exchange of information on negotiations and other processes in the search for a solution of the issues arising from the Guatemalan claim to Belize."[31]

In December 1985 the OAS decided to accept Belize as a member in 1990, regardless of the status of the territorial dispute with Guatemala. This was an exception to the normal OAS rules, which state that a nation will not be accepted as a member if it has unresolved territorial disputes with founding members. The decision was made with tacit Guatemalan acceptance.[32]

The coming to power in 1986 of a civilian administration in Guatemala after almost 30 years of military rule has helped to ease some of the tensions between the countries. Vincio Cerezo, Guatemala's president, has proved more accommodating and more conciliatory in his statements over the dispute with Belize than his military predecessors. President Cerezo lifted trade restrictions against Belize in 1986.

Guatemalan trade missions to Belize began shortly thereafter. Full diplomatic relations between Britain and Guatemala were restored on December 24, 1986, for the first time since 1963. Rather than claiming the whole of Belize as part of its territory, Guatemala changed its constitution in 1986 to allow the government to negotiate a settlement, which would be put to a referendum. While an official guest of the British government in December 1986, Alfonso Cabrara, President of the Guatemala Congress and Secretary-General of the ruling Christian Democratic Party, noted that their new constitution empowers the government to explore all possibilities in order to put forward alternative solutions to the problem of Belize. Cabrara said, "We are going to negotiate with Belize. . . . We are dealing with the problem of Belize as it should be dealt with — as a political problem that must be solved through negotiations and dialogue."[33] Earlier, at a meeting in West Germany, President Cerezo had announced that Guatemala was prepared to recognize Belize as an independent state.[34]

Given the more conciliatory statements and actions of the Cerezo government, Belizean officials had expected Guatemala to be more accommodating in formal negotiations, possibly settling for an agreement guaranteeing access to the Caribbean Sea. However, a joint communique issued after the first formal talks held between the foreign ministers of Belize and Guatemala in late April 1987 in Miami, with Britain serving as an observer, noted that "differences" were still great. In fact, Belize was surprised by the toughness of Guatemala's negotiating position. Guatemala insisted on ceding a substantial part of Belizean territory, a proposal completely unacceptable to Belize.[35] In adopting the harder line, the Guatemalan government could have been responding to the attacks of its opposition or bowing to the nationalist pressure against settlement pushed by its military. At any rate, Belize was troubled by Guatemala's hard line and immediately went on the diplomatic offensive, securing support from countries within the Caribbean and Central America.

By the end of 1987, however, Belize was viewing the April talks in a more positive light as a step forward in attempting to normalize relations between the two countries. Barrow agreed that "the attitude has been far less hostile." But in his address to the UN General Assembly that same year, Barrow warned that "there is no room in the contemplation of our continued existence for the encouragement of the pretension to all or part of our territory by another state."[36] He reiterated that Belize totally rejected Guatemala's demand of a portion of land guaranteeing access to the sea. Rather than land concessions Barrow said Belize could consider some form of access to the sea for Guatemala. He said that in the short term the best that could be hoped for would be piecemeal agreements that would lead eventually to a permanent settlement. He hoped to see economic cooperation agreements with work on joint projects, possibly with British or European Community backing. For its part Guatemala would like to fashion an agreement with Belize not only for the traditional reason of an adequate outlet to the Caribbean Sea, but also in order to further its desire to penetrate the Caribbean market. Guatemala's ability to enter the Caribbean market is impeded in part by the Caribbean countries' wariness of Guatemala's intentions toward Belize. Thus, in May 1988 the Guatemalan government initialed a joint accord with Belize to create a Belize-Guatemala Permanent Commission, with Britain as observer, to reach a compromise to resolve the conflict. Both countries have agreed to present any treaty proposal to the voters before signing it into law.[37]

The tripartite commission held its round of talks in Miami in October 1988. At that meeting the delegates established concrete mechanisms and criteria to continue negotiations.[38] Three subcommittees were formed: a political subcommittee to stipulate terms under which Guatemala would recognize Belize's independence and delineate territorial boundaries granting Guatemala an outlet to the Caribbean Sea; an economic subcommittee to fashion a binational development plan to be financed by the European Community; and a security subcommittee to deal with arms trafficking and drug control. Guatemalan officials state that until an accord is reached, Guatemala does not recognize the independence of Belize. Yet informally, the officials acknowledge that recovering Belize is a dream because it is now recognized by the international community. The only sector of Guatemalan society that is likely to oppose a treaty between Belize and Guatemala is the traditional far right. Before and after the round of talks in October 1988, members of the rightist National Liberation Movement (MLN) criticized the government for "handing over" Belize. So far, the government has ignored the protests of the MLN.

Although there may be some positive movement on the diplomatic fronts between Belize and Guatemala, the military threat from Guatemala is still viewed as very real by many Belizeans. With an aggressor that is so different in terms of size, ethnic composition, and its economy (see Table 6.1), it is perhaps understandable why some Belizeans fear Guatemala. Therefore both the Belize government and the opposition support the continued presence of British troops in Belize to defend the country against possible Guatemalan aggression.

TABLE 6.1
Guatemala and Belize Basic Data

	Guatemala	Belize
Population	8,831,000 (1988)	192,000 (1988)
Annual Growth Rate	2.5%	2.1% (1988)
Literacy	50.0%	93.0%
Ethnic Composition		
Ladino	54.0%	
Indian	44.0%	
Creole		39.7%
Mestizo		33.1%
Maya		9.5%
Garifuna		7.6%
White		4.0%
East Indian		2.1%
GDP	$9,600 million (1987)	$247 million (1988)

Sources: Tom Barry, *Belize: A Country Guide* (Albuquerque, N.M.: The Inter-Hemispheric Education Center, 1989), p. 69; and Tom Barry, *Guatemala: A Country Guide* (Albuquerque, N.M.: The Inter-Hemispheric Education Center, 1989), p. 139.

MAJOR ISSUES OF THE DISPUTE

Military Issues

Many Belizeans continue to fear that Guatemala will attempt to seize the country by force. Ultranationalists in Guatemala continue to threaten invasion and occasionally there are Guatemalan troop maneuvers along the Belize border. Upon independence Britain agreed to maintain a 1,600-man garrison in Belize for an appropriate period, to defend Belize against possible Guatemalan invasion. Britain refuses to state specifically how long its troops (now numbered about 1,800) will remain. Belize has asked that the troops stay until a negotiated settlement has been reached. The U.S. government would like Britain to commit troops to Belize until the Central American region is stable. The United States fears that once the British military presence has been withdrawn, Belize could become a staging ground for guerrilla strikes against Guatemala and, thus, another battleground for control of Central America. The British, however, are wary of being drawn into the Central American conflict and are even more eager to leave Belize.[39]

The troops plus four Harrier fighter jets are estimated to cost Britain $50 million annually.[40] British forces are rotated on a six-month basis, many coming directly from Northern Ireland. Apart from an occasional training accident, the British soldiers face little danger. Their major responsibility is to patrol the Belize-Guatemala border on a regular basis. They have established the main camp at the Belize International Airport in Belize City, but there are also several small encampments along the border. Their only responsibility is to help train the 700 Belize Defense Force (BDF), started in 1978 primarily to provide external security. British soldiers lecture regularly at the BDF training school, and BDF officers are sent to Britain for further training. It has been Belize government policy for British military presence to remain low key, but it is difficult to hide 1,600 to 1,800 soldiers within a small population. Soldiers in fatigues and personnel carriers rumbling through the streets have become common sights. On the whole, friction between the soldiers and the civilian population has been minimal.

The U.S. government has also increased its military presence in Belize. During the 1980s it sent U.S. advisers to train members of the BDF and sent Belize military students for training in Panama. Teams of U.S. Army engineers have been active during recent years, building roads and bridges under projects funded by the U.S. Agency for International Development (USAID). The United States continues to support the modernization of the Belize armed forces, including providing communications equipment, weapons, and training support. In 1981 the United States spent $748,000 for Belize; all the money went to the Peace Corps. In 1982, the figure was $11 million; $10 million went for promoting U.S. investment and trade under the Economic Support Fund program, $26,000 for training military personnel, and $985,000 for the Peace Corps.[41] In 1986 the United States allocated $14.6 million for Belize, $4 million of which came from the Economic Support Fund. An additional $9.3 million came from other economic assistance programs, including $6.8 million for development aid and $2.5 million for the Peace Corps.[42] In 1988 the United States spent $12.4 million on Belize. Of that amount $7.3 million was for development aid, $2.0 million was for the Peace Corps, and $1.07 million was for military assistance.[43]

The increased U.S. presence in Belize has not gone without its detractors in some quarters. Even the Peace Corps has received its share of criticism. Generally the volunteers are welcomed, but some local citizens accuse them of taking scarce jobs and involving themselves in areas better reserved for nationals. There is also the feeling that there are too many Peace Corps volunteers, which makes them quite visible. Belize has the highest number of Peace Corps members per capita in the world — about 180, or about one for every 1,000 citizens. By contrast,

Guatemala has roughly the same number of volunteers for 9 million people.[44]

Observers estimate there are approximately 120 U.S. troops in Belize. The U.S. troops, the 1,800 British troops, and the 700 troops in the Belize Defense Force add up to a significant military presence in a country with a population of only about 192,000. Under the rubric of maintaining external security, the country has experienced significant penetration by major powers. As we shall see below, that penetration has extended into internal affairs in important ways.

Political Issues

The history of nationalist politics in Belize has centered on differences in the external orientation of the government and opposition parties. Positions taken historically on the border dispute with Guatemala reflect most clearly the external orientations of the two parties.[45] The PUP, the party that governed Belize from the 1960s to 1984 and regained power in 1989, has claimed traditionally that Belize's "economy and way of life is interdependent with the United States and Central America" and not with the country's historic ties to Britain and the West Indies. Until the 1970s and the start of the internationalization campaign, PUP directed most of its efforts at trying to bolster its claim that Belize's economic and political future lay with Central America and, therefore, by extension, that some accommodation had to be reached with Guatemala.

The main plank of the opposition, from the 1960s to 1984 when they assumed government, had been that the country's constitutional advancement should be within the Commonwealth, in effect denying Belize's connection with Central America. Traditionally, the opposition party accused the PUP government of a willingness to violate the country's territorial integrity in its attempt to resolve the Anglo-Guatemalan dispute.[46] "No Guatemala!" became a rallying cry of the opposition. The opposition also demanded that Britain retain control over the country's external security until the dispute with Guatemala was resolved. Eventually their demand would be "No independence without a suitable guarantee," an issue that would delay independence for 18 years as Britain sought to grant independence without any defense obligations. From 1964, when Belize became internally self-governing, until independence in 1981, the PUP government expended vast amounts of its limited resources in trying to find a resolution to the crisis, a resolution that would respond to the needs of Guatemala and to its own opposition. In the end, Belize went on to independence without a resolution of the territorial dispute but with a defense guarantee from Britain for an unspecified period of time and without the full support of the opposition.

The dispute continues to have a decisive impact on the internal politics of Belize. One of the major issues in the 1984 general elections, in which the ruling PUP government was trounced by the UDP, was the role the United States should play in helping to resolve the territorial dispute. The PUP preferred to continue to rely on the nonaligned nations for assistance in resolving the dispute whereas the UDP opted for greater reliance on the United States. The UDP view was that the United States was best equipped to pressure Guatemala into resolving the dispute. Historically the United States has played an important role behind the scenes in trying to resolve Guatemala's claim to Belize. When the United States voted in 1980 for a UN resolution calling for Belizean independence with territorial integrity, which was effectively against the Guatemalan position, it was viewed as a major milestone in Belize's ultimately successful attempt to win independence with territory intact. Unlike the PUP, which feared that too close an alliance with the United States would harm its carefully orchestrated nonaligned image, the UDP openly embraced U.S. assistance.

During the UDP government, 1984–1989, the United States became an extremely influential and highly visible force in Belizean affairs. In 1985 the United States' $14.5 million balance-of-payments support loan to the new UDP government, which complemented a US$7 million International Monetary Fund (IMF) standby credit, was the predominant factor in pulling Belize out of foreign debt arrears and improving the country's short-term financial situation.[47] In less than two years the IMF ended its standby program, applauding Belize for its successful compliance with IMF demands for improvement in fiscal and trade deficits. USAID became heavily involved in the country's government operations, and the number of Peace Corps volunteers in the country increased dramatically. During the 1980s the U.S. strategy in Belize was designed to create a stable ally in a country with one foot in Central America and one foot in the Caribbean. The strategy, based largely on the conclusions presented in the 1984 Kissinger Commission Report on Central America, worked more smoothly under the UDP government. The UDP strategy of having the United States as a visible ally seemed to have been successful in keeping Guatemala from making its traditional bellicose statements about forcing the return of Belize to its rightful homeland. During the late 1980s, progress seemed to be made in resolving the dispute.

In a surprise victory in the 1989 general elections, the opposition PUP regained office with a 15 to 13 win over the UDP. Among the many charges leveled at the government by the PUP during the electoral campaign was the heavy U.S. presence in the country. The PUP promised to put "Belizeans first" and offered a vision of economic empowerment, political participation, and cultural dignity.[48] This vision is to be accomplished by putting Belizeans at center stage in the development process. It is expected that the U.S. presence in the country will be downscaled and that more emphasis will be placed on the support of the Non-Aligned Movement. However, the United States will continue to play a major role in the country's affairs as the PUP government grapples with a number of immediate issues, including the large influx of Central American refugees and the production and trade in illegal drugs.

Refugee Issues

Because of the Central American crisis, large numbers of refugees are entering Belize, both legally and illegally. While most Central American nations have a significant number of refugees, for Belize, with its population today of only about 192,000, the numbers are alarming. There is a feeling among many Belizeans that they are being "swamped by outsiders." A large number of those refugees, both legal and illegal, are from Guatemala. In 1985 there were 47,000 registered aliens in the country. According to the government, of those registered aliens, 10,853 (23 percent) are from Guatemala, 7,859 from El Salvador, and the remaining 28,288 from other areas. Although the government has done more than most other governments in the region for its refugee population, officials are very concerned about the drain on the country's social services budget because the more recent arrivals tend to be concentrated in enclaves and to speak little English. The Belize government is especially concerned that it lacks the resources to support the Guatemalan refugees because, without diplomatic relations between the two countries, there can be no official joint action on refugee relief. The UN High Commission on Refugees has been providing limited assistance for the Guatemalan and Salvadoran refugees in Belize.

During a period of amnesty in May and June 1984, 12,000 aliens took the opportunity to register their presence in Belize.[49] Because of these growing numbers, the government has begun to take a tougher stand on immigrants. In 1986 the government introduced a bill to make it harder for foreigners to obtain citizenship.[50] The government has charged that immigration is part of a "deliberate plan" to submerge Belize's identity, without suggesting who might be directing such a plan.

Officials from the Ministry of Home Affairs speak of 16,000 "illegal squatters," mainly from Honduras, Guatemala, and El Salvador, in addition to the 4,600 persons recognized by the UN High Commission for Refugees. Unofficial sources say the government figure is low (some suggest it is as high as 30,000), but even assuming it is correct, the total of 20,600 means that for every 15 Belizeans there are two aliens.[51] In a 1984 broadcast, then Home Affairs Minister Vernon Courtenay said the refugee situation "is unsatisfactory and poses a threat to our Belizean heritage."

Of great concern is the likely possibility that the ethnic composition of the country will change. Historically, the major ethnic group has been, and still is, black Creoles, but Mestizos are quickly gaining in number. With the influx of Central American refugees, Creoles could find their majority status eclipsed. The refugees contribute to making the population more Mestizo. The problem of the refugees coming in search of a more peaceful environment and a place to work is compounded by the fact that large numbers of Creole Belizeans have been emigrating for years to the United States, England, and Canada in search of work. In the late 1960s and early 1970s, ethnicity played a significant role in Belizean politics. Through a process of cooperation and isolation, ethnic politics at the time did not reach a level of violence, although fears of loss of jobs, housing, and status ran high among many Creoles. Out of that fear grew the country's Black Power Movement in 1968.[52] Whether more repressive measures might not be used this time if ethnicity becomes a significant political issue is a question that needs to be more fully considered.

Besides the social tension rising because of increased competition for scarce jobs, aliens are blamed for the rising crime rate. The government has charged that the upswing in the number of brutal murders and armed robberies is due to "strangers to Belize." Most of the incidents occur in the sugar belt in the north where there is the largest concentration of Central American refugees. Many of the aliens come originally as cane cutters with valid work permits. Eventually, however, they disappear into the jungles and are joined by relatives and friends who settle illegally. Many become involved in the lucrative business of marijuana cultivation in the dense jungle interior. The government alleges that these marijuana fields are often guarded by men heavily armed with automatic rifles and submachine guns.

It is the drug traffic, of course, that has authorities most concerned. The government is moving to control the existence of airstrips, many of which are now privately owned and not registered. Planes will be forbidden to land in unauthorized places. Blocking air traffic is only part of the solution. Belize's long uninhabited shoreline is ideal for small craft engaged in drug trafficking, and lately several boats have been caught, jammed with marijuana. In all of these operations the Belize Defense Force has played a primary role. From its inception the BDF has assisted the Belize police with the maintenance of law and order. However, the increasing stress on internal security amounts to being a code for combating drug activity.

In fact, one of the three major policy goals that the United States has for Belize in terms of its security assistance programs is suppression of narcotics traffic. Because Belize is estimated to be one of the largest marijuana suppliers to the United States, and because cocaine trafficking is increasing there, Belize has been under great pressure from the United States to pursue aggressively its antinarcotics activities. According to the U.S. Drug Enforcement Administration (USDEA) Belize has rapidly become the most important center of narcotics trafficking in Central America and the fourth largest supplier of marijuana to the United States (behind Colombia, Mexico, and Jamaica). There is also the potential for rapid expansion: the marijuana acreage has increased six-fold since 1982, and net production in 1894 was 1,100 metric tons.[53] Marijuana is not the DEA's major concern; there are fears that if the drug industry were allowed to flourish in Belize, the country could become an entrepôt for cocaine traffic en route from South America.

Knowing that the U.S. State Department has warned that it could be less generous with aid to countries that do not show a willingness to confront the drug issue, Belizean governments have bowed to the pressure. Not only have the security forces been going through the dense jungle on search-and-destroy missions; they are also using chemical warfare. With the assistance of the USDEA and the Mexican government, the Belize government began spraying fields in 1982 and continued in 1983. The offensive was discontinued during 1984 because of the general elections, but spraying was resumed in 1986. As a result of the earlier spraying, more than 3,000 plantations covering an area of 14,400 acres were destroyed in the late 1980s. The use of paraquat spray has caused quite a protest throughout the country from environmentalists, farmers, and others. Farmers in the north so hate the aerial spraying of marijuana fields that the spraying was one of the reasons given for the PUP government's losing the general elections in 1984. Yet the new government resumed the spraying after a year in office, with Prime Minister Manuel Esquivel calling the threat against drugs so serious that the country had to wage an all-out war against the menace. In a major address he called the drug industry a greater threat to the democracy and independence of Belize than the Guatemalan claim.[54]

There have been an increasing number of arrests and convictions for marijuana cultivation. Drug laws also have stiffened, including for the first time in Belizean history the provision for trials without juries. The crackdown on drugs may be necessary, but it is feared in some quarters that, under sanction from the United States, the Belize government may use the enforcement of drug laws to become more repressive toward its citizens. In November 1987 the UDP government established an independent Security and Intelligence Service (SIS) to deal primarily with espionage, sabotage, subversion, and terrorism both from internal and external sources. The identity of the members of the SIS as well as their work are to be kept secret. The director of the SIS is to have the same status as the commissioner of police, under direct ministerial control.[55]

There is speculation that the SIS will be mainly a mechanism to stem drug trafficking in and through Belize. According to the government the SIS is only a more updated, better organized version of the Special Branch of the Police Department, which had been operating for over ten years. The opposition charged, however, that the SIS will be used to punish those who speak out against the government. The opposition's anti-SIS stance was very strong. During the public debate on the bill, much discussion focused on the potential for SIS to be used to infringe upon civil liberties. Throughout the Caribbean there is concern that under the rubric of fighting drugs, government leaders are repressing their own people. In the name of the war on drugs, enemies of the government can be repressed with impunity, protests can be foiled, and dissent weakened.[56]

Economic Issues

Joint development of Guatemala's Peten area, the area adjoining Belize that is largely unexploited, could result in the kind of economic activity that is much needed by both countries. The vast area of El Peten constitutes about one-third of Guatemala, but its isolation hinders exploitation of its many resources. The Belize economy grew by 5 percent in the late 1970s but slowed to almost a standstill by the mid-1980s, due largely to poor prices commanded by agricultural commodities, the mainstay of the economy. With an infusion of multilateral and bilateral aid (especially from the United States) and an emphasis on private sector investment, the Belize economy improved dramatically in the late 1980s. The Guatemalan economy grew at the rate of 5 percent to 6 percent during the 1970s, but it lost speed in the early 1980s and registered negative growth. Reasons for the stagnating economy included not only the worsening political violence, but also undependable and low commodity prices, regional market instability, and decline in the tourist trade. Since the Cerezo government assumed power in 1986, the economy has grown by 2.5 percent to 4 percent each year. This rate does not, however, begin to recover the levels of national income achieved before the economic crisis set in during the late 1970s; it only matches the rate of population growth. By 1989, per capita income was no greater than it was in 1970.

Oil is regarded as the last chance for the Guatemalan economy; oil reserves, along with nickel and other minerals, have been found in the Peten but have not been fully exploited. Exploitation of the area requires improved access to the Caribbean Sea, which means in effect access through Belizean territorial waters. Guatemala's demand for an outlet to the sea is better understood within this context. A developed Peten would lead to extensive changes in the economy of Belize as well, creating a viability that has been unknown for years.

An additional economic factor for improved relations between the two countries is Guatemala's renewed interest in developing export markets in the Caribbean. Without normalized relations with Belize, the Caribbean Common Market (CARICOM) would remain closed to Guatemalan exporters. Belize also would be in a better position to expand its markets and to receive international aid from a wider variety of sources.

CONCLUSION

As a result of the territorial dispute with Guatemala, external actors have often intervened in the internal affairs of Belize. The rise of the Third World and its growing strength and influence in the international arena helped to neutralize the Guatemala threat and made it possible for Belize to achieve independence.[57] When, for various reasons, neither Britain nor the United States wanted to act as formal or primary guarantors of Belizean independence against Guatemala, the nations of the Third World supported Belize's claim to independence and in so doing rendered the Guatemalan claim suspect. Guatemala's claims have become more difficult to maintain and enforce in the face of a combination of United Nations pressure and Third World solidarity. Belize's diplomatic efforts to publicize its right to self-determination (what it termed independence with territorial integrity) eventually succeeded among Guatemala's staunchest supporters. In 1981 even the Organization of American States supported Belize's right to independence and in 1985 agreed to accept Belize as a member in 1990.

U.S. penetration into the affairs of Belize has been more questionable. The role of the United States in Belize has reflected its general policy in the Caribbean Basin — to ensure internal security and to exclude foreign domination. Since Britain granted Belize its independence in 1981, the U.S. presence in that country has grown larger. U.S. military and economic aid to Belize has been increasing. Even U.S. troops — approximately 120 — are mainly responsible for building roads and bridges under USAID sponsorship. The high number of Peace Corps volunteers per capita makes Americans very visible in Belize and has led to accusations that they have involved themselves in areas better reserved for nationals. Because Belize is estimated to be one of the largest marijuana suppliers to the United States, and because cocaine trafficking there is increasing, Belize has been under great pressure from the United States to pursue aggressively its antinarcotics activities. Knowing that the U.S. State Department has warned that it could be less generous with aid to countries that do not show a willingness to confront the drug issue, the Belizean government has bowed to the pressure, including agreeing to aerial spraying of marijuana fields. The U.S. presence in the country demonstrates the geographical importance of Belize. However, U.S. military and economic aid also leaves Belize vulnerable to further major power entanglements in its internal affairs and could intensify ethnic and economic tensions already present.

The growth in drug trafficking has made internal security more problematic. The crackdown on drugs may be necessary, but it is feared in some quarters that, under sanction from the United States, the Belize government may use the enforcement of drug laws to become more repressive toward its citizens. The uproar in 1987 over the newly created Security and Intelligence Service was an indication of that concern. The large number of Central American refugees entering Belize is having an impact on the ethnic composition of the country, on the level of violence, and on the provision of social services. The recent emphasis on greater economic cooperation between the two countries may lessen the Guatemalan threat but could lead to an economic union that spells the end of Belize as we know it today.

The time appears right for serious consideration of a negotiated settlement that would keep Belize sovereign with its territory intact and produce a constructive economic arrangement between Belize and Guatemala. Over the years Guatemala's demands have been downscaled, from seeking the whole territory of Belize to only the southern portion to the use of seabeds around two southern cay chains. Currently Guatemala's major objective appears to be free access to the sea through Belizean territorial waters, thus guaranteeing it access to a greater market. The Belizean government continues to be committed to territorial integrity. However, it seeks greater economic cooperation with Guatemala and other Central American markets. Joint development of the Peten, the Guatemalan area adjoining Belize that is largely unexploited, could result in the kind of economic activity that is much needed by both countries. Joint development requires, of course, that Guatemala gains an outlet to the sea, which means access through Belizean territorial waters. Economic development may fuel the resolution of this volatile territorial dispute. A resolution is sorely needed if Belize is not to be drawn into crises of insecurity that rage in Central America.[58]

The original impetus for a concern with security and military activity in Belize was the need for external defense to counter the Guatemalan claim. More recently, at U.S. urging, the military has been used for internal security — mainly to stem drug trafficking. The United States encourages the military presence also as a way of ensuring that Belize will not become another battleground for control of Central America: as a staging ground for insurgency against Guatemala. Until the territorial dispute is resolved, Belize has little chance of being able to chart its own future.

NOTES

1. See Alan J. Day, ed., *Border and Territorial Disputes* (Detroit: Gale Research, 1982); and J. Braveboy-Wagner, *The Venezuela-Guyana Border Dispute: Britain's Colonial Legacy in Latin America* (Boulder, Colo.: Westview Press, 1984).

2. See the discussion in Alma H. Young and Dion E. Phillips, eds., *Militarization in the Non-Hispanic Caribbean* (Boulder, Colo.: Lynne Reinner Publishers, 1986), pp. 4–6.

3. See Braveboy-Wagner, *Venezuela-Guyana Border Dispute;* see also Duke Pollard, "The Guyana-Surinam Border Dispute in International Law," in Leslie Manigat, ed., *The Caribbean Yearbook of International Relations* (St. Augustine, Trinidad: Institute of International Relations, 1977).

4. Peter Calvert, "Guatemala and Belize," *Contemporary Review* 228 (1976): 8.

5. G. M. Robinson and P. A. Furley, "Belize," in Robert B. Potter, ed., *Urbanization, Planning, and Development in the Caribbean* (London and New York: Mansell, 1989), pp. 212–13.

6. Ibid., pp. 220–21.

7. Ibid., pp. 222–23; also see Narda Dobson, *A History of Belize* (Trinidad and Jamaica: Longman Caribbean, 1973), pp. 126–34.

8. Calvert, "Guatemala and Belize," p. 8.

9. D. A. G. Waddell, "Britain and Central America in the Mid-Nineteenth Century," Paper presented at the International Congress of the Latin American Studies Association, Mexico City, September 29–October 1, 1983, p. 4.

10. Ibid., p. 4.

11. Ibid., p. 6. See also D. A. G. Waddell, *British Honduras: A Historical and Contemporary Survey* (London: Oxford University Press, 1983), pp. 34–37.

12. Donald Grunewald, "The Anglo-Guatemalan Dispute over British Honduras," *Caribbean Studies* 5 (July 1965): 33. For differing views on the interpretation of the treaty, see W. M. Clergern, "New Light on the Belize Dispute," *American Journal of International Law* 52 (1958): 280–97; and R. A. Humphreys, *The Diplomatic History of British Honduras, 1638–1901* (London: Oxford University Press, 1961), pp. 20–47. For conflicting legal analyses, see J. L. Mendoza, *Britain and Her Treaties on Belize*, trans. Lilly de Longh Osborne (Guatemala, 1947); and L. M. Bloomfield, *The British Honduras–Guatemala Dispute* (Toronto: Carswell Company, 1953).

13. For differing views on the interpretation see Bloomfield, *British Honduras*.

14. Grunewald, "Anglo-Guatemalan Dispute," p. 34.

15. Ibid., p. 35.

16. Ibid.

17. Ibid., p. 38; also see Guatemalan Ministry of Foreign Affairs, *White Book: Belize Question* (Guatemala City, 1968).

18. P. K. Menon, "The Anglo-Guatemalan Territorial Dispute over the Colony of Belize (British Honduras)," *Journal of Latin American Studies* 11 (November 1979): 365.

19. Bethuel Webster, "Draft Treaty between the United Kingdom of Great Britain and Northern Ireland and the Republic of Guatemala Relating to the Resolution of the Dispute over British Honduras (Belize)," New York, 1968.

20. *The New Belize*, June 1968, p. 3.

21. Ibid., November 1975; also see A. E. Thorndike, "Belize among Her Neighbors: An Analysis of the Guatemala–Belize Dispute," *Caribbean Review* 72 (1978): 16–18.

22. *The New Belize*, December 1975, p. 3.

23. Personal interview with Robert Leslie, Permanent Secretary in the Ministry of Home Affairs, Belmopan, Belize, February 20, 1988.

24. *The New Belize*, December 1980, p. 2.

25. Ibid., December 1981, p. 8.

26. "Heads of Agreement," *Hansard* 418 (1981), Cols. 656–61. See also "Government Explains the Heads of Agreement" (Belize: Government Information Service, 1981).

27. *The Beacon* (Belize), April 3, 1981.

28. *The New Belize*, August 1981, p. 8.

29. Ibid., August 1984, p. 12.

30. "Belize's Foreign Policy: Foreign Minister Dean Barrow Addresses 40th General Assembly of the United Nations" Belmopan: Government Information Service, October 8, 1985).

31. *The New Belize*, June 1986, p. 2.

32. *Central America Reports*, December 16, 1985.

148 / National Strategy and Security

33. *Latin American Reports/Mexico and Central America,* December 4, 1987, p. 4.

34. *Latin American Weekly Report,* November 6, 1986, p. 4.

35. *Amandala* (Belize), May 15, 1987, p. 5.

36. Statement by the Honorable Dean Oliver Barrow, Minister of Foreign Affairs and Economic Development of Belize, to the 42nd General Assembly of the United Nations, October 1, 1987 (Belmopan: Government Information Service).

37. *Central America Report,* June 3, 1988, p. 168.

38. Ibid., October 28, 1988, p. 333.

39. John Davie "Under the Volcano," *London Times,* October 2, 1983.

40. Ibid.

41. Tom Barry, Beth Wood, and Deb Preusch, *Dollars and Dictators: A Guide to Central America* (Albuquerque, N.M.: The Resource Center, 1982).

42. U.S. State Department, 1985.

43. Ibid., 1988.

44. *Arizona Daily Star,* June 15, 1986.

45. Alma H. Young and Dennis H. Young, "The Impact of the Anglo-Guatemalan Dispute on the Internal Politics of Belize," *Latin American Perspectives* 15 (Spring 1988): 6–30.

46. Ibid., 1988.

47. Alma H. Young, "Belize" in Abraham Lowenthal, ed., *Latin American and Caribbean Contemporary Record,* Vol. 7 (New York: Holmes and Meier Publishers, 1988).

48. *Belizeans First,* People's United Party Manifesto: 1989–1994, p. 27.

49. *The New Belize,* April 1985, p. 7; also see *Central America Report,* June 21, 1985.

50. *The New Belize,* October 1986, p. 10.

51. *Central America Report,* June 15, 1984, p. 180; also see John C. Everitt, "The Recent Migrations of Belize, Central America," *International Migration Review* 18 (Summer 1984): 319–25.

52. Alma H. Young, "Ethnic Politics in Belize," *Caribbean Review* 7 (April 1970): 32–36.

53. *Amandala* (Belize), July 19, 1985, p. 3.

54. As reported in *Amandala,* July 19, 1985, p. 1.

55. Security and Intelligence Bill, with Explanatory Notes (Belmopan: Government Printery, n.d.).

56. See Alma H. Young, "Peace, Democracy, and Security in the Caribbean," Paper presented at the Conference on Peace and Development, University of the West Indies, Kingston, Jamaica, 1988.

57. A. E. Thorndike, "Belize among Her Neighbors: An Analysis of the Guatemala–Belize Dispute," *Caribbean Review,* 72 (1978): 16–18.

58. See Alma H. Young, "The Central American Crisis and Its Impact on Belize," in Alma H. Young and Dion E. Phillips, eds., *Militarization in the Non-Hispanic Caribbean* (Boulder, Colo.: Lynne Reinner Publishers, 1986), pp. 139–57.

7   Guyana: The Military and the Politics of Change

Ivelaw L. Griffith

The death of Forbes Burnham in August 1985 and the rise to power of Desmond Hoyte have witnessed some dramatic changes in Guyana. These changes include privatization of the public sector, abolition of overseas voting, negotiations with the International Monetary Fund (IMF), and rapprochement with the United States. But the alterations since Burnham's death have been more in the broader context of personnel change and less in terms of institutional regime change. The dominant political force is still the People's National Congress (PNC), and the party is still dedicated to maintaining political hegemony. The military has been central to the exercise of political power by Burnham and the PNC. It is, therefore, appropriate to inquire into their role in the country's politics over the ensuing years.

The military is used here as a collective reference to the military and paramilitary institutions that are part of the security mechanism of the country and its ruling political elites. These are the Guyana Defense Force (GDF), the Guyana People's Militia (GPM), the Guyana National Service (GNS), and the Guyana Police Force (GPF). They are the key elements of the umbrella agency called the Disciplined Services of Guyana in which the Guyana Prisons Service and the National Guard Service are represented. The military agencies have varying official missions. For example, the primary objectives of the GDF are territorial defense against foreign aggression and assisting with internal order. The GPF is for internal security; the GPM is for civil defense and to complement the GDF in military defense. The GNS is to build a new political consciousness, aid economic self-reliance programs, and complement the GDF and the GPM in military defense.[1]

There have been both continuity and change in the operation of the military between 1985 and 1990. One way to appreciate this is to look at some of the role-areas in which the military have been featured, particularly over the last two decades. They have been security instruments in four main areas: regime political security; national military defense; economic security; and diplomatic security. But in order to appreciate the context in which these role-areas have developed, it is important to make a preliminary comment on Burnham era politics.

BURNHAM ERA POLITICS

Burnham era politics began in 1964 when Forbes Burnham became premier in a coalition government along with Peter D'Aguiar and the United Force (UF). Burnham's rise to power was occasioned by a combination of domestic and international factors. On the domestic side Guyana was in the throes of nationalist change featuring radical political prescriptions by two main political actors, Cheddi Jagan of the People's Progressive Party (PPP) and Burnham. Both leaders practiced racial politics, their parties being polarized along ethnic lines, with Indians supporting Jagan and Africans supporting Burnham.

The racial politics contributed to an anomaly in electoral representation. For example, at the 1961 general elections, while the PNC received 41 percent of the popular vote, it secured 11 legislative seats. The PPP, with 42.6 percent of the vote, received 20 seats. The UF won 4 seats, having secured 16.4 percent of the vote. Burnham called for a change in the First-Past-the-Post voting system to one that permitted representation to be more reflective of popular support. The British, then in colonial control of Guyana, conceded and later changed the voting system to proportional representation. This was ostensibly to secure more representative justice, but one reason was to accommodate Burnham.

On the international side, both the Americans and the British considered Burnham the lesser of two evils, the other evil being Jagan. Jagan, an avowed Marxist with a dogmatic pro-Moscow stand, had been premier in 1953 for 135 days and then again from 1957 until 1964. His unorthodox sociopolitical prescriptions during that time made the British and the Americans wary that his Marxist commitment would place an independent Guyana in the communist camp, possibly leading to a second Cuba. Thus on June 23, 1964, with the adoption of the British Guiana (Constitution) Order in Council, the nature and composition of the legislature and the system of voting were changed facilitating Burnham's rise to power in December of that year. Four years later, having led the country to independence in 1966, Burnham and the PNC consolidated power by winning the general elections. The coalition with the UF was dissolved, and the PNC began a conscious policy of transforming Guyana's political landscape.[2]

In 1970 Guyana was declared a cooperative socialist republic. The ruling political elites launched several major policy initiatives in what was said to be the beginning of a peaceful revolution. The first was the nationalization of foreign-owned property in pursuit of what Burnham called "control of the commanding heights of the economy." By 1976 U.S., Canadian, and European control over the sugar and the bauxite industries, banking, drug manufacture, the import and local trade, communications, and other areas was all transferred to the state. Compensation was paid, and agreements with the former owners provided for postnationalization technology and licensing, among other things.[3]

A second initiative was intended to make the cooperative sector the dominant one in a trisectoral economic structure, with the state and private sectors. Burnham explained what he had in mind:

> Ours is not the first or only government in the developing world to place major emphasis on the use and development of the cooperative as an instrument of development or in the thrust toward socialism.
>
> We, however, named Guyana a Cooperative Republic to highlight the fact that the cooperative will be the principal institution for giving the masses the control of our economy, to emphasize the fact that we aim at making the cooperative sector the dominant sector and that the cooperative is and will be the mechanism for making the little man a real man.[4]

A third key policy initiative was the Doctrine of Paramountcy. This doctrine, first enunciated at a special congress of the ruling party in 1973, made the PNC superordinate to all other institutions and organizations in the country; and the legislative, executive, and judicial branches of the government were declared to be the "executive arm" of the PNC. In 1975 Burnham further clarified the doctrine: "It is the Party that formulates policy on the basis of its ideology, strategy and tactics. It is the Party that mobilizes, educates and appeals to the people. . . . It is the Party that then selects the members of the political government to execute the former's policy."[5]

Central to the pursuit of this doctrine was the creation of a super agency through the fusion of the secretariat of the PNC with a government department in 1974. This new entity was called the Office of the General Secretary of the People's National Congress and the Ministry of National Development (OGSPNCMND or ND). It was a central part of the reorganization of the party, which began in 1973, and the party's political nerve center. It was responsible for the political socialization of government officials and the indoctrination program within the party; for mass rallies; for political campaigns for national and local government offices; and for the party's infiltration of political, labor, and civic organizations. A central task was the intimidation and harassment of critics and the political opposition. OGSPNCMND was also responsible for the international relations of the PNC. This led to several juris-dictional and operational conflicts with officials of the Ministry of Foreign Affairs who resented the undue politicization of the ministry and the dictation by "party comrades," many of whom were either novices or totally incompetent in international politics.

Burnham era politics thus witnessed the transformation of Guyana's political profile. In the quest for political power and the pursuit of "social-ist transformation," the PNC harassed critics, intimidated the opposition, and eliminated any major political threats; the best known case is the 1980 murder of Walter Rodney of the Working People's Alliance. The electoral process was subverted, and freedoms of speech and the press were curtailed. The human rights situation deteriorated. The regime became progressively authoritarian with the predominance of Burnham being increasingly patent.[6] It is in this larger context that the continuity and change in Guyana's civil-military relations may best be seen.

REGIME POLITICAL SECURITY

One role-area where there has been continuity of the military in politics is that of regime political security. The military is still central to the brokerage of power. This brokerage is not in the context of a prae-torian arrangement where military officers exercise a political veto or are direct political actors, as was the case in Surinam, Chile, or Panama until recently or as currently in Ghana, Nigeria, and Bangladesh. The civilian elites use the military in the context of civilian control of the military to guarantee their exercise of power. But there have been changes since 1985 — changes designed to enhance the image of the regime, but not necessarily to alter the centrality of the military as an instrument of power.

By Caribbean standards Guyana has been militarized over the last two decades. The indexes of the militarization are the number and size of the military and paramilitary agencies, the progressive increases in military expenditure until recently, and the overt and unapologetic use of military agencies for political purposes. This militarization was not solely to meet actual and potential territorial threats to the nation. Guyana has been one of those Third World societies where the political elites make little or no distinction between national security and regime security. Militarization ostensibly for national security is often designed to protect the ruling elites. As one Indian scholar observed:

> In most Third World countries ... hypothetical threats and the responsibility to preserve law and order are only convenient arguments for extravagant militarization. The desire for prestige and the determination to stay in power have been, more often than not, the true incentives of many governments to build up armed forces and acquire unnecessarily sophisticated military hardware.[7]

The territorial claims by Venezuela and Surinam once led to serious national security threats, especially in the mid-1960s and the early 1980s. The PNC has, therefore, not really used national security threats as an excuse to militarize in pursuit of regime security. Those threats provided an opportunity to do so. The regime political security role of the military was designed in the context of the Doctrine of Paramountcy mentioned above. Party paramountcy and the political security role of the military were demonstrated in various ways: intimidation of political opponents, the donning of military uniforms by Forbes Burnham, and the use of the military to help subvert elections.

The role of the military, particularly the GDF and the GPF, in undermining the electoral process at the instruction of the ruling elites became quite well known. For example, a team of international observers to the 1980 elections made a strong indictment against the military in the elections. In their report they noted, "The military presence in some areas was intimidating. The [ballot] boxes were collected by military personnel who prevented accredited officials of the opposition, sometimes by force or the threat of force, from accompanying or following the boxes." They also claimed, "Military personnel refused accredited representatives of opposition parties access to the count, at gun point in some cases."[8]

The conclusion of the team's report was a scathing commentary on democratic choice in Guyana and on the lengths to which the Burnham regime would go to further entrench itself.

> We came to Guyana aware of the serious doubts expressed about the conduct of previous elections there, but determined to judge these elections on their own merit and hoping that we should be able to say that the result was fair.

> We deeply regret that, on the contrary, we were obliged to conclude, on the basis of abundant and clear evidence, that the election was rigged massively and flagrantly. Fortunately, however, the scale of the fraud made it impossible to conceal it either from the Guyanese public or the outside world. Far from legitimizing President Burnham's assumption of his office, the events we witnessed confirm all the fears of Guyanese and foreign observers about the state of democracy in that country.[9]

Military personnel were also transported around cities to provide audiences at mass rallies where Burnham and other top PNC leaders spoke. This served several purposes. It allowed the ruling party to pursue its political and doctrinal socialization of members of the military, a classical stratagem of the penetration model of militarized politics. As Nordlinger explains, "the resulting congruity between the political ideas of civilians and officers frequently removes a potential source of conflict between them."[10] It also provided the party with a captive human pool with which to demonstrate an alleged mass support of the party and its policies. And further, it was a self-deception ploy used within the party. Party officials used it as evidence of their ability to "mobilize the masses" and to maintain the fiction of personal support and loyalty to the predominant leader.

In this context loyalty by the military was no longer to the constitution, to the office of president, and to the ideals of sovereignty and territorial integrity. Rather, it was to the paramount party and the predominant leader. This was not just demanded by the party, but was willingly offered by the leadership of the military. For example, in 1977, the then chief-of-staff of the GDF, speaking on behalf of the Disciplined Services of Guyana at the Second Biennial Congress of the PNC, offered this pledge:

> Comrade Leader, you have shown us the way. It is now for all of us who are interested in the revolution to show this in a tangible manner. We fulfill our security duties faithfully, because in doing so we are assured of the cooperation of the working class. We know that the road mapped out by the party and government is our road — the road the Disciplined Services will follow.[11]

Over the years since 1964, the PNC has been successful in broadening the racial composition of both the party and the government. People of Indian descent were placed in very influential or high-profile positions. Some of them, like Ranji Chandisingh, former PNC general secretary and state vice-president, now ambassador to Moscow, had been defectors from the PPP. Others, like Speaker of the National Assembly Sase Narain, had long been supporters of the PNC. But the one area where the PNC did not reach out meaningfully to Guyanese of Indian descent was the military. Military agencies have been dominated by Africans. The African dominance of the military has been an important dimension of the regime's security. For many Africans, their role in the empowerment of the PNC is part of a larger duty "to their people" to ensure the PNC's political power over a society where economic power is largely in the hands of the Indians. But things have begun to change. In 1988 Balram Raghubir became the first police commissioner of Indian descent. His tenure ended in July 1990 with a diplomatic appointment.[12] And with the retirement of Major General Norman McLean in February 1990, Colonel Joseph Singh, director-general of the GNS for eight years, became acting chief-of-staff of the GDF with the rank of brigadier general. He is the first professional head of the armed forces of Indian descent.

For another reason it would be unrealistic to expect the regime security role to have changed fundamentally since Burnham's death. The increasing economic deprivation over the recent years has led to a certain tenuousness of the country's political fabric. Although the relative deprivation has not translated into continuous mass violence — and this itself is a function of the PNC's control of the instruments of coercion — there has been a growing incidence of politically organized and socially driven protest and violence. Strikes in the bauxite and sugar industries have led to violent demonstrations and arrests; bombings in the capital, Georgetown; protests over stringent budgetary measures; and arson and vandalism in the sugar industry and in state-run commercial enterprises.

The current sordid economic state of affairs is expected to continue for some time. Therefore, the probability of related political instability is reasonable. The political power brokers will have every reason to apprehend danger to the maintenance of power if the military is not available to help shore up that power. But while the regime political security mission of the Burnham era continues, there have been changes in the tactical relationships between the military and the ruling party and in the political profile of the country.

One Guyana specialist describes the political circumstances of contemporary Guyana as "The Politics of Permanent Fear."[13] However, few Guyana watchers would deny that the circumstances of permanent fear of the Burnham era, partly a feature of the politicization of the military, have been changed. David de Caires, staunch PNC critic and editor-in-chief of the independent newspaper *Stabroek News* has acknowledged that

> The atmosphere of repression has lightened perceptibly and the style and language of politics were noticeably more responsive and less threatening. . . . Hoyte abolished overseas voting and the provisions for widespread proxy and postal voting. . . . Rabbi Washington, a notorious henchman of the Burnham regime, was prosecuted for murder. An independent newspaper has been permitted to open and there has been no interference with it. Political harassment has virtually ended.[14]

Human rights concerns in Guyana have centered on political intimidation, police brutality, press limitations, and questionable electoral processes. Military agencies have been involved in violations of all of these areas. And one gets some idea of the changes by comparing assessments of the country's human rights profile during one of the Burnham years with a more recent time.

The U.S. State Department survey for 1984 provides a marked contrast with that for 1989. There were no politically motivated killings in either year, but in 1984 there were well-supported allegations that the police killed sixteen individuals. As a result of political and interest group pressure, manslaughter charges were brought against two policemen and an intentional murder indictment was secured against another. Police harassment of opponents of the regime is not entirely a thing of the past. But the incidence and outlandish nature of this have both changed. Among the 1984 cases was the arrest, detention without charges, and interrogation of five people alleged to be involved in a plot to overthrow Burnham. One political leader, Paul Tennassee of the Democratic Labor Movement, was given what had become standard fare in the harassment menu: detention at the airport following a "tip" about an alleged infraction. Tennassee was held for five days during which he was questioned about an assassination plot against Burnham. He was later charged with failing to list 40 Guyana dollars on his currency declaration.

Two positive developments in 1989 were the passage of the Police Complaints Authority Act and the repeal of the 1966 National Security Act. The Complaints legislation provides for an institutional mechanism for the supervision of investigations into allegations of misconduct or illegality in the police force. While in force, the National Security Act permitted the detention, without charges for up to three months, of persons deemed to be acting "in any manner prejudicial to public safety or public order or the defense of Guyana." The opposition achieved a victory in 1990 with the tabling in the National Assembly of the Local

Authorities (Elections) (Amendment) Bill in April. A key feature of this legislation, first proposed by the Working People's Alliance, is the provision for a nonpartisan commission to supervise local government elections. The present law provides for a government minister to supervise these elections, and this has long been used to facilitate PNC control of local government positions.

Another boon to the opposition — one that would undoubtedly receive major applause by local and international critics — is the legislative provisions that officially sanction the scrutiny of national elections by international observers. In May Prime Minister Hamilton Green placed before the National Assembly the General Elections (Observers) Bill 1990. This legislation is to empower the president to invite foreigners "for the purpose of observing the democratic process of the State as enshrined in the Constitution, and more specifically, the conduct of any election." While welcoming this development, opposition leaders have criticized the power given to the president to name the observers and to the provisions that make "uninvited observers" subject to arrest and imprisonment if convicted.

The new law does something that was anathema to Burnham. It would allow observers to examine the list of electors, enter polling places and ballot counting centers, interview the chairman of the elections commission and other elections officials, and it obliges those officials to cooperate with international observers and comply with "any reasonable request" made by them. The bill goes further. It confers diplomatic privileges and immunities on observers and makes it an offense — punishable by a G$5,000 fine and an 18-month jail term — for anyone to interfere with or impersonate international observers. Two months after the tabling of the bill, President Hoyte announced that the Commonwealth Secretary-General had been invited to name a team of observers for the next general elections.[15] Hoyte also later agreed to have a U.S. team of observers. This team, from the Carter Center at Emory University, Atlanta, will be led by former President Jimmy Carter. Carter and other officials made a preliminary visit to Guyana during mid-October 1990. While in Guyana Carter was able to extract from Hoyte an agreement for preliminary ballot counts at polling places, something oppositions parties had been clamoring for over several years.[16]

MILITARY DEFENSE

The premier national defense agency is the Guyana Defense Force. The territorial claims against Guyana by Venezuela and Surinam, pressed even before independence, made the creation of the GDF in 1966 necessary. The GDF grew out of the Special Services Unit, a paramilitary group that had been part of the British Guiana Police Force before independence. It grew from an estimated 750 in 1966 to 5,000 currently. It is basically a ground force with air and maritime operations, all of which fall under an integrated command headed by a chief-of-staff. Troop strength and operational structure have expanded over the years, but the range and sophistication of weapons have not reached the levels desired by top military officials. There is no indigenous arms manufacture, and weapons come from several sources. Much of it was originally donated by the British and the Americans, but over the years, as Guyana adopted socialist and nonaligned postures, weapons equipment and training have been provided by Cuba, North Korea, East Germany, and Commonwealth countries, such as India.

Although the GDF has been the centerpiece of military defense, important roles have been identified for the GPM and the GNS. The GPM was established in 1976 to institute a popular mobilization strategy in the face of destabilization by the United States and intimidation by Venezuela. It has had the more politically wishful than logistically feasible mission of making "every citizen a soldier" through providing paramilitary skills to cross sections of the nation and using those trained for civic defense as a reserve for the GDF. Financial difficulties and changes in relations with both the United States and Venezuela since 1985 have led to the contraction of the GPM from 7,000 in 1977 to about 2,500 currently.

The GNS was formed in 1973 with defense and development objectives. These were to be accomplished through five corps: the Young Brigade; the National Cadet Corps; the New Opportunity Corps; the Pioneer Corps; and the Special Service Corps. A National Reserve Corps was also contemplated. As the parliamentary paper on the subject explained: "This will be the last Corps to come into operation. It is envisaged that all groups of the Pioneer Corps will be given an opportunity to sign up as reservists to be on call for work in any area vital to the stability, security or productivity of the country."[17] The military defense role of the GNS was intended to revolve primarily around the Pioneer Corps and the National Reserve Corps. But the Reserve Corps was never created.

Guyana and Venezuela have developed a new and productive cordiality over the past five years, but the territorial controversy is yet to be settled.[18] There are still staunch advocates of the "military solution" in Venezuela. And Venezuelan domestic crises might well precipitate use of the dispute as a political expedient to deflect attention away from pressing domestic issues. There is no doubt that the military in Guyana are no match for those in Venezuela. The security capability of Guyana pales in comparison with that of Venezuela. Guyana has an area of 214,969 square kilometers whereas Venezuela has 912,050. Its total armed forces number 8,950; Venezuela's is 49,000. Its population is 815,000 compared with Venezuela's 19 million, and its GNP per capita is US$380 as proposed to US$3,230 for Venezuela. Moreover, unlike Guyana, Venezuela has an army with light and medium tanks, a navy with submarines and frigates, and an air force with American-made F-16s and French-made Mirage combat aircraft.[19]

The nonresolution of the territorial dispute and the security capability gaps between the two countries are themselves reasons why a military defense role for Guyana's Disciplined Services will continue to be pursued. Altering or abandoning this would be both politically suicidal for the political elites and psychologically destabilizing for the nation at large. Moreover, it should be remembered that Guyana also has an unsettled territorial dispute with Surinam.[20] Guyana's security capability compares well with that of Surinam. Surinam is smaller, with an area of 163,265 square kilometers. It has a population of 395,000, armed forces numbering 2,690, and GNP per capita of US$2,360. In addition to this, the GDF and the GPF demonstrated their superior capability over the Surinamese forces in 1966 and 1967 following clashes along the Guyana-Surinam border.

It should also be remembered that Third World nations like Guyana do not maintain military defense entities only because they may have hegemonic designs or to provide for credible defense. They also do this for symbolic purposes. Guyana's military will continue to have a military defense role even in the absence of specific threats because the political elites there pay close attention to the symbolism of sovereignty. The military defense role of the GDF, the GPM, and the GNS is an important symbol of an intent by the political elites to defend national sovereignty even in the face of capability limitations and powerful antagonists. What may change — and evidence already suggests this — is the operationalization of this role: the manner in which force deployments are made, from whom arms are purchased and military assistance secured, and with whom joint military exercises are held.

ECONOMIC AND DIPLOMATIC SECURITY

Another role-area designed for the military in Guyana is that of economic security. The designation of the GDF as "the people's army" was partly intended to indicate the multiple roles of the army. Forbes Burnham made it clear to the GDF in 1970 that "while standing ready to carry out the two primary tasks of assisting civilian authorities and defending the borders, [the GDF] must be an army . . . identified and identifiable with the community." Part of this identification was to be in practical application of manpower and technical and organizational skills in areas of economic development and community building.

In this respect elements of the military have made valuable contributions in constructing roads, schools and other public buildings, airstrips, and parks and in developing and maintaining agricultural ventures. This economic security role has often assumed explicitly political contexts. The GDF and the GNS in particular have been used as scab labor during industrial disputes in the sugar and bauxite industries. This was both to shore up the economic opposition of the industries and to bolster the political position of the government. There is, however, another aspect of the link between the economic and the political missions in that the government uses the military to help fulfill political promises of economic improvement in a cost-efficient manner, allowing it to deploy resources elsewhere.

The Burnham era created the foundations for the economic decline that has become precipitous over recent years. Guyana now finds itself in very dire economic straits, even by the admission of its political and technical managers.[21] The economic circumstances create a very tenuous political situation. It also necessitates the use of every cost-efficient measure and potentially useful strategem to help keep the economy afloat. The military, especially the GDF and the GNS, are prime candidates in the search for such measures. Thus, even if only out of necessity, the military will continue to be used as an instrument of economic security.

This economic security role may be placed in the context of the increasingly widening debate about the political economy of the military in the Third World, particularly regarding the value of militarization to modernization and the nexus between militarization and economic growth.[22] The growth of military budgets and military forces — indexes of militarization — is said to have significant opportunity costs: diversion of resources away from other sectors of society, creation of psychological tensions, and the violation of civil and political liberties, among other things. The counterargument is that with militarization comes the prospect for expanded employment, education, and health care, and a general spillover from the military to the civilian sectors, to the benefit of the entire society.

Benoit's 1973 study of 44 countries found that higher defense burdens — military expenditure as a percentage of GDP — were positively associated with higher growth. Although he recognized that a shift in resources to the military sector could result in negative economic growth, he pointed to several off-setting effects, each of which can enhance the potential for growth: importation of technical skills through military training, construction of basic infrastructure such as roads and bridges likely to benefit civilian production, and adoption of more expansionary monetary and fiscal policies. Lebovic and Ishaq found that higher military burdens actually suppressed economic growth in the Middle East between 1973 and 1982. The adverse impact of high military burdens was reflected in several things: decreased private consumption because fewer resources are available to the civilian sector, increased inflation because of increased budgetary deficits, and income distribution in favor of the military and against civilian sectors, among other things.

There are studies on Guyana that give militarization indexes in terms of total military expenditure and force size.[23] But there is no study on the (net) economic value of the military or the cost-efficiency of military institutions that would allow concrete assessment of Guyana in terms of the militarization-modernization debate. And such is beyond the purview of this chapter. Even though there is reason to believe that the cost-efficiency is very low, little evidence suggests that the present government plans to abandon this role.

The uses of the military by the post-Burnham elites seem to suggest a new role: that of diplomatic security. This new role is suggested by the consistency with which detachments from the GDF and the GPF have been utilized in the foreign policy arena recently. A contingent of 30 soldiers with special skills along with aircraft and supplies were sent to Jamaica in September 1988 in the wake of Hurricane Gilbert; a joint-services detachment, with GDF, GPM, and GNS personnel, was sent to the Eastern Caribbean in 1989 following the destructive trail of Hurricane Hugo; and a detachment of 30 members of the GPF were in Namibia from June 1989 to April 1990, as part of the United Nations Special Monitoring Force.

A 31-member Joint Services Relief Task Force composed of servicemen from the GDF, the GPM, and the GNS were also in Montserrat from February to April 1990. They built 32 houses and repaired a school as a followup to a similar mission in 1989. And in August 1990 a 40-member contingent from the GDF's First Infantry Battalion led by Captain Andrew Pompey spent two weeks in Trinidad in the wake of the July–August coup attempt there. The GDF officers joined security detachments from Jamaica and member countries of the Regional Security System (RSS) in helping to provide internal security in Trinidad.[24]

Guyana's foreign policy conduct over the past two decades has been one of activism, particularly within CARICOM, the Non-Aligned Movement, the Commonwealth, and in certain pursuits of the United Nations.[25] It could be argued that Guyana's participation in the Namibia Monitoring Force was a logical and natural continuation of its work in the United Nations Council for Namibia, of which it was once president. One might also contend that the security assistance to other Caribbean countries is a reflection of Guyana's well-known commitment to regionalism. However, military assistance has never been central to the country's foreign policy pursuits. This is not to suggest that military assistance has never been offered or given to other countries. For example, Trinidad was offered, but declined, military assistance in 1970 during the time of its military crisis. The Bishop government was given military technical assistance, and Dominica received military assistance during the tenure of Patrick John. These were however different in scope and apparent intent than the present pattern.

The current pattern seems to be part of larger foreign policy shifts and emphases since the death of Burnham.[26] There has been a rapprochement with the United States and with the IMF and the World Bank. The number and frequency of visits to the United States by Hoyte since 1985 is a marked contrast to the disdain shown by Burnham in not even wanting to transit there while making foreign trips. There has been a marked improvement in relations with contiguous states — Brazil, Surinam, and Venezuela. There has been a desperate renewal of harmonious relations with CARICOM states, beginning with the 1986 meeting of Desmond Hoyte with the other Caribbean leaders in Mustique, just off St. Vincent. The relations with Cuba and the Soviet Union have cooled. President Hoyte took two years before acting on Fidel Castro's 1987 invitation to visit Cuba. He went there from January 26–30, 1989, while on his way to Venezuela for the inauguration of Carlos Andres Perez as president. Castro and Hoyte tried to smooth several rough edges in the relations between their countries. And as a sign of good intentions, Hoyte was invested with the Jose Marti Award. Curiously enough, the Soviets made a radical departure from their posture on the country's domestic politics. In November 1990 for the first time they publicly called for free and fair elections in Guyana while endorsing electoral reforms introduced by Hoyte.[27] This is obviously a reflection of their own political and economic "new thinking."

The use of the military in pursuit of an altered foreign policy agenda allows the government to accentuate its cooperative relations in a way that polishes the image of the regime.[28] It simultaneously allows the bonds of friendship between Guyana and other nations to develop in another dimension, secures commendation for Guyana as a nation that offers humanitarian assistance to others even with its own stringencies, and makes a positive political gesture to the Caribbean and the international community.[29] This is precisely what the acting chief-of-staff of the GDF hopes would result. Brigadier Joe Singh addressed the troops who went on the Trinidad mission on August 3, 1990, at Camp Stephenson, shortly before their departure for Port-of-Spain. Among the things he emphasized was the need for them "to be good ambassadors of Guyana, but also of the GDF."

A critical target area is the Caribbean because CARICOM offers the much desired political support in dealing with the Surinam and Venezuela claims, among other things. And CARICOM states, especially Trinidad and Barbados, have in recent times become vital to Guyana's efforts at maintaining economic viability. The United States is also critical as a potential investment resource and aid source. Guyana also can ill afford the kind of U.S. hostility of the 1970s that was politically and economically destabilizing.

In the context of the altered foreign policy agenda, the GDF has been collaborating with the U.S. military. This collaboration has involved visits to Guyana by top U.S. military officials, including one by General Fred Warner of the U.S. Southern Command in Panama during July 1988; reciprocal visits by top GDF officials, including one led by then Chief-of-Staff Major General Norman McLean to the Southern Command Headquarters in October 1988; and joint military exercises, including one with the U.S. Army 44th Medical Brigade in March 1989.[30]

There had been minimal contact between the GDF and the U.S. military before 1988. For example, there were no military sales to Guyana between 1982 and 1987. Between 1984 and 1988 there was no assistance to Guyana under the International Military Education and Training (IMET) program. The last time before 1989 that Guyana secured IMET assistance was in 1983 — 10 places. This is compared with 22 for Barbados; 19 for Belize; 73 for Jamaica; and 20 for the Organization of Eastern Caribbean States (OECS). The 1989 IMET assistance proposal was Guyana — 4; Bahamas — 17; Barbados — 13; Belize — 22; Jamaica — 56; Trinidad and Tobago — 10; and OECS — 67.[31]

The United States hopes that Guyana's shifting policies will facilitate renewed contacts with the Guyana military, ultimately to pursue its own security interests. This much is clear from Pentagon submissions to Congress in 1988:

> The IMET program tentatively proposed for Guyana would improve the professional military skills of the Guyana Defense Force (GDF) and enhance the GDF awareness and observance of human rights. We would like to restart the program at the earliest opportunity. This would give us important access to the GDF and enable us to impart and reinforce shared values such as respect for civilian rule and human rights. It would also discourage the GDF from seeking military assistance and/or training from the Soviet bloc.[32]

CONCLUSION

Recent studies on Third World military-political relations have been stressing disengagement by the military and democratization of the polity, in some places as political desires, in others as welcome accomplishments. Within the last decade the military has withdrawn from political control in Paraguay, Burma, Surinam, Argentina, Chile, and South Korea, to name a few places. And the democratization process has proceeded in most places with relatively little political fallout.[33] These twin concepts — disengagement and democratization — are best analyzed in situations where military-political relations are praetorian in nature, where military officers are major or predominant political actors by virtue of their actual or threatened use of force.

Guyana's circumstances are not praetorian. They fit Nordlinger's penetration model of civilian control under which:

> Civilian governors obtain loyalty and obedience by penetrating the armed forces with political ideas (if not fully developed ideologies) and political personnel. Throughout their careers officers (and enlisted men) are intensively imbued with the civilian governors' political ideas. In the military academies, training centers, and mass-indoctrination meetings, and in the frequent discussions that take place within the smallest military units — at these times and places intensive efforts are made to shape the political beliefs of the military.

According to Nordlinger:

> The resulting congruity between the political ideas of civilians and officers consequently removes a potential source of conflict between them. Moreover, the officers' acceptance of currently orthodox political ideas is employed as a

significant promotional criterion, along with military abilities and experience. . . . Along with the downward dissemination of political ideas, civilian supremacy is maintained by the extensive use of controls, surveillance, and punishment. . . . Political penetration thereby turns the army into an officially recognized organ of the single ruling party.[34]

Under these circumstances it is more appropriate to talk about the desire for depoliticization and democratization than about disengagement and democratization in Guyana. Because of Guyana's circumstances, initiatives to depoliticize and democratize have to come from the civilian political elites, not from the military. Such initiatives have direct implications for some of the role-areas discussed above. For one, the regime political security role would have to be abandoned. But such initiatives are not incompatible with the roles of military defense and economic security.

Some of the ruling elites are aware that these initiatives are not merely desirable but necessary for the country's economic recovery and its political stability.[35] Others, however, seem prepared to sacrifice these in an effort to maintain the political status quo. The new direction in which the country seems to be heading suggests that it is merely a matter of time before the former are completely victorious over the latter, thereby bringing about the full depoliticization of the military and democratization of society.

NOTES

A version of this paper was presented at the 15th Annual Convention of the Caribbean Studies Association, Port-of-Spain, Trinidad, May 22–26, 1990. I am grateful for comments by Humberto García Muñiz and Dennis Bassier on the conference draft.

1. For more on the military institutions and their roles, see George Danns, *Domination and Power in Guyana* (New Brunswick, N.J.: Transaction Books, 1982), esp. Chs. 3 and 5; Humberto García Muñiz, *La Estrategia de Estados Unidos y la Militarización del Caribe* (Puerto Rico: Institute of Caribbean Studies, 1988), pp. 131–61; and David Granger, *A Short History of the Guyana Defense Force* (Georgetown: GDF, 1975).

2. For more on preindependence politics and Burnham's rise to power, see Leo Despres, *Cultural Pluralism and Nationalist Politics in British Guiana* (Chicago: Rand McNally, 1967); Cheddie Jagan, *The West on Trial*: (Berlin: Seven Seas, 1966); and Forbes Burnham, *A Destiny to Mould* (London: Longman, 1970).

3. For more on nationalization and economic strategy in general, see Mohamed Shahabuddeen, *Nationalization of Guyana's Bauxite* (Georgetown: Ministry of Information, 1981); Norman Girvan, "The Guyana-Alcan Conflict and the

Nationalization of Demba," *New World Quarterly* 5 (1972); Kemp Hope, Wilfred David, and Aubrey Armstrong, "Guyana's Second Development Plan, 1972–1976: A Macroeconomic Assessment," *World Development* 2 (1976); and C. Y. Thomas, "From Colony to State Capitalism: Alternative Paths to Development in the Caribbean," *Transition*, No. 5, 1982, pp. 1–20.

4. Forbes Burnham, *Declaration of Sophia* (Georgetown: PNC, 1975), p. 9. For evaluations of the cooperative and of cooperative socialism, see C. Y. Thomas, "Guyana: The Rise and Fall of Cooperative Socialism," in Anthony Payne and Paul Sutton, eds., *Overcoming Dependence: The Political Economy of the Commonwealth Caribbean* (Manchester: Manchester University Press, 1984); and Perry Mars, "Cooperative Socialism and Marxist Scientific Theory," *Caribbean Issues* 4 (1978): 71–106.

5. Forbes Burnham, *Toward the Socialist Revolution* (Georgetown: PNC, 1975), p. 8.

6. For example, Burnham's birthdays became major national events. People working with state agencies were obliged to make contributions to the purchase of birthday gifts, and their attendance at rallies where he spoke became compulsory.

7. Jagat Mehta, *Third World Militarization: A Challenge to Third World Diplomacy* (Austin, Tex.: LBJ School of Public Affairs, 1985), p. 17.

8. "Something to Remember," Report of the International Team of Observers at the Elections in Guyana, December 1980, Cited in Latin American Bureau, *Guyana: Fraudulent Revolution* (London, 1984), p. 83.

9. Ibid.

10. Eric Nordlinger, *Soldiers in Politics: Military Coups and Governments* (Englewood Cliffs, N.J.: Prentice Hall, 1977), p. 15.

11. Cited in Danns, *Domination and Power in Guyana*, p. 175.

12. The acting commissioner, Laurie Lewis, is expected to be confirmed in the position.

13. See Festus Brotherson, Jr., "The Politics of Permanent Fear: Guyana's Authoritarianism in the Anglophone Caribbean," *Caribbean Affairs* 1 (1988): 57–76.

14. David de Caires, "Guyana after Burnham," *Caribbean Affairs* 1 (1988): 194–95.

15. See U.S. Department of State, *Country Reports on Human Rights Practices for 1984*, Washington, February 1985, pp. 558–67; *Country Reports on Human Rights Practices for 1989*, Washington, February 1990, pp. 611–19; "Electoral Commission for Guyana," *Sunday Guardian* (Trinidad), May 27, 1990, p. 4; Courtney Gibson, "Elections Observers for Guyana," *New York Carib News*, June 12, 1990, p. 4; Gibson, "Elections Observers for Guyana," *New York Carib News*, July 17, 1990, p. 5. Elections are due constitutionally by March 1991, but irregularities with the voters list and developments during early 1991 suggest that the elections will not be held until September 1991.

16. See "Carter to Advocate More U.S. Aid for Guyana," *New York Carib News*, October 23, 1990, p. 36.

17. *State Paper on National Service of the Cooperative Republic of Guyana*, Sessional Paper No. 3/1973, Third Parliament of Guyana, presented to the National Assembly December 20, 1973, by Prime Minister Linden Forbes Sampson Burnham, p. 11.

18. During March and April 1990 the Good Offices Representative of the United Nations Secretary-General held discussions with Venezuelan Foreign Minister Dr. Reinaldo Figueredo Planchart and with Guyanese Foreign Minister Rashleigh Jackson. The representative is Alister McIntyre, former CARICOM Secretary-General, former UN Assistant Secretary-General and now University of the West Indies Vice-Chancellor. His role is to help the parties decide on a peaceful method of resolving the dispute. For a discussion of the dispute, see Ivelaw Griffith, *On the Western Front* (Georgetown: Ministry of Information, 1981); and Jacqueline Braveboy-Wagner, *The Venezuela-Guyana Border Dispute: Britain's Colonial Legacy in Latin America* (Boulder: Westview Press, 1984).

19. See entries on Guyana and Venezuela in *Europa World Yearbook 1989* (London, 1989). For a very good discussion of Venezuela's security capability, see David Myers, *Venezuela's Pursuit of Caribbean Basin Interests*, Rand Corporation, R-2994-AF, 1985.

20. For a discussion of this dispute see Ministry of External Affairs, Guyana, *Friendship with Integrity* (Georgetown, 1969); and Duke Pollard, "The Guyana-Surinam Boundary Dispute in International Law," in Leslie Manigat, ed., *The Caribbean Yearbook of International Relations* (St. Augustine: Inst. of Int'l Relations, 1977).

21. See, for example, "Budget Speech by Carl Greenidge, Minister of Finance," Parliamentary Sessional Paper No. 1 of 1990.

22. See, for example, Emile Benoit, *Defense and Economic Growth in Developing Countries* (Lexington: Lexington Books, 1973); Alfred Maizels and Machiko Nissanke, "The Determinants of Military Expenditure in Developing Countries," *World Development* 14 (1986): 1125–40; James Lebovic and Ashfaq Ishaq, "Military Burden, Security Needs, and Economic Growth in the Middle East," *Journal of Conflict Resolution* 21 (1987): 106–38; Nicole Ball, *Security and Economy in the Third World* (Princeton: Princeton University Press, 1988).

23. See George Danns, "Militarization and Development: An Experiment in Nation-Building," *Transition* 1 (1978): 23–41; García Muñiz, *La Estrategia de Estados Unidos*, esp. pp. 140–50; and Ball, *Security and Economy in the Third World*, Appendixes 1, 4.

24. See "Guyana to Send More Soldiers," *Barbados Advocate*, October 6, 1988, p. 8; "Guyana Police Contingent Leaves for Namibia," *Guyana Chronicle*, June 27, 1989, p. 1; "GDF Contingent Returns from Montserrat," *New Nation*, April 5, 1990, p. 15; "GDF Troops Leave for Trinidad," *Guyana Chronicle*, August 4, 1990, p. 1.

25. For discussions of Guyana's foreign policy, see Georges Fauriol, *Foreign Policy Behavior of Caribbean States: Guyana, Haiti, and Jamaica* (Lanham: University Press of America, 1984); Festus Brotherson, Jr., "The Foreign Policy of Guyana 1970–1985: Burnham's Search for Legitimacy," *Journal of Inter-American Studies and World Affairs* 31 (1989): 3–36; Rashleigh Jackson, *The International Question* (Georgetown: PNC, 1981); Henry Gill, "Domestic Political Competition and Foreign Policy: Guyana's Changing Relationships with the Communist World with Special Reference to Cuba, China, and the Soviet Union," in Leslie Manigat, ed., *The Caribbean Yearbook of International Relations* (St. Augustine: Inst. of Int'l Relations, 1977); and Ivelaw L. Griffith, "Guyana in World Affairs," *Chronicle Annual*, December 1981.

26. See, for example, Desmond Hoyte, "The Economy: The Diplomatic Effort," Address at Heads of Mission Conference, Georgetown, July 11, 1986; and "Good

Neighbors," Presidential Address to the Fourth Sitting of the First Session of the Second Supreme Congress of the People, April 3, 1987. The winds of change blowing across many parts of the world make studies on foreign policy changes both practically necessary and theoretically challenging. For some useful theoretical analyses and case studies, see Gavin Boyd and Gerald Hopple, eds., *Political Change and Foreign Policies* (New York: St. Martin's Press, 1987). Theoretical discussions are provided by Charles Hermann, "Changing Course: When Governments Choose to Redirect Foreign Policy," *International Studies Quarterly* 34 (1990): 3–21; and, particularly relevant to small states like Guyana, by Maria Papadakis and Harvey Starr, "Opportunity, Willingness, and Small States: The Relationships between Environment and Foreign Policy," in Charles Hermann, Charles Kegley, Jr., and James Rosenau, eds., *New Directions in the Study of Foreign Policy* (Boston: Allen and Unwin, 1987).

27. Soviet Ambassador to Guyana Michail Sobolev made the statement on November 7, 1990, while toasting the 73rd anniversary of the 1917 revolution at a reception. See "Soviet Ambassador Welcomes Fair Elections," *Stabroek News,* November 11, 1990, pp. 1, 2.

28. One new practice is the placement of military officials in the diplomatic establishment. In April 1990 Commandant of the GPM Colonel Carl Morgan was named Ambassador to Surinam. The following month Police Commissioner Balram Raghubir was named High Commissioner to India, effective July 1990.

29. See, for example, "Montserrat Official Lauds Guyana's Contribution," *Guyana Chronicle,* April 24, 1990, p. 1., where the GDF, in particular, and Guyana, in general, are showered with praise by Montserrat's Chief Minister John Osborne and other top officials.

30. See *Guyana Chronicle,* "U.S. Army Team Arrives Tomorrow," March 3, 1988, p. 1; *New York Carib News,* "U.S. Army for Exercise in Guyana," January 24, 1989, p. 3.

31. U.S. Department of Defense, *Congressional Presentation for Security Assistance Programs Fiscal Year 1989,* Washington, 1988.

32. *Congressional Presentation for Security Assistance Programs,* p. 176.

33. See, for example, Claude Welch, Jr., *No Farewell to Arms?* (Boulder: Westview Press, 1987); and Larry Diamond, *Democracy in Developing Countries* (Boulder: Lynne Rienner, 1988).

34. Nordlinger, *Soldiers in Politics,* pp. 15, 17.

35. See, for example, "The Philosophy of the Party Has Undergone Tremendous Change," President Hoyte's interview with *Stabroek News* editor-in-chief David de Caires on the fifth anniversary of his presidency. *Stabroek News,* August 12, 1990, pp. 11–14.

8 Security and Self-Determination in the U.S. Virgin Islands

Jannette O. Domingo

On March 31, 1917, pursuant to the 1916 treaty between the United States and Denmark, the three small islands of St. Thomas, St. John, and St. Croix, along with approximately 50 cays and islets became the United States Virgin Islands, an unincorporated territory of the United States. In the midst of World War I, the Danish islands were perceived by U.S. policy makers as a critical strategic asset that should not be allowed to fall into hostile German hands. Thus, after 245 years, the Danish West Indies were transformed from subjects of a distant, minor European power into a colony of the ascendant power of the hemisphere. The new metropole's domestic and foreign policies would henceforth dominate socioeconomic and political change and reshape the Caribbean identity of these islands.

Divergent world views and contrasting concepts of security in the Caribbean are reflected in the historical relationship between the U.S. Virgin Islands and the United States, on the one hand, and in the current efforts to reexamine that relationship and redefine the political status of the United States Virgin Islands, on the other.

Historically, the relationship between the U.S. Virgin Islands and the United States has been largely determined by the latter's geostrategic paradigms. This world view has been embodied in the revered Monroe Doctrine since the 1820s and in such twentieth-century corollaries as Teddy Roosevelt's big stick policy, dollar diplomacy, the characterization of the Caribbean as the American Mediterranean, and the current Caribbean Basin reformulation of that concept. From this perspective, continued U.S. hegemony, supported by local stability, is the key to both regional and U.S. security. Change and development, in general, and in the Caribbean, in particular, have been perceived by U.S. policy makers primarily in relation to the United States' national security concerns, particularly East-West — or earlier European–United States — conflict and competition. Development issues such as poverty, income and resource distribution, democratization, and social justice have been subordinated to U.S. security concerns and other U.S. policy objectives.

In contrast, Virgin Islanders' efforts to redefine their relationship to the United States imply a renewed interest in self-determination and, ultimately, a correspondingly self-centered notion of security. To some extent, the status debate also reflects a recognition of the need for an economic and political structure more fully empowered to address socio-economic problems and, hence in the long run, dynamic Virgin Islands stability, through social, political, and economic change and development. However, the fervor of the debate and the extent to which such a national development perspective fuels it are limited by the dependency and the ambiguous Virgin Islands identity that are legacies of the relationship currently being challenged.

GEOPOLITICAL CONSIDERATIONS

The U.S. Virgin Islands were initially perceived neither as a colony for exploitation nor as a colony for settlement, but rather as a fueling station, a Caribbean foothold, and later as a naval base protecting access to the Panama Canal. National security concerns, heightened by World War I, were the immediate impetus for the 1917 purchase of the then Danish West Indies. But their acquisition was also an integral part of contemporary U.S. imperialism in the Pacific and the Caribbean.

The United States first gave serious consideration to acquiring the Danish West Indies during the Civil War. At that time, the primary consideration was the potential strategic value of the St. Thomas/St. John harbor as a naval base and coaling station, which would put the United States on an equal footing with the European powers that already controlled such territories in the Caribbean. Although in economic decline, St. Thomas was still an important commercial and transportation hub in the Eastern Caribbean. In addition, there was an even more enduring preemptive motivation for acquisition of the Danish West Indies. Concern that the Danish West Indies might fall into more powerful and potentially less friendly European hands was most instrumental in moving negotiations forward. The Treaty of 1867 between the United States and the Danish kingdom was promptly ratified by the Danish Rigsdag. However, in the midst of impeachment proceedings against President Andrew Johnson, the United States Senate failed to ratify it immediately. After several postponements, the treaty was finally rejected in 1870.[1]

U.S. interest in the Danish West Indies at that time was not an isolated phenomenon. Other efforts were also made to act upon the Monroe Doctrine's assertion of U.S. hegemony in the Western Hemisphere and to discourage European expansion within that sphere of influence. Thus, the United States was also engaged in such endeavors as the attempt to purchase Cuba in 1857 and 1859, to annex the Dominican Republic in 1871, and to impose U.S. arbitration in the boundary dispute between Venezuela and Britain over British Guiana in 1895.[2]

The next major effort to acquire the Danish West Indies also coincided with renewed U.S. expansionism and Roosevelt's big stick elaboration of the Monroe Doctrine that closed out the nineteenth century and ushered in the twentieth. As a result of the Spanish American War, Puerto Rico was acquired and Cuba was forced to allow an essentially permanent U.S. military presence. The importance of the Danish West Indies as a potential naval station was thus greatly reduced. However, persistent rumors of Denmark's desire to sell the financially burdensome islands to Britain or France, or to trade them to Germany in exchange for the disputed North Schleswig territory, provided a strong rationale for U.S. intervention. Negotiations led to the Treaty of 1902. This time, however, the treaty was not ratified by the Danish legislature. It was quickly passed by the lower house. There the main concern seemed to be that of taking the opportunity to dispose of the insolvent islands. However, business interests in the upper house resisted losing control of the St. Thomas harbor. Moreover, resentment of the U.S. rejection of the 1867 Treaty and vestigial imperialist pride of possession also colored the discussion. The United States' unwillingness to include provisions for a plebiscite among the local population may also have been a factor.[3]

The United States finally succeeded in acquiring the Danish West Indies during World War I. By that time, Roosevelt's big stick and the dollar diplomacy corollary to the Monroe Doctrine were well established. The U.S. involvement in Panama — encouraging its secession from Columbia in 1903, guaranteeing its independence from Columbia and taking over construction of the canal — had cemented that stance. Safeguarding the canal became the ultimate rationalization for dollar diplomacy. No potentially dangerous influences could be allowed to gain a foothold near the canal, nor could political or economic instability that might invite foreign intervention be tolerated. Imposition of a naval protectorate in Nicaragua in 1912 was legitimized by the same logic.[4]

German naval bases and coaling stations in Haiti and the Dominican Republic helped justify U.S. military occupation of those countries in 1915.[5] By then, the German Hamburg-American Steamship Line was headquartered in St. Thomas and employed 20 percent of the island's labor force loading and unloading coal and cargo and administering the company even while the dispute between Germany and Denmark over North Schleswig continued in Europe.[6] Thus the sale of the Danish West Indies was expedited by the very believable threat of U.S. seizure of the islands in the event of German absorption of Denmark and, hence, of the Danish possessions. Another important factor was the generous purchase price of $25 million.

The Virgin Islands have played a minimal role in U.S. military affairs and security concerns since World War I. Their strategic importance was eclipsed by the proximity of Puerto Rico and its cultivation as the major site of U.S. military presence in the region. Thus, although the Virgin Islands were administered by the U.S. Navy from 1917 to 1931, there was no significant effort to fortify them. The small submarine and air bases built during World War II were as much a form of economic aid to the depressed islands as a reflection of their strategic importance.[7] The bases have since reverted to civilian uses. However, the United States retains the right to reoccupy the former naval base if needed.[8] Currently, the U.S. military presence in the Virgin Islands consists of a navy radar and sonar calibration station, a water tracking range, and frequent port calls by warships. There are also permanent Virgin Islands National Guard installations. The National Guard responds with disaster relief in the Virgin Islands and in neighboring islands. The National Guard has also been used to support NATO maneuvers and engages in training exercises with defense forces on other islands.[9]

The potential importance of Virgin Islands involvement in such activities is increased by the fact that they have occurred during a period in which U.S. control of the Panama Canal has been challenged and in which the specter of East-West conflict has been raised by revolutionary regimes in Grenada and Nicaragua. The renegotiation of the Panama Canal Treaty in 1977 made it clear that although Panamanians wish to reassert their sovereignty over the canal, many Americans will resist the loss of control over this strategic asset. The 1989 invasion of Panama was more easily justified within this context. In an assessment of the motivations for U.S. support of militarization in the Eastern Caribbean, it has been noted that "diminishing control over the canal itself ... doubtlessly demanded increased monitoring and munitioning of the causeway's front and back approaches."[10] Thus, the Eastern Caribbean — including the Virgin Islands — once again assumes a heightened strategic importance because of the proximity of the canal.

In the late 1950s and early 1960s, when anti-Communism was the most strident component of U.S. foreign policy and security concerns, immigration and labor policies in the Virgin Islands were adjusted in order to help U.S. capital develop the tourism economy that made the Virgin Islands a minor "showcase for democracy" until the recessionary 1970s. The 1980s Caribbean Basin reformulation of the concept of the U.S. sphere of influence led to both the trade initiative, which reduced the Virgin Islands advantage with the United States, and to the invasion of Grenada, which was publicly supported by the Virgin Islands' Congressional delegate.[11]

In 1982 Barbados took the lead in organizing members of the Organization of Eastern Caribbean States (OECS) into a Regional Security System. Within months, this group was called upon to support the U.S. invasion of Grenada. Since then, the United States has increased its funding of the training and equipping of special service units among such friendly Eastern Caribbean states.

Despite the peripheral role of the Virgin Islands in U.S. regional policy, U.S. domestic and foreign policies have been major determinants of the nature and extent of growth and development in the islands. Federal priorities — domestic and international — assumed a central role in the evolution of the local economic and political systems. Although a paradoxical "denial of empire" meant that there was no consistent colonial policy or development strategy, some early influences nevertheless reoriented and "Americanized" the Virgin Islands in the first three decades of U.S. sovereignty.[12] Among these were the principle of nonincorporation of territories, Prohibition, the restrictions associated with World War I and the opportunities of World War II, a restrictive federal immigration policy, New Deal public enterprises, and minimum wage legislation.[13]

The Virgin Islands' more recent relationship to the United States has also fostered an ambivalent socioeconomic identity among Virgin Islanders and distorted their participation in the Eastern Caribbean region. The immigration and labor practices fostered by federal policy during the "Development Decade" of the 1960s and the early 1970s led to explosive growth in the population and labor force and to unprecedented growth in domestic product and per capita income. However, these policies also generated an economic and social structure polarized by race, ethnicity, place of birth and class — one in which native Virgin Islanders too often felt themselves economically and politically endangered not only by whites, but also by Eastern Caribbean immigrants.[14]

THE CONTEXT OF THE STATUS ISSUE:
A LIMITED NATIONALISM

Since the Development Decade of the 1960s, the U.S. Virgin Islands have attempted, unsuccessfully, to exercise greater self-determination through constitutional change and, more recently, through proposed changes in their formal political and economic relationship with the United States. The options under consideration range from continuation of the current unincorporated status to independence. The extent of decolonization sought and achieved will have important implications for the nature of future growth and development, for regional cooperation, and for the evolution of the concept of security. However, both the status chosen and its ultimate impact will be strongly influenced by the ambivalence of the Virgin Islands' Eastern Caribbean identity, an ambivalence that has been fostered by the historical relationship between the United States and the Virgin Islands.

In Puerto Rico there has been an intense debate among supporters of statehood, enhanced commonwealth status, and independence. Congress has also heatedly argued the language of the bill that will present these options to the Puerto Rican electorate and provide for implementation of the results of the referendum. The fate of U.S. military installations in Puerto Rico has been an important issue for all sides in the debate. In contrast, in the Virgin Islands, seven official status options have generated a relatively muted public debate.[15] Moreover, Congressional interest has also been minimal. Despite over a decade of discussion in the Virgin Islands, there has been no Congressional activity to provide for implementation of the results of the eventual referendum.[16] Expectations for real change in the Virgin Islands appear to be low.

Unique History

The development of Virgin Islands nationalism and of an identification with the region have been undermined by the islands' unique history, relative affluence, and so-called "special relationship" with the United States. The quest for self-determination and a self-centered concept of national security has been severely limited.

Nearly 250 years as a Danish colony and another 74 years as a U.S. colony have estranged the Virgin Islands from the rest of the Caribbean politically and helped engender a rather ambivalent identity. Virgin Islanders as a group are not mainstream Americans culturally (or racially). Neither are they fully identified with the rest of the English-speaking Caribbean. At the same time, while the Virgin Islands are dependent on U.S. capital and special economic relations with the federal government, they have also been dependent on the Eastern Caribbean for expansions of the population and labor force.

Moreover, not only has the historical affiliation of the Virgin Islands as a group differed significantly from that of their Eastern Caribbean neighbors, but the specific experiences of each of the islands have also distanced them somewhat from each other. On St. John, the smallest of the three major islands, the plantation economy never recovered from a slave rebellion in 1733 in which a number of whites were killed and many of the slaves were either killed or committed suicide.[17] Subsistence farming, handicrafts, minor exports like bay leaves and limes, and commuting a few miles by boat to work in St. Thomas were the main sources of livelihood until the current tourism era. The population remained below 2,000 until the 1980s.

In a very different scenario, plantation agriculture was also abandoned early in the colonial history of St. Thomas. There it was abandoned partly because of the island's extremely hilly terrain and, more important, in favor of a commercial economy based on an excellent harbor and central location for international trade. By the early 1800s, St. Thomas was a cosmopolitan, relatively urban center. By the mid-1800s, it was the main source of employment for the nearby British Virgin Islands as well as for St. John. Even before Emancipation, there was a large free black population and emigration of free blacks from other islands. A highly stratified social structure was enforced by law and custom. The tremendous value placed on status symbols and disdain for manual labor (and manual laborers) became key cultural attributes.[18] St. Thomas's early prosperity ended with changing maritime and communications technology and trade patterns long before the United States acquired the islands from Denmark in 1917. Nevertheless, invidious social and cultural distinctions and friction between St. Thomians and Crucians have continued.

St. Croix is about 40 miles away from St. Thomas and St. John. It is the largest of the three islands and the best suited to agriculture. Although its brief golden age of plantation-based prosperity ended in the 1700s, St. Croix remained primarily agricultural until the 1950s. St. Croix had had a relatively undifferentiated slave society with little opportunity for manumission and few alternatives to agricultural work before or immediately after Emancipation. It was on St. Croix's sugar plantations that the critical slave rebellions occurred, including the 1848 rebellion that precipitated the Emancipation of slaves in the Danish West Indies and where Danish West Indian labor unions were initiated in the early 1900s. Soon after Emancipation, St. Croix's white landowners began importing contract labor from the Eastern Caribbean, and later from Puerto Rico, in order to maintain the balance of power in the labor market.[19] More recent relocations of Puerto Ricans to St. Croix were caused by the U.S. Navy's appropriation of most of the land on the Puerto Rican islands of Vieques and Culebra for use as a major naval base and testing range. Puerto Ricans are now a significant percentage of the population of St. Croix.

Reinforced by recent development, each island retains a degree of individuality. The disparate ways in which each has been involved in economic development have reflected and have been superimposed on the traditional contrasts in economic and social lifestyles. Thus, St. John remains sparsely populated with only two major resort complexes and 40 percent of the island reserved as a national park. St. Thomas has experienced the most hotel and condominium construction and almost all of the massive cruise ship traffic. St. Croix has hosted the large-scale industrial projects by Amerada-Hess Oil (refinery) and Martin Marietta, formerly Harvey Alumina (bauxite processing), and a smaller hotel-based tourism industry.

Costs of Affluence

Although historical differences have weakened the unity of the Virgin Islands, interest in self-determination has also been reduced by the fact that the Virgin Islands are rather well off by Caribbean standards. The Virgin Islands receive about $200 million a year in federal aid for housing subsidies, education grants, welfare, and food stamps. Even though the income of one-third of the Virgin Islands population falls below the official (U.S.) poverty line and per capita income is only half that of the United States, at approximately $9,000, it is among the highest in the Caribbean, surpassed only by that of the off-shore banking centers of Bermuda, the Bahamas, and the Cayman islands.[20]

The current Virgin Islands economy is largely a product of the unprecedented restructuring and explosive growth that occurred during the 1960s and early 1970s. During that era, tourism became the economy's leading sector. It was based on the beauty of the islands, but perhaps more important, on mainland prosperity and demand for leisure. Improved transportation to the Virgin Islands, freeport status, customs exemptions, tax exemptions, and unlimited supplies of Eastern Caribbean labor were also critical factors. A new petroleum refinery and bauxite processing facility on St. Croix also contributed to rising incomes in the territory. Between 1960 and 1970, the population more than doubled, and employment tripled as people from other Eastern Caribbean islands — especially St. Kitts-Nevis, Antigua, and the British Virgin Islands — filled most of the service and blue-collar positions generated by the booming tourism based economy. In addition, mainland whites filled most of the private sector's new professional, technical, and managerial positions. By 1970, only 46.5 percent of the Virgin Islands population was Virgin Islands born.[21]

In the 1960s, mainland prosperity helped fuel the Virgin Islands tourism boom and the expansion of light industry, but the recessionary environment of the 1970s led to a sharp downturn in the local economy. Visitor arrivals, exports, population, and employment stagnated. Thousands of undocumented aliens were expelled as the demand for labor fell. Propelled by the mainland business cycle, tourism and other economic indicators improved at the end of the 1970s, lagged again in the early 1980s, and regained their 1980 levels by 1985.

Affluence has imposed some heavy social and economic costs. With an area of only 136 square miles and a population of approximately 103,000, the Virgin Islands receives more than 1.8 million visitors a year.[22] It is an extremely open, "flow through" economy in which imported goods are sold to transient consumers, and much of the income generated leaks out of the local system. Overburdened infrastructure — roads, electric power, telephones, and water — and degradation of the environment are serious concerns.

Heightened racial tension has accompanied the large number of mostly white tourists and the even more disturbing increase in the resident white population of "continentals" who have become an increasingly important political as well as economic force.[23] Intraracial conflict also accompanied the influx of Eastern Caribbean workers. The Virgin Islands' nineteenth- and early twentieth-century experience of oppressive social stratification, coercive labor relations, and ambivalent identification with the Eastern Caribbean was reproduced by the immigration process of the 1960s and early 1970s that was essentially a modern contract labor system. Old patterns were updated and reinforced. The bargaining power of labor was again undermined by its fragmentation into indigenous and foreign segments, by the initially temporary status of most of the new labor force, and by the many illegals created by the system. Moreover, because of their numbers, these new arrivals threaten the political and social hegemony of the indigenous population, and ultimately challenge the very definition of "native Virgin Islander."

Local labor and capital have been only marginally involved in the private sector expansion that began in the 1960s. Local government became the main employer of the indigenous labor force, and both local and federal government policies focused on "inviting" mainland capital to the islands. As a result, the overall ratio of black to white income has remained only about 40 percent. Although indigenous blacks have moved up into white-collar public sector employment, the percentage of business ownership by blacks has decreased, and low wage private sector occupations are dominated by black Eastern Caribbean immigrants. Moreover, at the same time, the occupational distribution of whites has become more heavily professional, administrative, and managerial; whites also command higher wages than their black counterparts in the same occupational category.[24] This white employment advantage along with expatriate capital continues to reproduce traditional colonial socioeconomic power relations.

Thus, the social and economic costs of this expanded economy have become increasingly evident and have engendered efforts to exercise greater local control over the development process through planning and legislation. Many of these concerns are also reflected in the status debate as some Virgin Islanders seek an economic and political structure more fully empowered to adopt a national development perspective.

A Special Relationship

These developments have taken place within the context of a so-called special relationship between the Virgin Islands and the United States. As U.S. citizens, Virgin Islanders are free to live and work anywhere in the United States and to travel between the mainland and their home islands at will. Virgin Islanders also have access to the broad range of social services and other opportunities available only to citizens, qualified, of course, by the same limitations of race, class, and gender that apply throughout the society. They bear all the responsibilities of citizens — subject to a military draft, to federal laws and the limitations of the Constitution, paying federal taxes, etc. — but do not enjoy all of the rights and privileges of citizenship with respect to local autonomy or to full participation in the national political system.

The U.S. Constitution (Article IV, Section 3) empowers Congress to make all needful rules for territory or other property of the United States. Thus, the Virgin Islands territorial government exists only by virtue of an act of Congress and is under the administrative tutelage of the Department of Interior. Congress claims the ultimate authority to establish the legislative and policy parameters within which economic, political, and social development take place in the Virgin Islands. Within this special relationship, Congress has granted the Virgin Islands tax and trade concessions not available to states or to independent Caribbean countries. Such concessions have largely determined the fiscal capability of the public sector as well as the tourism and light industry focus of the private economy.[25] As an unincorporated territory, Congressional determination, not self-determination, has limited the extent of local control of these processes.

The policy of nonincorporation imposed U.S. geopolitical priorities at the expense of a national development perspective. Nonincorporation was first applied to the Philippines, Guam, and Puerto Rico, the territories acquired by the United States in 1898 as a result of the Spanish-American War, and then to Hawaii, which was annexed in 1898, to American Samoa in 1899, and to the Virgin Islands in 1917.[26] These noncontiguous insular possessions were regarded in a very different light from earlier acquisitions on the North American mainland. For them, the 1787 Ordinance for the Government of the Northwest Territory had established the concept of territories as extensions of the nation with their citizens entitled to the same civil rights as residents of the states, and the territories were expected to become states at some future time. In contrast, it was widely viewed as inappropriate to attempt to fully integrate these alien, mainly nonwhite peoples into the body politic.[27] They had been acquired in the context of various international power struggles, as strategic assets, not as colonies of settlement.

At the same time, efforts by Presidents Roosevelt and Taft to centralize administration of the insular possessions in a single department had been resisted by Congresses unwilling to fully acknowledge U.S. imperialism by establishing a colonial office and an explicit colonial policy.[28] Thus, the nonincorporation doctrine deprived Virgin Islanders of the traditional presumption of movement toward local autonomy, and the denial of empire meant that no coherent colonial policy was established in its stead.

Within the context of the special relationship of nonincorporation, Virgin Islanders were subject to military rule for 15 years (1917–1931), did not become U.S. citizens until 1927, did not have a local constitution

(Organic Act) until 1936, and did not elect their own governor until 1970. The Virgin Islands still have no voting representative in Congress, do not vote in national elections, and must still have Congressional approval for any changes in the structure of local government, and of course, for any change in their status.

The Organic Act

The Organic Act provides the basic legislative framework of the special relationship between the Virgin Islands and the United States. It was enacted by Congress in 1936 and revised in 1954. Rather than a Constitution of their own devising, it is the Organic Act that defines the civil rights of Virgin Islanders, as well as the structure, powers, and revenues of the territorial government and its relationship to the federal government. The Revised Organic Act and other important federal legislation and policy changes adopted by Congress in 1954 were key determinants of the kind of development that has since occurred in the Virgin Islands.

In contrast to the growing international emphasis on self-determination, the 1954 Revised Organic Act actually reduced the relative power of the elected legislature in the Virgin Islands and increased that of the presidentially appointed governor and, therefore, of the president and Congress. Moreover, an attempt was made to guarantee minority (i.e., white) representation in the legislature through restructuring and a complicated at-large voting procedure.[29] Most important, however, the Revised Organic Act set the stage for U.S. capital to begin economic development in the context of a political framework restructured to heighten the preeminence of executive decision makers and hinder the development of legislative constraints.

The revenue provisions of the Revised Organic Act gave the Virgin Islands government the fiscal capability to assume a more active economic role. All federal income taxes of Virgin Islands residents would be paid into the Virgin Islands treasury. In addition, excise taxes on most Virgin Islands products sold in the United States are returned to the Virgin Islands. This includes almost $27 million in rum excise taxes but arbitrarily excludes the much larger revenues from petroleum products. At approximately $200 million a year, such revenues now amount to almost two-thirds of the territorial government's operating budget.[30]

Increased revenues allowed the Virgin Islands government to become the major employer of indigenous labor while the private sector imported cheaper labor from the Eastern Caribbean and management from the mainland. This broader revenue base was also used to support private development through infrastructure expansion and local tax incentives to tourism (mostly hotels) and export manufacturing, especially watch assembly, and later petroleum products and bauxite.

At the same time that the Revised Organic Act allowed the Virgin Islands the flexibility to "invite" foreign capital through tax incentives, Congress also supported U.S. investment in export-oriented light industry in the territories of Guam, Samoa, and the Virgin Islands by revising the United States Tariff Act. The revision liberalized the definition of the territories' products and allowed duty free entry into the United States of products, such as watches, in which dutiable foreign materials comprised as much as 50 percent of their value.[31]

The year 1954 also marked the beginning of a new era with respect to applying federal immigration policy in the U.S. Virgin Islands. The large-scale tourism projects that began in the 1950s were undertaken by major U.S. capitalists like the Rockefellers. Congress responded to their demands for low-wage service workers with an extremely liberal interpretation of the "temporary worker" concept. This interpretation allowed a rapid and large-scale influx of Eastern Caribbean workers into the Virgin Islands labor market. Hess Oil and Harvey Alumina, two relative giants who entered the Virgin Islands economy in the mid-1960s, also benefitted from this transnational labor market.

Thus, 1954 was a critical turning point for the Virgin Islands. In that year, Congressional determination was very evident. Several Congressional committees gave separate attention to various aspects of the relationship between the Virgin Islands and the United States. These were ad hoc attempts to lighten the burden on the U.S. treasury while providing what was then referred to as a "showcase for democracy" by fostering development led by U.S. capital. As a result, for each of the soon to be leading sectors of the Virgin Islands economy — tourism, export manufacturing, and government — federal policies created new growth parameters: an elastic labor supply for tourism, tax incentives for exports, and revenue sources for local government.

A NEW INTEREST IN SELF-DETERMINATION

Since the 1954 revision of the Organic Act, continued efforts have been made to persuade Congress to improve the various components of the special relationship between the Virgin Islands and the United States. Within this framework, election of the territorial governor in 1970 and the

House of Representatives' admission of a nonvoting Virgin Islands delegate in 1972 have been the major accomplishments.

However, the current concern with status has been aroused by the confluence of a variety of long-standing issues and recent trends and events that are not addressed by such reforms. Among these oft cited factors are the following: the Virgin Islands' inability to adopt a constitution; the lack of local control of immigration and of the alienation of land; federal court rulings reaffirming the limited nature of the powers of the government of an unincorporated territory; federal declarations of willingness to entertain change in the status of territories; actual changes in the status of the U.S. Pacific territories; regional decolonization; and the global decline in the legitimacy of colonialism. Thus, the Virgin Islands' struggle to define their own priorities and to exercise greater control over local resources is occurring within the context of regional and global developments that challenge the U.S. geostrategic perspective by making self-determination and national development more critical concerns.

Constitutional development has been an important part of recent efforts to exercise greater self-determination in the Virgin Islands.[32] Four constitutional conventions were held in the Virgin islands between 1964 and 1980. The first convention's frame of reference was actually that of influencing Congressional legislation. The objective was to increase the autonomy of the territorial government through further revision of the Organic Act. A Second Revised Organic Act was drafted and submitted to Congress. Congress responded in a piecemeal fashion, implementing many of the convention's proposals over the next several years but failing to address other key issues.[33]

Subsequent conventions submitted draft constitutions to the Virgin Islands electorate. Small percentages of eligible voters narrowly approved one draft in 1972 but rejected — by a widening margin — two subsequent drafts in 1979 and 1981. Because of the small vote in favor of the second convention's draft, it was not submitted for Congressional approval, and a third effort was mounted. The third convention's defeat was largely due to concerns about the cost of implementing the proposed expansion of local government and to opposition to the increased fragmentation implied by the proposed proliferation of island based (rather than territorial) governmental units.[34]

Principles established by the previous conventions were further developed in the fourth convention's 1981 draft constitution. They included broadening the scope of constitutionally protected civil rights, expanding and further differentiating the rights and privileges of Virgin

Islanders, as opposed to those of other residents, protecting the culture and tradition of the Virgin Islands and of the environment, and enhancing the autonomy of local government. Building on recommendations of the previous convention, this draft provided for constitutional recognition of civil rights commonly protected only by the courts or by statute. Such recognition is not normally found in constitutional charters. Among these are Miranda rights, provision of legal counsel by the state, no penalty for exercise of the fifth amendment right against self-incrimination, exclusionary rule for illegally seized evidence, and the right to privacy in the conduct of one's personal affairs. The proposed constitution also recognized new rights not generally guaranteed in U.S. law or practice such as collective and individual labor rights and the right to know. Protection of the culture and traditions of Virgin Islanders and of the environment was also emphasized.[35]

The negative presidential review, and subsequent Congressional concern, focused on such provisions as the proposed concept of Virgin Islanders as those born in the Virgin Islands or whose parents were born in the Virgin Islands, extended residency requirements for certain elected officials, the proposed court structure, issuance of bonds and other financial provisions, the Bill of Rights, and environmental protection.[36] The federal criticism reflected the limitations imposed on Virgin Islands constitutional development by the supremacy of the United States Constitution. The chilling effect of the ever present constraint of federal oversight, in addition to the growing political influence of nonindigenous residents, particularly white Americans, contributed to the defeat of the last two draft constitutions.[37]

Both the third and fourth conventions went beyond the scope of their enabling legislation in considering the status issue and advocating that the Virgin Islands address the framework of federal relations within which the proposed constitutions would have to function. A 1980 reformulation of federal territorial policy also supported a broadening of the discussion. In 1982, soon after the fourth convention's proposed constitution was defeated, a referendum endorsed consideration of political status before any further attempts to draft a constitution.

As a territory of the United States, the Virgin Islands cannot independently restrict immigration nor impose controls on the alienation of land. The lack of local autonomy in these areas is of particular public concern. Inflated real estate prices reflect the impact of explosive tourism development and a greatly expanded population. Many indigenous Virgin Islanders are prevented from acquiring land. A growing white (American) population with complete freedom of access to the Virgin Islands, which exercises both economic and political power,[38] along with both first and second generation Caribbean immigrant populations increases the probability of continued social and economic segmentation.

Other highly visible reminders of the limitations of local land use policies include the federal government's ownership of an entire small island in the St. Thomas harbor (Water Island); the national park status of 40 percent of the area of St. John, an arrangement engineered by David Rockefeller to provide a buffer to his Caneel Bay resort development; and the continued control of submerged lands by the West Indian Company. This control is based on the Danish law whose provisions were incorporated into the Organic Act. Thus empowered, the company has developed those lands in violation of local environmental regulations.

Recent federal court rulings and reports of federal agencies also underscore the limitations of territorial government under the current unincorporated status. In September 1987 the United States Third Circuit Appeals Court struck down the Virgin Islands' one-year residency requirements for voting and practicing law. These requirements had been explicitly designed to reduce the political impact of the islands' many short-term residents. However, because of the 30-day precedents established by states, the Virgin Islands were denied the right to determine their own residency requirements based on their own local conditions.

In November 1987, the same court declared that "the local government does not exist by virtue of a Constitution, as does the federal (U.S.) Government [but] only by legislative grace of Congress."[39] The government of the Virgin Islands is, therefore, in effect, a federal agency exercising delegated powers and is, therefore, subordinate to the Department of Interior. This decision echoed the characterization of the governments of the Virgin Islands, Guam, and American Samoa published earlier that year in a report by Congress' Office of Technology Assessment. At the same time, the General Accounting Office's recommendation that the arrangement allowing the Virgin Islands to retain federal income tax revenues ($127 million annually) be ended highlighted the tenuous nature and unilateral determination of the relationship between the United States and the Virgin Islands.

Nevertheless, some dimensions of federal territorial policy have been permissive of increased self-determination. Policy initiatives early in the Carter administration explicitly encouraged greater autonomy within a limited context. Public Law 94-584 of 1976, "an Act to provide for the establishment of constitutions for the Virgin Islands and Guam," specifically allowed local self-government within the existing federal-territorial relationship, that is, consistent with U.S. sovereignty, the supremacy of the U.S. Constitution, treaties, and laws. In contrast, in a 1980 statement to Congress, President Carter articulated a reformulated policy: "In keeping with our fundamental policy of self determination, *all options* for political development should be open to the people of the insular territories." However, self-determination would still be limited by the U.S. perception of national security. Thus, it could occur "so long as their choices are implemented when economically feasible and *in a manner that does not compromise the national security of the United States.*"[40] This new federal attitude led directly to the creation of a Virgin Islands Status Commission and the beginning of formal consideration of redefining the relationship between the Virgin Islands and the United States.

The consummation of this process by the U.S. Pacific territories further encouraged the debate in the Virgin Islands. This was particularly true with respect to Guam's 1987 referendum in favor of commonwealth status, subsequent adoption of a constitution, and then recognition as a commonwealth by Congress in 1989. Like the Virgin Islands, and unlike the Pacific Trust Territories, Guam had also been an unincorporated territory, acquired during the same expansionist era, and governed by an Organic Act. It was also outside the U.S. customs zone, retained federal taxes paid by its residents or on its products, and had experienced population inflows that threatened the political, economic, and cultural dominance of the indigenous people. Indeed, Guam had been considered the Virgin Islands' Pacific counterpart, and federal legislation generally addressed both Guam and the Virgin Islands. This affinity and the contribution of the Guamanian experience to the Virgin Islands debate were reflected in the visits of Guam's Senate speaker and governor to the Virgin Islands in 1988 and 1989, respectively. They shared information on a range of issues and encouraged the Virgin Islands to actively pursue their own change of status and to press Congress to act expeditiously in implementing the expressed will of the people.[41]

At the same time that events have proceeded in the Pacific, Eastern Caribbean regional developments have also contributed to the context of decolonization and increased self-determination. Over the past 15 years, several smaller and/or poorer Eastern Caribbean islands have gained their independence, including those from which most of the Virgin Islands' recent population increases have come, such as Antigua, St. Kitts-Nevis, and Dominica. In addition, the Virgin Islands' interest in regional organizations such as the OECS and the Caribbean Community (CARICOM) reflects an increased regional identification. However, it also exposes the limitations on Virgin Islands' participation in the region given their current political status.

These local, national, and regional events and trends that have encouraged the Virgin Islands' current focus on redefining their political status have taken place within the larger context of a global decline in the legitimacy of colonialism. Since World War II, 80 countries have been removed from the UN list of non–self-governing territories. Eighteen remain on it, including the U.S. Virgin Islands and six other Caribbean territories.

The United Nations has played a key role in institutionalizing this new world view. The 1960 United Nations Declaration on Decolonization asserted the right of all people to self-determination. In 1961, the Special Committee on Decolonization was established as a mechanism for monitoring and encouraging implementation of this perspective. This committee, known as the Committee of 24, reviews the political, economic, social, educational, and constitutional progress of non–self-governing territories.

The United Nations has also played a more direct role in shaping the context of U.S. policy toward the Virgin Islands and its other territories. In the early 1960s, the committee urged that U.S. territories be allowed to elect their own governmental leaders. UN support of local initiatives contributed to the enactment of the Elective Governor's Act of 1968 in which the Virgin Islands and Guam were granted the right to elect their governors.

General Assembly resolutions in the early 1970s expressed concern with the "limited political and constitutional development" in dependent areas. Administering powers were urged to consult with local elected representatives in order to establish specific timetables within which they would determine their own political status.[42] During this period, formulation and adoption of a local constitution was sanctioned by the Carter administration and Congress, although with the explicit limitation of working within the existing territorial-federal relationship.

Between 1977 and 1979, UN resolutions exhorted the United States to "encourage further and meaningful discussion regarding the political and constitutional status of the Territory."[43] Heightened UN attention led to the first — and so far, only — site visit to the Virgin Islands by the Committee of 24 allowed by the United States. It also encouraged the reformulation of U.S. policy with respect to the permissible scope of self-determination in the Virgin Islands discussed above. In the 1980s, an increasingly detailed and intense UN debate on the Virgin Islands led to a number of statements in which the United States acknowledged the right of the people of the Virgin Islands to determine their own political status.[44] However, although the United States is thus on record in support of self-determination, there has been no Congressional activity to provide for implementation of the results of an eventual referendum, and few resources have been made available to assist the local educational effort.

STATUS OPTIONS

To varying degrees the status options being considered respond to a perceived need for an economic and political structure more fully empowered to address socioeconomic problems and, hence, to address the Virgin Islands' long-term stability. However, as a member of the Status Commission noted, despite the various commissions, reports, and educational efforts of the pat decade, there is a relative lack of public passion in the status debate, which may well reflect a widespread perception of change in political status as an isolated phenomenon unrelated to, or unable to address, social and economic problems.[45] Indeed, of the seven options, only three — independence, free association, and integration (statehood) — are recognized by international organizations as expressions of complete self-determination. The other four options are versions of continued territorial, non–self-governing status.

In July 1989, a few months before the scheduled November referendum, the Virgin Islands legislature attempted to rationalize the selection process by grouping the seven options into three categories:

continued or enhanced territorial status — unincorporated territory (status quo), compact of federal relations, and commonwealth options;
complete integration into the United States — incorporated territory and statehood options;
greater or complete autonomy — free association and independence options.

If no category received a majority vote, a runoff would be held between categories. A final vote would then choose a specific option from the winning category.

The referendum was postponed indefinitely because of Hurricane Hugo. However, a survey of voters in the 1988 election conducted by the Caribbean Research Institute of the University of the Virgin Islands indicated the following preferences:

compact	4%
unincorporated territory	7%
commonwealth	11%
subtotal, first category	22%
statehood	19%
incorporated territory	14%
subtotal, second category	33%
independence	10%
free association	6%
subtotal, third category	16%
not sure	29%

Although no category received a majority vote, those options representing integration into the United States clearly made the strongest showing, with one-third of those polled indicating this preference. The various forms of continued territorial status were preferred by a total of 22 percent of those polled, with the more autonomous commonwealth most popular in this category. Sovereignty through independence or free association attracted 16 percent of those polled. Thus, a 1988 runoff between categories would have been between integration and continued territorial status.

Compact of Federal Relations

Of the official options, the "compact of federal relations" is the least definitive, and perhaps for that reason received the least support (4 percent) in the 1988 survey. Nevertheless, this option has been supported by the governor and by prominent members of the Virgin Islands legislature.[46] The governor may well see the compact as a means of renegotiating the unincorporated territory, a status that he is also on record as having endorsed.[47] However, a compact has more often been a framework for negotiations leading to free association or commonwealth.

Rather than an actual status, a compact is an agreement, or process by which changes in the relationship between the Virgin Islands and the federal government would be negotiated. Congress would thus agree not to exercise its power to make unilateral changes in the relationship. However, as with status quo and commonwealth, the other options in the continued territorial status category, the Virgin Islands would still be a territory subject to U.S. sovereignty, the supremacy of the U.S. Constitution and laws, and the authority of the federal courts to interpret them.[48] Compact proponents propose the return of federal taxes collected on all Virgin Islands products, including currently excluded petroleum products, authorization of the Virgin Islands government to enter into agreements with Eastern Caribbean governments, and regular consultation between the federal and Virgin Islands governments on matters affecting their relationship. However, the compact option emphasizes that such matters are to be negotiated by the Virgin Islands and federal governments. Thus, a vote in favor of a "compact of federal relations" would still leave unanswered the question of exactly what those "federal relations" would ultimately be.

Commonwealth

Although there is no standard definition of commonwealth, in the context of the U.S. territories, a commonwealth is a territory that is governed by its own locally devised constitution and is, therefore, not under the supervision of the Department of Interior. Commonwealth status allows greater internal autonomy than that enjoyed by an unincorporated territory.

As with the special relationship between the unincorporated territory of the Virgin Islands and the United States, the people of the Commonwealths of Puerto Rico, Guam, and the Northern Mariana Islands retain their U.S. citizenship and have nonvoting delegates to the House of Representatives. Commonwealth residents also pay no federal taxes, or have them remitted to the local treasury, and the commonwealths enjoy a variety of tax breaks and incentives to U.S. investment.

Puerto Rico has been a commonwealth since 1952, but the extent of its autonomy is still not clearly defined, prompting some critics in the Virgin Islands to describe commonwealth as a meaningless "distinction without a difference" and to urge its exclusion from consideration in the status referendum.[49] Indeed, the official voter education literature initially emphasized the ambiguity of the concept.[50] Some of the same critics, however, later attempted to have commonwealth placed in the autonomous status category along with independence and free association rather than grouping it with the status quo.[51] It is not clear how the 11 percent of the 1988 voters who preferred commonwealth actually perceived it.

Under new locally drafted constitutions, the recently established Commonwealths of Guam and the Northern Mariana Islands do have more explicit guidelines with respect to the scope of self-government.

Their constitutions also reflect local culture and concerns in such areas as recognizing indigenous languages and controlling immigration and the alienation of land. The Pacific commonwealths also control their own foreign affairs in nonmilitary matters. These are the very kinds of enhancements to its commonwealth status that Puerto Rico has sought, unsuccessfully so far, and that advocates of a Virgin Islands commonwealth finally had written into the official description of that option. They make commonwealth a meaningful alternative.

In the Virgin Islands, such provisions have drawn heated criticism as "an affront to Americanism."[52] They have been attacked on the basis of what would appear to be an excessive concern for their "legality," that is, constitutionality, given that such provisions have already been enacted in the Pacific territories.[53] Such patriotic challenges have been directed primarily at the commonwealth option whereas independence and free association, which offer the greatest opportunity to escape the limitations of the U.S. Constitution and complete domination by U.S. policy priorities, have received little critical attention. Perhaps they are not seen as serious contenders.

Free Association

Although only 6 percent of Virgin Islands voters polled in 1988 preferred free association, there are several precedents for this status among former U.S. territories. Free association has recently been adopted by most of the former Pacific Trust Territories — the Federated States of Micronesia and the Marshall Islands.[54] As such, they are now sovereign states with their own presidents, congresses, and citizenship. They exercise full internal autonomy emphasizing their own individuality and culture. Vibrant national identities, and resistance to cultural imperialism have played an important political role in the Pacific, counterbalancing the economic dependence on the U.S. military presence.[55] The free associated states also conduct their own foreign relations. However, the United States maintains authority and responsibility for military affairs. In exchange for military rights, the United States provides economic aid and other assistance.

The greater autonomy of free association seems a natural development in the Pacific. The United States assumed administration of the Trust Territories in 1947 with an explicit UN mandate to foster self-determination. In contrast, the Virgin Islands were acquired in an era in which the legitimacy of colonialism was hardly questioned. They were then governed under a debilitatingly paternalistic administrative tutelage.

Independence

In 1965, the Virgin Islands' first constitutional convention explicitly rejected independence in favor of the greatest degree of autonomy possible within the existing unincorporated territory status.[56] Nevertheless, a 1981 Harris poll found that 13 percent of those surveyed favored independence. The 1988 survey found that 10 percent of voters preferred independence. Although too small and, thus, far too quiet a minority to impose their preference, these percentages actually compare favorably to the *independentista* showing of only about 5 percent in Puerto Rico where some supporters of independence may be voting for commonwealth in order to block statehood.[57]

There is no institutionalized independence party in the Virgin Islands, nor is there the tradition of highly visible pro-independence activism that enlivens and broadens the scope of the Puerto Rican struggle for self-determination.[58] New pro-independence organizations have been established in response to the opportunity presented by the current status debate. However, they appear to concede the immediate vote and focus instead on continued activism after the referendum in order to develop the "mental emancipation" needed to make independence a conceivable alternative.[59]

Many observers have noted that Virgin Islanders generally appear to fear the loss of U.S. economic support and to doubt their ability to govern themselves. The administrative tutelage imposed on the Virgin Islands by Congressional determination has taken a heavy toll. Nevertheless, the Virgin Islands are actually comparable in size, population, and resources to other recently independent Caribbean nations. Postindependence economic assistance from the United States would depend on the terms of the independence agreement and on the amicability of the separation. The same factors would condition the reactions of private investors.

The Philippines, the only territory to gain independence from the United States, was allowed a 10-year transition period during which they received foreign aid to compensate for lost domestic aid. However, with major U.S. military installations, the Philippines has remained a key element in U.S. geostrategic considerations and a prime example of the impact of the U.S. equation of stability with security at the expense of the national development perspective. Their relative insignificance militarily might allow an independent Virgin Islands at least partial escape from this syndrome.

The most serious impediment to independence for the Virgin Islands, however, may well be the limited sense of nationalism and, therefore, the lack of priority assigned to national objectives that require greater self-determination.

Incorporated Territory/Statehood

In spite of the recent independence of most of their Eastern Caribbean neighbors and the assumption of free association and commonwealth status in the Pacific, statehood is still a more familiar and more attractive concept to those Virgin Islanders who identify strongly with the United States. In the 1988 survey, one-third of those polled preferred either immediate or future statehood — 19 percent for statehood and another 14 percent for incorporated territory status.

An incorporated territory can be characterized as "an incipient state," that is, a territory that Congress has indicated will eventually be fully integrated as a state. However, unless there is a very explicit Congressional mandate, there is no guarantee that an incorporated territory will become a state. Neither is there a timetable for statehood. It took decades for Hawaii and Alaska to become states after they were recognized as incorporated territories.

An incorporated territory would be treated like a state in many ways without actually being one or being represented as one. Thus, special concessions from the federal government that are not available to states would be eliminated. In the Virgin Islands this would mean, for example, that over $200 million in federal income taxes, customs duties, and excise taxes would no longer be paid into the Virgin Islands treasury. This equals approximately two-thirds of the operating budget of the territorial government. Greater access to federal grants could not compensate for such a revenue loss to an incorporated Virgin Islands or a Virgin Islands state. Nor could state taxes be expected to duplicate these revenues. Inclusion in the U.S. customs zone would also disallow the reduced duties that currently encourage tourism sales.

Moreover, although local self-government would be expanded along with full representation in national government, this inclusion would also imply the full application of the U.S. Constitution, laws, and precedents regardless of their applicability or impact on the particular needs of a small, extremely open economy with a distinct cultural heritage. Thus, local control of resources such as population inflows and land use, and of residency requirements would remain severely limited.

In any case, despite the apparent preference of many Virgin Islanders for closer integration into the United States, the debate in Congress over the conditions of Puerto Rico's statehood option raises questions about the actual willingness of Congress to accept the territories as future states. Their racial composition, relative poverty, and population size are divisive issues.[60] There is also a related concern that precedents might be established that could be applied by advocates of statehood for the District of Columbia.[61] Congress' rejection of Spanish as an official language of the proposed Puerto Rican state has also highlighted Congressional unwillingness to respect cultural differences in the Caribbean.[62]

CONCLUSIONS

The questions that must ultimately be addressed with respect to the future status of the Virgin Islands are, first, what areas of autonomy are most important to the Virgin Islands and, second, which of the various status options best provides the desired aspects of self-determination? Greater Virgin Islands autonomy has been sought in external relations, particularly in the form of increased participation in regional and other international organizations, and might also conceivably take such form as independent negotiation of trade agreements, and even the exercise of an independent Caribbean foreign policy. Thus, the quest for greater self-determination in the Virgin Islands has indeed included seeking autonomy that might ultimately prove to be inconsistent with the U.S. geostrategic view of the Caribbean and impinge on the presumption of a U.S. monopoly in establishing the terms of discourse in the region.

However, the issues that most arouse Virgin Islanders appear to be those that reflect a concern for local security through development based on a more narrowly defined autonomy. The focus has been on empowerment that would allow self-determination in areas such as control of immigration and establishment of local residency requirements and prerogatives for native Virgin Islanders, restrictive land ownership and use policies, environmental protection policies, and preservation of such cultural expressions as local holidays, landmarks, education, and language. Nevertheless, the tenuous connection perceived between the status options and the solution of such problems — along with the ambivalence of the Virgin Islands' identification with the rest of the Caribbean — has apparently led to a paradoxically strong preference for greater, rather than less, integration into the United States. Thus, there is an implicit willingness to subordinate local objectives to the U.S. geostrategic perspective and federal policy priorities.

NOTES

1. For a more detailed description of the negotiations and of U.S. and Danish political considerations surrounding the various treaties for the sale of the Danish West Indies, see Isaac Dookhan, *A History of the Virgin Islands of the United States* (Epping, Essex: Caribbean Universities Press in association with Bowker Publishing, 1974), pp. 243–64.

2. See Eric Williams, *From Columbus to Castro: The History of the Caribbean, 1492–1969* (New York: Harper & Row, 1970), pp. 415–17.

3. See William Boyer, *America's Virgin Islands: A History of Human Rights and Human Wrongs* (Durham: Carolina Academic Press, 1983), pp. 81–82.

4. William Boyer, "The Navy and Labor in St. Croix, U.S. Virgin Islands, 1917–1931," *Journal of Caribbean History* 20 (1985/86): 82.

5. Williams, *From Columbus to Castro*, pp. 423–25.

6. Herbert D. Brown, *Report on Political, Social and Economic Conditions in the Virgin Islands, 1930*, Unpublished manuscript, Records of the Bureau of Efficiency (1913–1933), 19.V7; Record Group 51, National Archives, p. 29.

7. Gordon K. Lewis, *The Virgin Islands: A Caribbean Lilliput* (Evanston: Northwestern University Press, 1972), p. 72.

8. Dion Phillips, "A New 'Special Relationship' for the U.S. Virgin Islands?" *Trans-Africa Forum* 5 (1988): 44.

9. Dion Phillips, "Reflections on Independence for the U.S. Virgin Islands," *Bulletin of Eastern Caribbean Affairs* 10 (1984): 53, n. 21.

10. Frank K. Taylor, "'Peace-Keeping' in Paradise: The Arming of the Eastern Caribbean," *Trans-Africa Forum* 3 (Spring 1986): 51.

11. Cited in Douglas Dunkel, "Tourism as a Form of Demographic Imperialism: A Comparison of the Bahamas and the Virgin Islands," Ph.D. dissertation, Michigan State University, 1985, p. 218.

12. For the origin of the concept of "denial of empire," see Whitney Perkins, *Denial of Empire: The United States and Its Dependencies* (Leyden: A. W. Sithoff, 1962).

13. For an analysis of the impact of these early influences, see Jannette O. Domingo, "U.S. Domestic and Foreign Policies and the Virgin Islands Labor Market, 1917–1950," *Cimarrón*, forthcoming.

14. See Jannette O. Domingo, "Employment, Income, and Economic Identity in the U.S. Virgin Islands," *The Review of Black Political Economy* 18 (1989): 37–57.

15. The seven status options are status quo (unincorporated territory), commonwealth, compact of federal relations, incorporated territory, statehood, free association, and independence. The options are discussed further below.

16. A select committee of the Virgin Islands legislature recommended that a referendum be conducted along with the November 1986 election. However, it was postponed to 1988 and then postponed again to November 1989 in order to allow more time for voter education. The devastation wreaked by Hurricane Hugo in October 1989 led to a further indefinite postponement.

17. John Knox, *A Historical Account of St. Thomas, W.I.* (St. Thomas: College of the Virgin Islands, 1966 [1852]), p. 76.

18. See Albert A. Campbell, *The St. Thomas Negroes: A Study of Personality and Culture* (Evanston: American Psychological Association, 1943); and Edwin

Weinstein, *Cultural Aspects of Delusion: A Psychiatric Study of the Virgin Islands* (New York: The Free Press, 1962).

19. For explicit statements of the repressive intent of the planters' immigration schemes, see Immigration Committee Correspondence, 1860–1871, Record Group 55, National Archives.

20. For Virgin Islands data, see Virgin Islands Department of Economic Development and Agriculture, Bureau of Economic Research, *U.S. Virgin Islands Economic Indicators, 1988.* For comparative data, see Carmen Deere et al., *In the Shadows of the Sun: Caribbean Development Alternatives and U.S. Policy* (Boulder: Westview Press, 1990), pp. 5–6.

21. U.S. Department of Commerce, Bureau of the Census, *Census of Population, 1970.*

22. U.S. Virgin Islands Department of Economic Development and Agriculture, Bureau of Economic Research, *U.S. Virgin Islands Tourism Indicators, 1988.*

23. See Paul M. Leary and Klaus de Albuquerque, "The Other Side of Paradise: Race and Class in the 1986 Virgin Islands Election," *Caribbean Affairs* 2 (1989): 51–63.

24. Domingo, "Employment, Income, and Economic Identity," pp. 46–49.

25. For example, federal income and excise taxes are returned to the Virgin Islands treasury. They comprise the bulk of the territorial government's revenues. Being outside the U.S. customs zone, the Virgin Islands can impose minimal import duties. The tourist shopping industry is supported by the "freeport" status as well as by the higher duty exemptions the United States allows tourists returning from the Virgin Islands. In addition, Virgin Islands products are imported into the United States duty free. The U.S. Tariff Act defines products of the Virgin Islands so liberally as to include goods assembled or otherwise finished in the Virgin Islands with only a small value added. At the same time, the Virgin Islands are exempt from the Jones Act's expensive requirement that only U.S. vessels be used in interstate commerce. This exemption helped attract major industrial projects to St. Croix.

26. The doctrine of nonincorporation was established by the Supreme Court in the Insular Cases [Downes v. Bidwell, 182 U.S. 244 (1901) and Dorr v. U.S., 195 U.S. 138 (1904)] in which the court found, in effect, that the rights, privileges, and protections of the constitution do not automatically follow the flag but must be specifically legislated by Congress.

27. See Isaac J. Cox, "The Era of Overseas Expansion," in William Haas, ed., *The American Empire* (Chicago: University of Chicago Press, 1940), pp. 1–24.

28. Perkins, *Denial of Empire*, p. 342.

29. James A. Bough, "General Introduction to the Constitutional Development of the Virgin Islands," in James A. Bough and Roy C. Macridis, eds., *Virgin Islands — America's Caribbean Outpost: The Evolution of Self-Determination* (Wakefield, Mass.: William F. Williams Publishing, 1970), pp. 124–25.

30. U.S. Virgin Islands Department of Economic Development and Agriculture, *Economic Indicators, 1988.*

31. The tariff revision was supposed to encourage diversification and economic development of the insular possessions by encouraging light industry. However, along with the local tax incentives, it actually subsidized marginal investment by U.S. firms employing a small labor force of low wage, often imported, labor. The indigenous employment, income, and public revenue benefits were minimal.

32. The first draft constitution was actually submitted to Congress during the 1923–1924 session. This early effort was spearheaded by local labor leader Rothschild Francis with the support of the New York-based American Civil Liberties Union. Oppressive working conditions and repression of the labor movement in the Virgin Islands had led to a political struggle centered on labor's demands for universal suffrage, a fully elected local government, and freedom of speech and of the press. The economic elite opposed such political development and instead proposed appeasement through ineffective economic reforms unsupported by political empowerment. This struggle reflected the contemporary working class's belief in, and insistence on, political reform as a necessary foundation for economic reform. There was a similar perception on the part of the economic elite and the allied naval administration. See Isaac Dookhan, "Labour Relations in St. Croix, United States Virgin Islands: A Case of Administrative Failure," *Journal of Caribbean History* 18 (1984): 91–98.

33. Key proposals that have not yet been addressed include the right to vote in presidential elections, local appointment of the comptroller, and designation of the Virgin Islands as an "autonomous territory" with the greatest degree of self-government consistent with its status as an unincorporated territory.

34. William C. Gilmore, "The Search for Constitutional Change in the U.S. Virgin Islands," *Social and Economic Studies* 33 (1984): 149.

35. Ibid., pp. 150–51.

36. See House Doc. 375, 96th Cong., 2d Sess., 1980.

37. See, for example, *New York Times,* November 5, 1981, Part II, p. 19, for conflicting responses of native born Virgin Islanders and others to draft provisions.

38. See Leary and de Albuquerque, "The Other Side of Paradise."

39. Cited in Carlyle Corbin, *Dependency and Change: Political Status Options for the United States Virgin Islands* (St. Thomas: Aaronsrod Communications, 1988), p. 3.

40. House Doc. 268, 96th Cong., 2d Sess., 1980, at 3. Emphasis added.

41. *St. Thomas Daily News,* December 10, 1988, pp. 3, 12; July 29, 1989, pp. 1, 12; August 1, 1989, pp. 1, 12.

42. Corbin, *Dependency and Change,* pp. 13–15.

43. Ibid., p. 15.

44. United Nations documents cited in Phillips, "A New Special Relationship," pp. 44–45; United Nations documents and U.S. responses cited in Gilmore, "The Search for Constitutional Change," p. 154; and in Corbin, *Dependency and Change,* pp. 15–16.

45. Status Commission member David Jones, cited in *St. Thomas Daily News,* August 18, 1989, p. 10.

46. *St. Thomas Daily News,* March 18, 1989, p. 10; May 9, 1989, p. 12; June 6, 1989, pp. 3, 12; June 9, 1989, p. 11; July 13, 1989, p. 1; July 20, 1989, p. 12.

47. Cited in Bette A. Taylor, *Territorial Political Development: An Analysis of Puerto Rico, Northern Mariana Islands, Guam, Virgin Islands and American Samoa, and the Micronesian Compacts of Free Association* (Washington, D.C.: Congressional Research Service, Library of Congress, October 17, 1988), p. 28.

48. U.S. Virgin Islands Commission on Status and Federal Relations, *The Compact of Federal Relations: Questions and Answers* (St. Thomas: University of the Virgin Islands, n.d.).

49. *Report of the Select Committee on Status and Federal Relations of the Sixteenth Legislature of the Virgin Islands,* St. Thomas, January 14, 1985, p. 5. See also comments of Status Commission Co-Chair, Virgin Islands Senator Lorraine Berry, *St. Thomas Daily News,* December 12, 1988, p. 12.

50. U.S. Virgin Islands Commission on Status & Federal Relations, *Brief Descriptions of the Seven Political Status Options* (St. Thomas: University of the Virgin Islands, n.d.).

51. *St. Thomas Daily News,* July 6, 1989, p. 1; July 8, 1989, p. 1; July 20, 1989, pp. 1, 10, and 12.

52. See comments of Status Commission member Fred Vialet in *St. Thomas Daily News,* May 5, 1989, p. 1.

53. See comments of Status Commission Co-Chair, Virgin Islands Senator Lorraine Berry in *St. Thomas Daily News,* June 6, 1989, p. 3.

54. Only the Northern Mariana became a commonwealth. Their objective in so doing was to allow for possible reintegration with the Commonwealth of Guam. See Corbin, *Dependency and Change,* p. 38.

55. For a brief but useful summary of developments in the Pacific territories, see Taylor, *Territorial Political Development,* pp. 11–24, 29–39.

56. Resolution of the 1965 Constitutional Convention cited in Bough and Macridis, *Virgin Islands,* p. 126.

57. Alan Weisman, "An Island in Limbo," *New York Times Magazine,* February 18, 1990, p. 32.

58. The United People's Party (UPP) was formed in 1973. The UPP advocated political, economic, and social independence. In the 1974 election, the now defunct party was unable to win even a single seat.

59. *St. Thomas Daily News,* September 6, 1989, pp. 1, 12.

60. *St. Thomas Daily News,* May 10, 1989, p. 2; *New York Times,* July 10, 1989, p. B9.

61. *St. Thomas Daily News,* February 14, 1989, p. 4; *Congressional Quarterly,* August 5, 1989, p. 2024.

62. Weisman, "An Island in Limbo," pp. 32, 34.

Selected Bibliography

Adkin, Mark (1989). *Urgent Fury: The Battle for Grenada.* Lexington: Lexington Books.

Axline, Andrew (1988). "Regional Cooperation and National Security: External Forces in Caribbean Integration," *Journal of Common Market Studies,* Vol. 27, No. 1, pp. 1–25.

Barry, Tom, et al. (1984). *The Other Side of Paradise.* New York: Grove Press.

Braveboy-Wagner, J. (1989). *The Caribbean in World Affairs.* Boulder: Westview Press.

Bryan, Anthony, ed. (1986). *The Organization of American States and the Commonwealth Caribbean: Perspectives on Security, Crisis, and Reform.* St. Augustine, Trinidad: Institute for International Relations.

Bryan, Anthony, J. E. Greene, and Timothy Shaw, eds. (1990). *Peace, Development, and Security in the Caribbean.* New York: St. Martin's Press.

Commonwealth Study Group (1985). *Vulnerability: Small States in the Global Society.* London: Commonwealth Secretariat.

Corbin, Carlyle (1988). *Dependency and Change: Political Status Options for the United States Virgin Islands.* Road Town, Tortola: Aaronsrod Communications Co.

Danns, George (1982). *Domination and Power in Guyana.* New Brunswick: Transaction Books.

Deere, Carmen, et al. (1990). *In the Shadows of the Sun: Caribbean Development Alternatives and U.S. Policy.* Boulder: Westview Press.

Domingo, Jannette O. (1989). "Employment, Income, and Economic Identity in the U.S. Virgin Islands," *The Review of Black Political Economy,* Vol. 18, No. 1, pp. 32–57.

Fauriol, Georges, ed. (1989). *Security in the Americas.* Washington, D.C.: National Defense University Press.

García Muñiz, Humberto (1988). *La Estrategia de Estados Unidos y la Militarización del Caribe.* Río Piedras: Institute of Caribbean Studies.

____. (1988). "Defense Policy and Planning in the Caribbean: An Assessment of Jamaica on its 25th Independence Anniversary," *Journal of Commonwealth and Comparative Politics,* Vol. 27, No. 1, pp. 74–102.

Gilmore, William C. (1984). "The Search for Constitutional Change in the U.S. Virgin Islands," *Social and Economic Studies,* Vol. 33, No. 3, pp. 143–61.

Griffith, Ivelaw L. (forthcoming). "Asia and the Caribbean: Security Comparisons," in J. Braveboy-Wagner et al., *The Caribbean in the Pacific Century.* Boulder: Lynne Rienner, forthcoming 1992.

____. (forthcoming). *The Quest for Security in the Caribbean.* Armonk, N.Y.: M. E. Sharpe, forthcoming 1992.

Harden, Sheila, ed. (1985). *Small Is Dangerous.* New York: St. Martin's Press.

Heine, Jorge, and Leslie Manigat, eds. (1988). *The Caribbean and World Politics.* New York: Holmes and Meier.

Hudson, Rex (1989). "Strategic and Regional Security Perspectives," in Library of Congress, *Islands of the Commonwealth Caribbean.* Washington, D.C.

Ince, Basil, et al., eds. (1983). *Issues in Caribbean International Relations.* Lanham: University Press of America.

Jackson, Rashleigh (1982). *Safeguarding the Security of Small States.* Georgetown: Ministry of Foreign Affairs.

Knight, Franklin W., and Colin Palmer, eds. (1989). *The Modern Caribbean.* Chapel Hill: University of North Carolina Press.

Lacey, Terry (1977). *Violence and Politics in Jamaica: 1960–1970.* Manchester: Manchester University Press.

Mehta, Jagat, ed. (1985). *Third World Militarization: A Challenge to Third World Diplomacy*. Austin, Tex.: LBJ School of Public Affairs.

Oxaal, Ivor (1971). *Race and Revolutionary Consciousness*. Cambridge, Mass.: Schenkman.

Payne, Anthony (1984). *The International Crisis in the Caribbean*. Baltimore: Johns Hopkins University Press.

Phillips, Dion E. (1988). "The Creation, Structure, and Training of the Barbados Defense Force," *Caribbean Studies*, Vol. 21, Nos. 1 and 2, pp. 125–57.

___. (1988). "A New Special Relationship for the U.S. Virgin Islands," *Trans-Africa Forum*, Vol. 5, No. 2, p. 39–58.

Rodríguez Beruff, Jorge (1985). "Puerto Rico and U.S. Militarization," *Contemporary Marxism*, Issue 10, pp. 68–91.

___. (1989). "U.S. Caribbean Policy and Regional Militarization," in Augusto Varas, ed., *Hemispheric Security and U.S. Policy in Latin America*. Boulder: Westview Press.

Schoultz, Lars (1987). *National Security and United States Policy towards Latin America*. Princeton: Princeton University Press.

Searwar, Lloyd (1987). *Peace, Development, and Security in the Caribbean Basin: Perspectives to the Year 2000*. Conference Report for Canadian Institution for International Peace and Security, No. 4.

Serbin, Andres (1990). *Caribbean Geopolitics: Toward Security through Peace?* Boulder: Lynne Rienner, 1990.

Stone, Carl (1986). *Power in the Caribbean Basin*. Philadelphia: Institute for the Study of Human Issues.

Sutton, Paul (1988). "The Caribbean as a Focus for Strategic and Resource Rivalry," in Peter Calvert, ed., *Central American Security System: North-South or East-West?* Cambridge: Cambridge University Press.

Thomas, Clive Y. (1988). *The Poor and the Powerless*. New York: Monthly Review Press.

Young, Alma H., and Dion E. Phillips, eds. (1986). *Militarization in the Non-Hispanic Caribbean*. Boulder: Lynne Rienner.

Young, Alma H., and Dennis H. Young (1988). "The Impact of the Anglo-Guatemalan Dispute on the Internal Politics of Belize," *Latin American Perspectives*, Vol. 15, No. 2, pp. 6–30.

Index

Adams Doctrine, 110–11, 119
Adams, Tom, 10, 103, 106–8, 111–13, 117, 120
Alleyne, Sidney-Burnett, 107–9, 112, 116, 119
Anguilla. *See* St. Kitts-Nevis
Antigua. *See* Antigua-Barbuda
Antigua-Barbuda, 9, 12, 27, 29, 31, 36, 39, 41, 46, 108, 111, 118, 185

Bahamas, 9, 12, 14–15, 20, 27, 29, 36, 39, 40–41; and drugs (*See* drugs)
Bakr, Abu, 10–11, 64
Barbados, 8, 31, 35; Barbados Labor Party, 21, 101, 103, 106–7, 109–13, 116–19; Coast Guard, 103, 105, 108, 119; defense policy, 101–20; Democratic Labor Party, 21, 101, 103, 105–6, 109, 112, 120
Barbados Defense Force, 108–11, 113–15, 117–20
Barbados Regiment, 103, 105, 108
Barrow, Errol, 4, 6, 103–5, 109, 112–15, 117, 118, 120
Belize, 5, 20, 103; British troops (*See* United Kingdom); dispute with Guatemala (*See* territorial disputes); economic issues, 143–44; Heads of

Agreement, 131–32, 133; internationalization, 130–31; People's United Party, 132, 138–40; United Democratic Party, 132, 133, 139, 143; U.S. military (*See* United States); Webster Proposals, 129–30
Belize Defense Force, 132, 137–38, 142
Bermuda, 9, 27, 29–30, 39–41
Bird, Vere, Sr., 4, 6, 18–19
Bishop, Maurice, 12, 19, 66, 106–8, 111, 118
Blaize, Herbert, 88–89, 118
Braithwaite, Nicholas, 5, 18–19
Britain. *See* United Kingdom
British Guiana. *See* Guyana
Burnham, Forbes, xiv, 4–7, 12, 19, 31, 61, 104, 106, 149–57, 160–62

Caribbean Community and Common Market, 12–13, 17, 41, 77–78, 92, 162–63
Caribbean Democratic Union, 21
Caribbean Development Bank, 17
Caribbean Peace Keeping Force, 111
CARICOM. *See* Caribbean Community and Common Market
Castro, Fidel, 9, 112
Cayman Islands. *See* Turks and Caicos

About the Contributors

IVELAW L. GRIFFITH is Assistant Professor of Political Science at Lehman College, New York, where he also teaches in the Latin American and Caribbean Studies Program. He is author of *The Quest for Security in the Caribbean* (forthcoming) and contributor to *The Caribbean in the Pacific Century* (forthcoming).

JANNETTE O. DOMINGO, Chair of the Department of African American Studies at John Jay College of Criminal Justice, New York, is an economist who specializes in the economics of crime and in Virgin Island Politics. She has published in *The Review of Black Political Economy, Journal of Contemporary Criminal Justice, Blacks in Criminal Justice,* and elsewhere.

NEVILLE C. DUNCAN is Senior Lecturer in Government at the University of the West Indies, Cave Hill, Barbados. He specializes in Caribbean Political Sociology and International Politics. Dr. Duncan has published numerous articles and several books and monographs, including *Women in Barbados Politics* (1978) and *Public Finance and Fiscal Issues in Barbados and the O.E.C.S.* which he edited in 1989.

HUMBERTO GARCÍA MUÑIZ, Associate Researcher at the Institute of Caribbean Studies, University of Puerto Rico, is author of *La Estrategia de Estados Unidos y la Militarización del Caribe* (1988) and *Boots, Boots, Boots: Intervention, Regional Security, and Militarization in the*

Caribbean (1986). His research has also appeared in Latin American and European journals.

CLIFFORD E. GRIFFIN is Assistant Professor of Political Science at North Carolina State University. Dr. Griffin, author of *Democracy in the English-Speaking Caribbean* (forthcoming), is a 1991–1992 National Fellow at the Hoover Institution on War, Revolution, and Peace at Stanford University.

DION E. PHILLIPS is Associate Professor of Sociology at the University of the Virgin Islands. He is co-editor (with Alma H. Young) of *Militarization in the Non-Hispanic Caribbean* (1986) and has published in *Caribbean Studies, Latin American Perspectives, Trans-Africa Forum,* and elsewhere.

ALMA H. YOUNG, Professor of Urban and Regional Planning at the University of New Orleans, is co-editor (with Dion E. Phillips) of *Militarization in the Non-Hispanic Caribbean*. She has contributed to seven editions of *Latin America and Caribbean Contemporary Record* and to *The Dutch Caribbean* (1990).